Petro-Aggression

Oil is the world's single most important commodity, and its political effects are pervasive. Jeff Colgan extends the idea of the resource curse into the realm of international relations, exploring how countries form their foreign policy preferences and intentions. Why are some but not all oil-exporting "petrostates" aggressive? To answer this question, a theory of aggressive foreign policy preferences is developed and then tested, using both quantitative and qualitative methods. *Petro-Aggression* shows that oil creates incentives that increase a petrostate's aggression, but also incentives for the opposite. The net effect depends critically on its domestic politics, especially the preferences of its leader. Revolutionary leaders are especially significant. Using case studies including Iraq, Iran, Libya, Saudi Arabia, and Venezuela, this book offers new insight into why oil politics has a central role in global peace and conflict.

JEFF D. COLGAN is an Assistant Professor at the School of International Service at American University in Washington, DC, where his research focuses on international security and global energy politics. He has published work in several journals, including *International Organization*, the *Journal of Peace Research*, *Review of International Organizations*, and *Energy Policy*, and his article on petro-aggression in *International Organization* won the Robert O. Keohane award for the best article published by an untenured scholar. Dr Colgan has previously worked with the World Bank, McKinsey & Company, and The Brattle Group.

Petro-Aggression

When Oil Causes War

JEFF D. COLGAN

CAMBRIDGE UNIVERSITY PRESS
Cambridge, New York, Melbourne, Madrid, Cape Town,
Singapore, São Paulo, Delhi, Mexico City

Cambridge University Press
The Edinburgh Building, Cambridge CB2 8RU, UK

Published in the United States of America by Cambridge University Press, New York

www.cambridge.org
Information on this title: www.cambridge.org/9781107654976

First published 2013

Printed and bound in the United Kingdom by the MPG Books Group

A catalogue record for this publication is available from the British Library

Library of Congress Cataloguing in Publication data
Colgan, Jeff, 1975– author.
    Petro-aggression : when oil causes war / Jeff D. Colgan.
        pages   cm
    Includes bibliographical references and index.
    ISBN 978-1-107-02967-5 (hardback) – ISBN 978-1-107-65497-6 (paperback)
    1. Petroleum industry and trade.   2. War–Economic aspects.   I. Title.
    HD9560.5.C576 2013
    355.02'73–dc23
    2012035321

ISBN 978-1-107-02967-5 Hardback
ISBN 978-1-107-65497-6 Paperback

For January

Contents

Figures

Tables

Acknowledgments

It takes a village. So they say about raising a child, but it applies equally well to writing a scholarly book. As with raising a child, there is someone who is ultimately responsible, but it just cannot be done without a lot of help.

The genesis of this book was my PhD dissertation at Princeton University, where I was lucky enough to be guided by a helpful, wise, and engaged committee of advisors: Professors Robert Keohane (who served as chair), Christina Davis, Thomas Christensen, and Jennifer Widner. The transformation from dissertation to book was a significant one, in this case: I added several new chapters, deleted another, and revised all the rest. So my advisors cannot be blamed for any flaws in the product you see before you; but they can be proud of the lasting contributions they made to my work and my intellectual outlook.

After I completed a draft of the book manuscript and thought I was on the final stretch, I decided to hold a manuscript workshop to get a new round of feedback from a group of accomplished scholars. Boaz Atzili, Andrew Bennett, Ken Conca, Charles Glaser, Joseph Grieco, Tamar Gutner, Rose Kelanic, Michael Ross, and Elizabeth Saunders each read the entire manuscript and came to a one-day workshop at my new home, American University. Their critique profoundly shaped my thinking; indeed, in some sections of the manuscript, they sent me back to the drawing board. I am incredibly grateful. Many of the participants have helped me also outside of the workshop, and here Charlie Glaser deserves special mention, as he generously welcomed me into his working group on energy and international security at George Washington University. In addition, I owe deep thanks to James Goldgeier for funding the workshop, for attending it and giving substantive suggestions, and for his ongoing support of my work. I also appreciate the help of Mana Zarinejad, David Parker, and the staff of the Washington Institute for International and Public Affairs Research for managing the workshop.

A number of colleagues provided helpful comments on my work at various stages. Special thanks go to David Bosco, Målfrid Braut-Hegghammer, Sarah Bush, Ashley Conner, Joanne Gowa, Jessica Green, Thomas Hegghammer, Steffen Hertog, Michael Horowitz, Sikina Jinnah, Kristina Johnson, Mareike Kleine, Michael McKoy, Michael Miller, Gwyneth McClendon, James Morrison, Margaret Peters, Ed Rhodes, Margaret Roberts, Michael Ross, David Steinberg, Jordan Tama, David Victor, Inken von Borzyskowski, Jessica Weeks, and Sharon Weiner. They are more than just excellent colleagues, they are friends and supporters.

I feel I must highlight the help I received from three good friends whom I met at Princeton: Sarah Bush, Jessica Green, and Jordan Tama. All of them read and critiqued large parts of my work, often more than once, and delivered incisive, constructive comments. Sarah has probably read more of my work, more times, than anyone except me. Together, they have consistently pushed my work to become better than I could have made it on my own.

In addition, my work benefited from participant comments at the Princeton University International Relations Colloquium; presentations at Georgetown University, the University of Michigan, and the University of Toronto; and various panels at APSA, ISA, IPES, MPSA, and elsewhere. John Haslam and three anonymous reviewers at Cambridge University Press provided a valuable critique, and they will no doubt see significant changes as a result. My editor Carrie Parkinson offered helpful advice and support, while Rob Wilkinson of Out of House Publishing ensured the book was published without any hitches. I received excellent research assistance from Summer Lopez, Tom Scherer, Lamis Abdel-Aziz, Neslihan Kaptanoglu, Laina Stuebner, and David Parker. I thank Francisco Monaldi and others at IESA in Caracas for hosting me during my stay in Venezuela. I also thank Dan Byman, Marc Busch, James Vreeland, and others at Georgetown University for welcoming me in Washington while I finished up my dissertation. Financial support from the American University, the Lynde and Harry Bradley Foundation, the Niehaus Center for Global Governance, the Woodrow Wilson School of International and Public Affairs (Princeton), the Woodrow Wilson International Center for Scholars (Washington), and the Social Sciences and Humanities Research Council of Canada is gratefully acknowledged. I also thank

Cambridge University Press for permission to use material drawn from my 2010 article in *International Organization*.

My deepest thanks go to my wife January, my mother Valerie, and my brother Andrew. They provide support and encouragement when it is needed. The rest of the time, they are remarkably patient listeners as I prattle on about global oil politics. They always help to give me a sense of perspective. Thank you for everything.

1 | *Introduction*

Oil is the single most valuable commodity traded on international markets. The total value of its trade is many multiples larger than the trade of any other natural resource, including natural gas, diamonds, timber, or coffee. Not surprisingly, its political effects are pervasive. Oil helps define the relationship between the Persian Gulf countries and the rest of the world. It underlies the "resource curse" in oil-producing states, the symptoms of which include poor economic growth, authoritarianism, and civil war. It is a source of both tension and cooperation between China, India, and the West. It affects the flows of foreign aid. And it shapes military alliances and troop commitments all over the world. As oil supplies become more difficult to access in the future, the relationship between oil and international security is increasingly important.

This book makes the case that global oil consumption is a significant cause of international war. Under certain conditions, oil income enables aggressive leaders to eliminate political constraints, reduce domestic accountability, and take their countries to war. I call this "petro-aggression." This concept is quite different from the conventional notion of petro-competition: i.e., the idea that states commonly go to war to own "the prize" of oil. Such wars do happen, but they are relatively rare. I argue that petro-competition is only one way in which oil and international security are linked, and it is probably not the most important link. Petro-aggression is a big part of what makes oil so dangerous for world politics.

At its broadest level, this book explores how states form their foreign policy preferences and intentions. For those who study the causes of war, the formation of preferences (especially aggressive preferences) is a fundamental topic. Over the last several decades, scholars have significantly advanced our understanding of how various domestic political factors affect the formation of state preferences. This book focuses on a state's endowment of natural resources, specifically oil resources.

1

I seek to understand what makes a state aggressive by extending our understanding of the resource curse into the realm of international relations.

Two puzzles

Petrostates – states in which revenues from net oil exports constitute at least 10 percent of gross domestic product (GDP) – are among the most violent states in the world.[1] Such states show a remarkable propensity for militarized interstate disputes (MIDs): on average, they engage in MIDs at a rate more than 50 percent higher than non-petrostates.[2] This was not always true: until about 1970, petrostates were just about as likely to get into international conflicts as non-petrostates. Yet the modern age of oil, which began in earnest after the Arab oil embargo of 1973, created a world in which petrostates play an oversized role in global military affairs. Indeed, the relatively small group of petrostates has accounted for almost a quarter of all of the world's international conflicts since 1970.

This pattern of petrostate conflict generates two puzzles that lie at the heart of this book. First, what explains petrostates' propensity for aggression and international conflict? Second, what accounts for the variation in that propensity among the petrostates? While some petrostates have repeatedly instigated conflicts, others such as Saudi Arabia, Indonesia, or Nigeria, have had relatively peaceful international interactions over the past half-century (setting aside their domestic violence).

Existing research does not adequately answer these questions. Few scholars have looked deeply at the link between oil and international conflict, and most of those who have focus on petro-competition.[3] Petro-competition is consistent with the view that conflict is more likely

---

[1] This definition of a petrostate follows a standard one used by scholars of *rentierism*, e.g., T. Karl, 1997. There are alternative definitions of a petrostate: see Chapter 3 for more details.

[2] For petrostates, the rate is an average of 0.69 MID per year, compared to 0.44 per year for non-petrostates. The figures given here are based on the Correlates of War (COW) dataset (1945–2001) and the author's analysis. See Figure 1.1.

[3] N. Choucri and R. North, 1975; T. Homer-Dixon, 1999; M. Klare, 2002, 2004, 2008; R. Mandel, 1988; A. Westing, 1986. See also W. Engdahl, 2004; J. Ghazvinian, 2008; S. Pelletiere, 2004; S. Randall, 2007; C. Singer, 2008; D. Yergin, 2008 [1991]; A. Zalloum, 2007.

when a contested territory contains economically valuable resources such as oil.[4] The Iraqi invasion of Kuwait in 1990 seems to provide a textbook example of a resource war, proving beyond all doubt that oil acts as a prize of war. In reality, Saddam Hussein likely had multiple motivations for invading Kuwait, but still it is plausible that the opportunity to seize control of Kuwait's oil fields was an incentive for the invasion. Thus many people see petro-competition as the key to understanding the role of energy in international struggles.

Yet the idea of petro-competition cannot account for the actual historical pattern of conflicts. As I will show, the link between oil and conflict is driven largely by petrostates that are aggressive in international conflicts. Examples of such actions are not hard to find: Iraq's invasion of Iran and Kuwait; Libya's repeated incursions into Chad in the 1970s and 1980s; Iran's long-standing pattern of hostility and conflict; Venezuela's mobilization for war against Colombia in 2008. This is puzzling. If states are simply fighting over access to the oil, it is not clear why the states that are already oil-rich should be so aggressive. It suggests that petro-competition is incomplete as an explanation for oil and international conflict.

Moreover, there is an unresolved debate in the literature about the extent to which oil actually leads to more frequent international conflict at all. Skeptics correctly point to the lack of a clearly articulated theory linking oil and war, backed by systematic historical evidence.[5] A single event like Iraq's invasion of Kuwait does not mean that there is a systematic link between oil and war. After all, many other petrostates produce oil without suffering international invasions, and many international conflicts occur for reasons that have nothing to do with oil. The absence of a clear theory linking oil to international conflict represents a major gap in the study of war. I aim to address that gap.

The core argument: petro-aggression

This book develops and tests a theory of petro-aggression. Petro-aggression is the idea that, under certain circumstances,

---

[4] P. Hansel in J. Vasquez, 2000; P. Huth, 1998; J. Maxwell and R. Reuveny, 2000.
[5] N. Gleditsch, 1998; E. Meierding, 2010; I. de Soysa *et al.*, 2011; D. Victor, 2007.

oil-exporting states are systematically more likely to act aggressively and instigate international conflicts. Rather than being simply a magnet for greed and international competition, oil has multiple effects. Oil creates some incentives to increase a petrostate's aggressiveness and some incentives to decrease it. The net effect of oil for a petrostate's foreign policy depends on how the oil income interacts with the state's domestic politics. Oil income has its most negative consequences for international peace when it flows into a state that is led by a government with aggressive preferences. Such leadership often arises in the wake of a domestic political revolution.

Crucially, not all petrostates are affected by petro-aggression. A common misperception about oil politics is that it has a uniform, monolithic effect on politics. This book argues that this is simply not true, and that in fact the net political effect of oil varies dramatically depending on the nature of the petrostate. One should not look for a single, simple answer about how oil affects international affairs; instead, one should seek to understand the conditions under which oil makes conflict more or less likely.

Large-scale oil income generates multiple political incentives that affect a petrostate's foreign policy. One of the more important but subtle incentives is that oil facilitates risk-taking by petrostate leaders. Oil income is easily controlled by the central government, thereby giving the leader an independent source of financial resources that can be redistributed to buy political support. Consequently, a petrostate leader often faces very little domestic political accountability, and thus a low risk of being removed from office for risky and potentially unpopular actions. In non-petrostates, one of the reasons that leaders tend to avoid international conflicts is because they know that if they lose, they are very likely to be removed from office, either peacefully or violently. Yet a leader with huge financial resources to redistribute to purchase political support can afford to take risks, including those involved in aggressive foreign policy adventurism.

The net impact of oil's multiple effects on a state's foreign policy depends critically on its domestic politics, especially the preferences of its leader. Governments that have come to power by way of a domestic revolution are especially significant. Revolutionary governments are more likely to have aggressive preferences for two reasons. First, revolutionary politics tend to select leaders that are systematically more risk-tolerant and ambitious to revise the status quo than non-revolutionary leaders. Second, revolutions tend to eliminate domestic political constraints that might otherwise restrain an aggressive leader from taking a state into conflict or war. Thus, in general, revolutionary states have a higher propensity for aggression than comparable non-revolutionary states, regardless of whether they have oil.

These two factors – oil income and revolutionary government – lie at the heart of this book's story. For states in which a revolutionary government has taken power, oil amplifies the state's propensity to instigate international conflicts. The combination of a risk-tolerant revolutionary leader, financial resources for military activities, and a high degree of political autonomy generated by oil income, creates a toxic mix that facilitates state aggression, which in turn leads to conflict. In non-revolutionary petrostates, the net effect is quite different. Oil still provides incentives for aggression, but these are balanced by the incentives to avoid international conflict, such as the opportunity cost of any potentially disrupted oil exports.

Multiple links between oil and global violence

Interstate war is not the whole story when it comes to oil and violence. Broadly speaking, there are two additional connections. First, a substantial and growing body of academic research demonstrates that petrostates have a higher propensity for civil wars and domestic violence than non-petrostates.[6] Oil and other resources are believed to promote civil war in three possible ways: by providing finances for warring parties, especially rebels; by increasing the financial value of victory in a civil war, and thus the motivation to fight; and by encouraging corruption and weakening the institutions of the exporting state.[7] Second, oil is linked to terrorism and transnational violence by non-state actors, especially in association with radical Islam. Some petrostates have

---

[6] P. Collier and A. Hoeffler, 2004; J. Fearon and D. Laitin, 2003; H. Hegre and N. Sambanis, 2006; M. Humphreys, 2005; P. Lujala, 2010; M. Ross, 2012. But see also B. Smith, 2004; C. Thies, 2010.

[7] P. Le Billon, 2007. These are related to, but distinct from, the mechanisms that produce international conflict. In both civil and international conflict, oil appears to alter the costs of fighting, but not in the same way. As Chapter 2 argues, oil affects the costs of international fighting for the state as a whole (e.g., by disrupting oil sales) and for the leader as an individual (by lowering the leader's risks of domestic punishment for his foreign policy).

used their oil wealth to fund the teaching of a radical version of Islam that has fueled global jihadism. Separately, Osama bin Laden and Al Qaeda have highlighted the oil industry in the Middle East as one of their chief grievances. The connection between oil, Islam, and violence perpetrated by non-state actors is not yet well understood.[8] It deserves to be the topic of intense scholarly research.

Still, this book focuses on the relationship between oil and inter-state conflict. The causes of such conflicts have been a primary concern for scholars of international relations dating back to the days of Thucydides. In recent years, international wars seem to be less frequent than they were in the past.[9] While this is certainly excellent news, it does not mean that such conflicts have disappeared, nor that the downward trend will continue. Even if it does, petro-aggression can help us understand why some conflicts persist even in the face of a global shift away from interstate conflict.

Future shifts in the pattern of global oil production and consumption could raise the salience of oil in international security. Over the next few decades, a number of states will begin to produce oil for the first time or will experience an influx of oil revenues totally different than what they have experienced before. These new or changing petrostates are geographically diverse and include Brazil, Ghana, Uganda, and Kazakhstan to name just a few. As many as sixteen countries could become petroleum exporters in the near future.[10] While these states might be relatively small players in the global oil market, the role of oil in their domestic economies is likely to be huge. Understanding the conditions under which oil increases a state's propensity for international conflict is even more important in the face of these trends.

Petro-aggression and petro-competition are not the only potential links between oil and interstate conflict. The role of oil in internationalizing some civil wars, such as those in Angola and Libya, is a worthy topic for investigation. Likewise, the role of pipeline politics and transit routes in international security would benefit from systematic

---

[8] Though see T. Hegghammer, 2010.

[9] J. Goldstein, 2011; J. Mueller, 1989; S. Pinker, 2011.

[10] Ross (2012) reports that Cuba, Ghana, Guinea, Guinea-Bissau, Guyana, Israel, Liberia, Mali, Sao Tome and Principe, Senegal, Sierra Leone, Tanzania, Togo, and Uganda could become new oil or gas exporters in the coming years. Indonesia and Tunisia, former exporters that had become net importers, may once again become petroleum exporters.

research.[11] Elsewhere, I argue that there is a whole set of potential causal pathways linking oil to international conflict.[12]

In this book, I focus specifically on petro-aggression. Iraq, Iran, Venezuela, and Libya are far better characterized as instigators of aggression than as passive targets of resource conquest, and that behavior requires explanation. Moreover, even some of the most famous cases of 'oil wars' could benefit from thinking about petro-aggression. For example, it could be that the Iraqi invasion of Kuwait in 1990 was as much about Iraq's oil as it was about Kuwait's. While there is little doubt that capturing Kuwait's oil fields represented a tempting prize of war for Iraq, it is also clear that that can be said of any major oil patch in the world in relation to any country with sufficient military power to fight for it. On its own, the existence of Kuwait's oil fields do not explain Iraq's invasion. As subsequent chapters will show, it is fruitful to refocus our attention on the oil in Iraq. Saddam Hussein's access to oil income allowed him to buy-off and repress domestic political opposition, thereby eliminating mechanisms of accountability that might otherwise have deterred him from risky foreign policy maneuvers. Unlike leaders in most non-petrostates, Saddam was able to take his country into two costly wars, fail to achieve any significant gains, and nonetheless remain in office after those costly failures.

The first step toward reconsidering the role of oil is suggested by Figure 1.1. Figure 1.1 graphs the average annual rate of the onset of international military conflicts. The data for this graph are drawn from the Correlates of War project's dataset of militarized interstate disputes (MIDs).[13] More will be said about MIDs in subsequent chapters, particularly Chapter 4. For now it suffices to say that the military conflicts are divided into two categories: those in which the state was the attacker, and those in which the state is the defender or the target of an attack.[14]

Figure 1.1 reveals an interesting pattern: petrostates are more likely to attack than to defend in military conflicts. This idea contrasts sharply with the conventional wisdom about petro-competition.

---

[11] Such research could build on B. Jentleson, 1986.

[12] J. Colgan, "The Pathways from Oil to War." See also C. Glaser, 2011.

[13] Correlates of War database, based on F. Ghosn *et al.*, 2004.

[14] This is done using the COW coding of whether or not the state was acting as a "revisionist" party in the dispute – that is, the state that seeks to revise the status quo by force. For more details, see Chapter 4.

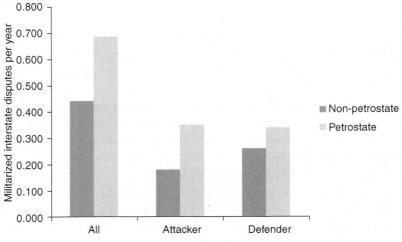

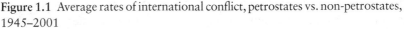

Figure 1.1 Average rates of international conflict, petrostates vs. non-petrostates, 1945–2001

Note: Count of MID onsets per state-year. All differences between petro and non-petrostates are statistically significant.

The data show that while petrostates are more likely to participate in military conflicts than non-petrostates overall – which is consistent with the idea of petro-competition – the primary reason for that result is that, on average, petrostates are highly likely to instigate such conflicts. Indeed, this simplified comparison shows that petrostates instigate conflicts at a rate that is almost twice as large as the rate of non-petrostates, on average. Petrostates are the targets of attack 30 percent more frequently than non-petrostates. Thus while petrostates are substantially more likely to be both the attacker and the defender in conflicts, it is their behavior as attackers that accounts for the largest portion of their high conflict rate.

The simple analysis reflected in Figure 1.1 does not isolate the causal impact of oil income on international conflict propensity. For a variety of reasons, the graphs could be masking real differences between the groups, or suggesting differences that disappear once other factors are properly accounted for. Nonetheless, the graphs are intriguing, and cry out for an explanation. The development of such an explanation is the task of the chapters to come.

The stakes are high. Some of the conflicts involving petrostates have cost thousands of lives and have been extraordinarily damaging to millions of others. For the United States and its allies, these wars are politically impossible to ignore, meaning that a substantial amount of public wealth – and human lives – is spent on military deployments that are directly or indirectly connected to the global oil industry. So long as industrialized economies remain dependent on oil, there is no reason to expect that the need for these operations will disappear.

Oil and the broader causes of war

The theory I develop in this book focuses on how and why petrostates develop aggressive preferences and capabilities. In political science, state preferences are taken as inputs to many of the rational choice models on the causes of war, and often no effort is made to try to explain the origin of those preferences.[15] Charles Glaser points out that a rational choice approach to the causes of war, focusing on the strategic interactions of unitary state actors, is only the "middle layer" of a comprehensive explanation.[16] This middle layer of theory should be preceded by a layer that explains the inputs to strategic choice theory, including state preferences. It could also be followed by an additional layer of theory that explains the sources of suboptimality that lead states to engage in war even when it might have been rationally avoidable.[17] My argument is about preference formation, and thus it logically precedes a theory of strategic interaction.

As such, my research joins a growing body of scholarly work that considers the multiple ways in which domestic political factors affect the formation of state preferences.[18] One example is Jack Snyder's work on the "myths of empire" which can create domestic preferences for aggression and over-expansion.[19] The work by Daniel Byman, Hein Goemans, James Goldgeier, Stephen Rosen, Elizabeth Saunders, and others on the role of leaders in international security is a second

[15] J. Fearon, 1995; D. Filson and S. Werner, 2004; C. Glaser, 2010; R. Powell, 1999.
[16] C. Glaser, 2010: 15.
[17] R. Jervis, 1976.
[18] Any list of citations to this literature is bound to be incomplete, but some important books in this area include: T. Christensen, 1996; S. Van Evera, 1999; M. Fravel, 2008; W. Howell and J. Pevehouse, 2007; A. Johnston, 1998; C. Kupchan, 2010; J. Legro, 2005; P. Katzenstein, 1996; R. Schweller, 2006; P. Senese and J. Vasquez, 2008; A. Stam, 1999. See also the citations in the notes that follow this one.
[19] J. Snyder, 1991.

example.[20] A third is the research by Stephen Walt, Zeev Maoz, and others on the impact of domestic revolutions on international conflict, which is of special importance to my argument in this book.[21]

A sizeable portion, perhaps even a majority, of the research on domestic influences on international security over the last two decades focuses on the democratic peace and related questions. Many have focused on the ways in which established democracies are or are not different from autocracies in conflict behavior.[22] One branch of this work focuses on the development of selectorate theory pioneered by Bruce Bueno de Mesquita and others.[23] Somewhat separately, the effect of the process of democratization on international conflict has been investigated by Edward Mansfield, Jack Snyder, and others.[24]

Without denying the importance of the democratic peace, the extent to which scholars have focused on regime type at the expense of other factors affecting international conflict and peace is remarkable. Purely by way of illustration, Figure 1.2 compares the influence of democracy, revolution, and oil on states' propensity for international conflict. The figure plots the average number of MIDs initiated within a pair of states (known as directed-dyads). The rate of conflict is plotted depending on whether both, either, or neither of the states within the pair are democratic, revolutionary, or a petrostate.

As Figure 1.2 indicates, the differences between revolutionary and non-revolutionary states, or petrostates and non-petrostates, are at least as large as those between democracies and non-democracies. This is true even in percentage terms.[25] I hasten to add that this graph is not

---

[20] V. Bunce, 1981; D. Byman and K. Pollack, 2001; G. Chiozza and H. Goemans, 2011; H. Goemans, 2000; J. Goldgeier, 1994; M. Horowitz *et al.*, 2005; S. Murray, 2006; J. Post and A. George, 2004; S. Rosen, 2007; E. Saunders, 2011.

[21] J. Goldstone, 1997; T. Gurr, 1988; Z. Maoz, 1996; T. Skocpol, 1988; R. Snyder, 1999; S. Walt, 1996.

[22] B. Bueno de Mesquita *et al.*, 2004; A. Downes, 2009; M. Doyle, 1986; E. Gartzke, 2000, 2007; J. Gowa, 2000; P. Huth and T. Allee, 2003; C. Layne, 1994; C. Lipson, 2003; J. O'Neal and B. Russett, 2001; J. Owen, 1997; D. Reiter and A. Stam, 2002; S. Rosato, 2003; B. Russett, 1994; K. Schultz, 2001; J. Weeks, 2008.

[23] B. Bueno de Mesquita *et al.*, 2004.

[24] E. Mansfield and J. Snyder, 2005; V. Narang and S. Nelson, 2009.

[25] Directed-dyads with no democracies have 160 percent more MIDs than directed-dyads with two democracies. Directed-dyads with two revolutionary states have 232 percent more MIDs than directed-dyads with no revolutionary

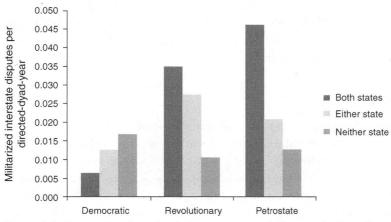

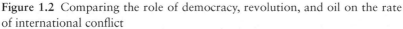

Figure 1.2 Comparing the role of democracy, revolution, and oil on the rate of international conflict

intended to prove which factor is most important, or to support any causal inference. I should also add that Figure 1.2 is different in several respects from Figure 1.1.[26]

My point is simply that the empirical pattern makes further investigation of factors like oil and revolution well worth the effort. Curiously, academic scholars have relatively little to say about how oil affects international security. This paucity is made more noticeable by the fact that energy is a central theme for political analysts, military commanders, journalists, and policymakers. It is not that scholars have ignored oil altogether.[27] Yet scholars who study the causes of war largely ignore the role of oil, and those who study oil politics say little about international conflict. For instance, much valuable research

states. Directed-dyads with two petrostates have 266 percent more MIDs than directed-dyads with no petrostates. Admittedly, there are more democratic states than there are petrostates or revolutionary states, which is relevant for their total importance for world politics.

[26] For instance, Figure 1.1 is based on a monadic analysis, whereas Figure 1.2 is dyadic (directed-dyads). Figure 1.2 focuses exclusively on the MIDs in which the state is the "attacker," and only includes politically-relevant dyads. For more detail about how the data for Figure 1.2 were generated, see the dyadic analysis in Chapter 4.

[27] Some recent research focusing on oil and security includes J. Duffield, 2007; E. Gholz and D. Press, 2010; C. Glaser, 2011; M. Klare, 2004; C. Talmadge, 2008.

has investigated the domestic consequences of the resource curse.[28] To date, however, scholarly analysis has yet to take our understanding of the resource curse into the realm of international relations. One of my aims is to help do just that.

Scope of inquiry

The study of oil in international relations invites tantalizing comparisons to other natural resources. The argument just sketched about the behavior of petrostates might conceivably apply to states dominated by other natural resource sectors, such as diamonds, metal mining, natural gas, or timber. It might even apply to other sources of non-tax revenues like foreign aid. However, this book focuses primarily on oil, for three reasons. First, the sheer importance of oil to the modern global economy makes it the logical starting point of any inquiry into the role of natural resources on foreign policy. The global trade of oil generates revenues that are somewhere between ten and a hundred times larger than the next largest natural resource. While the political effects of other natural resources are worthy of study, oil is in a league of its own. Likewise, the value of oil dwarfs the total global flows of foreign aid.[29]

Second, oil has specific economic characteristics that are not necessarily shared by other natural resources. These characteristics (e.g., ease of centralization and control of revenues; high capital intensity; low demand for labor), if not shared by other resources under investigation, could introduce unforeseen heterogeneity in the analysis. Indeed, existing scholarship suggests that oil has special effects on domestic political conditions such as authoritarianism and civil war, and that these effects are not necessarily shared by other natural resources.[30] The differences between oil income and foreign aid are potentially even

---

[28] N. Barma *et al.*, 2011; H. Beblawi and G. Luciani, 1987; E. Bellin, 2004; P. Collier and A. Hoeffler, 2004; T. Dunning, 2008; M. Humphreys *et al.*, 2007; P. Luong and E. Weinthal, 2010; K. Morrison, 2009; M. Ross, 2012; J. Sachs and A. Warner, 1995; P. Stevens and E. Dietsche, 2008.

[29] According to the BP Statistical Review of World Energy, global oil production was worth approximately $2.3 trillion in 2010. The OECD's website reports that total Official Development Assistance in 2010 was $120 billion. While OECD aid is not the same as the global total, it is the probably the largest part.

[30] M. Humphreys, 2005; M. Ross, 2012.

larger (e.g., oil does not come from a donor, and a donor has interests). The potential explanatory factors in the analysis may be specific to oil, so it is prudent to restrict the analysis solely to petrostates.

Third, any bias created by focusing on oil to the exclusion of other natural resources will have a conservative effect on the analysis presented here. Suppose that some non-petrostates actually behave similarly to petrostates, because of similar dynamics involving their non-oil natural resources. If so, this would make it more difficult to observe a difference between petrostates and non-petrostates. Thus if this book can show that petrostates are substantially different from non-petrostates despite this bias, it ought to only enhance our confidence that the observed propensities of petrostates actually do exist.

For these reasons, this book focuses principally on oil and petrostates. Nonetheless, the role of other natural resources is investigated briefly in Chapter 4.

Structure of the book

The book proceeds as follows. Chapter 2 develops the core theory that explains the linkages between oil, revolutionary government, and international conflict. It argues that when a state leader has aggressive preferences, as is likely under a revolutionary government, the political autonomy provided by oil income makes it more likely that the leader will decide to launch an international conflict. Thus petro-revolutionary states are more likely to instigate international conflict than comparable non-petrostates, even though oil on its own (in the absence of a revolutionary government) does not have the same impact. Chapter 3 explains my research strategy for testing the theory empirically, combining both quantitative and qualitative methods.

Chapter 4 then uses statistical analysis to test the hypothesis that revolutionary and non-revolutionary states have significantly different propensities for initiating international conflict, and that oil exacerbates this difference. (Chapter 4 is based primarily on an article I published in *International Organization* in 2010, but there is some new material. The key differences are described at the start of the chapter.) The analysis uses cross-national data on militarized interstate disputes (MIDs) over the period 1945–2001. The findings suggest that revolutionary petrostates have a high propensity for international conflict: *almost 250 percent higher than that of a typical state.*

Chapters 5–9 provide historical case studies of individual petrostates. Chapter 5 focuses on Iraq. Saddam Hussein emerged as a leader from the revolutionary turmoil that began with the fall of the monarchy in 1958 and ultimately led to Saddam's ascension to the presidency in 1979. Iraq's initiation of two costly wars, against Iran in 1980 and then Kuwait in 1990, had much to do with Saddam's risk-tolerance and ambition as a leader, but it also had to do with the way in which oil clientelism distorted the domestic politics of Iraq and eliminated effective political accountability for Saddam's actions. Chapter 6 considers Libya under King Idris and then Muammar Qaddafi. As expected by the theory, Libya's foreign policy was highly aggressive under Qaddafi. Oil income played a central role in expanding Qaddafi's opportunities for aggression, both by allowing him to override domestic resistance to his foreign policy adventurism, and by increasing his military capability far beyond what it would otherwise have been. Chapter 7 focuses on Iran under the Shah and then the Ayatollahs, showing how the revolutionary regime dramatically changed the nature of Iran's foreign policy. The chapter also considers implications of my argument for contemporary global politics and interactions with today's Iran.

Chapter 8 studies Venezuela, taking on the question of the geographic portability of my argument outside of the Middle East. The so-called "Bolivarian Revolution" led by Hugo Chávez gave Venezuela a moderately revolutionary government, and the theory predicts a moderately aggressive foreign policy. This is indeed observed in Venezuela's militarized disputes with Colombia, its support of revolutionary groups such as FARC, and its wider program within Latin America of destabilizing existing international institutions. This contrasts with the cooperative foreign policy behavior of previous governments in Venezuela.

Chapter 9 looks at the Kingdom of Saudi Arabia, which remained non-revolutionary for the entire period of study. The process by which it managed its foreign policy and potential international conflicts is seen in stark contrast to the behavior of revolutionary petrostates. Saudi foreign policy has been dominated by two themes: first, its use of financial and economic power to achieve foreign objectives rather than direct military conflict; and second, its extensive cooperation with the United States and other oil importers. The incentives generated by oil money underpin both themes. This chapter also compares Libya and Saudi Arabia, which in the 1960s were quite similar. The emergence of a revolutionary government in one but not the other provides a useful basis for analytic comparison.

Chapter 10 addresses the question of whether oil causes revolutionary government, which could generate an alternative account of the empirical pattern we observe. This question is important because in the rest of the book the emergence of a revolutionary government is treated as independent from the country's oil income. The question is addressed both quantitatively and qualitatively. Although a comprehensive investigation into the causes of revolutions is far outside the scope of this book, there does not appear to be any evidence to suggest that oil causes revolutionary governments to emerge.

Chapter 11 concludes the book by considering future research and policy implications. This chapter examines how some recent changes in the Middle East, most notably the political movements known as the Arab Spring, might influence the international politics of the region. I also consider the implications of my findings for energy policy in the United States and elsewhere. A certain kind of energy independence, which emphatically does not require energy autarky, is a policy goal that is both feasible and desirable. Indeed, a significant reduction in oil dependence could represent a major step forward in the interests of global peace.

2 | A theory of oil, revolution, and conflict

The oil can is mightier than the sword.

— Everett Dickson

As Chapter 1 notes, petrostates show a remarkable propensity for instigating international conflict. What explains the relationship? This chapter develops the core of my answer to that question, which is then tested empirically in subsequent chapters. My argument draws on existing research on the resource curse, which suggests that oil erodes domestic political accountability due to the ease with which oil revenues can be centralized and controlled by the state's leadership. I show that the resource curse extends into international politics, and use it conceptually as a building block for the theory of petro-aggression developed in this chapter.

My theory focuses on how state preferences for aggression are formed. Existing research identifies revolutionary states as highly conflict-prone.[1] I extend previous work by arguing that revolutions tend to select risk-tolerant, ambitious leaders who increase their state's propensity for instigating conflict. I then theorize that oil generates multiple incentives that affect a state's foreign policy, some of which increase the costs of conflict, and some of which reduce those costs. The net effect of oil depends crucially on the underlying preferences of the state's leaders. Oil makes revolutionary states even more aggressive than comparable revolutionary states without oil. In non-revolutionary states, however, oil tends not to cause state aggression. In sum, I argue that the effect of oil depends on the state's domestic politics.

The primary dependent variable in this inquiry is a state's propensity to instigate international conflict. This focus is not to discount the

---

[1] J. Goldstone, 1997; T. Gurr, 1988; Z. Maoz, 1996; T. Skocpol, 1988; S. Walt, 1996.

importance of petrostates' propensity to be the targets of aggression
in international conflicts. However, much has already been said about
that aspect of the problem, particularly with respect to resource competition.[2] My goal is to shed new light on a part of the puzzle which
has gone largely unnoticed: international conflicts in which the petrostate is acting as an aggressor.

Each section of the chapter describes a link in the chain of logic of
my argument. First, I argue that the probability of international conflict increases when at least one of two conditions holds: the costs of
fighting decrease, or a state's risk-tolerance increases. Second, I argue
that a domestic revolution makes a state more likely to instigate conflict, due to changes in the two conditions just identified. Third, I argue
that the net effect of oil income is to amplify the effect of a domestic revolution. Thus oil and revolutionary politics interact to increase
the propensity of the state to instigate international conflict. Having
painted the theory in broad brushstrokes, the last section of this chapter addresses some important questions arising from the theory, such
as how political constraints differ from political accountability, what
other effects revolutions and oil income have on a state's international
relations, and whether oil causes revolutions.

Domestic politics shape the state's propensity for international conflict

The first link in my chain of logic is that domestic politics shape the
state's propensity for international conflict. My argument joins a
growing body of research that focuses on the causes of international
conflict arising from domestic- or individual-level factors ("monadic
factors").[3] One common question for all such theories is how monadic
factors relate to strategic interaction between two or more states.
The question arises because rationalist models of war suggest that if
states are fully rational, all information is public, and there are no

---

[2] W. Engdahl, 2004; J. Ghazvinian, 2008; R. Goralski and R. Freeburg, 1987;
P. Huth, 1998; M. Kaldor *et al.*, 2007; M. Klare, 2002, 2004, 2008; R. Mandel,
1988; J. Maxwell and R. Reuveny, 2000; S. Pelletiere, 2004; S. Randall, 2007;
C. Singer, 2008; A. Westing, 1986; A. Zalloum, 2007.
[3] B. Bueno de Mesquita *et al.*, 2004; G. Chiozza and H. Goemans 2011;
K. Gleditsch *et al.*, 2008; E. Mansfield and J. Snyder, 2005; S. Rosen, 2007;
I. Salehyan, 2009; E. Saunders, 2011; J. Weeks, 2012.

commitment problems, the states ought to be able to reach a peaceful bargain that reflects the balance of power between them, thus rendering monadic factors irrelevant.[4] In this account, the potential for conflict arises when the rationalist model's initial assumptions break down. Even for fully rational state leaders, private information and uncertainty generates one possible route to war.[5] Another possibility is that state leaders are boundedly rational and make imperfect judgments about a complex world.[6] In either case, the range of potential bargaining outcomes that could satisfy both parties is important: the larger the range, the lower the probability of conflict.[7]

With this model in mind, I highlight two conditions which increase the probability of international conflict. The first is a decrease in the costs of fighting.[8] The second is a reduction in a state's risk-aversion, or equivalently, an increase in a state's risk-tolerance.[9] Either condition makes fighting relatively more attractive as a way to settle a dispute,

---

[4] The avoidance of war stems from the anticipated costs and risks of the conflict, which creates a bargaining space known as a "win set": a range of outcomes that ought to satisfy both parties. For concreteness, we can think of two states bargaining over a territory, and the win set represents the range of places where the border can be drawn that are acceptable to both sides. If the parameters of the win set are known perfectly to both sides, there is no need for conflict. See J. Fearon, 1995; D. Filson and S. Werner, 2004; J. Morrow, 1989; R. Powell, 1999.

[5] K. Schultz, 2001: 3–4; J. Fearon, 1995.

[6] J. Kirshner, 2000.

[7] Whether leaders are fully or boundedly rational, the size of the win set is important for the probability of conflict. If the win set is large, the probability of conflict remains low because leaders would have to grossly miscalculate in order to fail to perceive an acceptable peaceful bargain. But when the win set is small, the likelihood of war increases because even small miscalculations or a small amount of uncertainty could mean that the parties are no longer able to find a mutually agreeable bargain to avoid war. In an extreme case, the perceived win set collapses entirely, and the states have incentive to go to war.

[8] The costs of fighting determine the size of the win set. In the canonical model developed by Fearon, two states consider the division of territory in proportion to their probability of victory in an armed conflict (the parameter "p"). The size of the win set is determined by the parameter "c," where c is the state's utility for the costs of fighting a conflict. Importantly, the c term "captures not only the states' values for the costs of war but also the value that they place on winning or losing on the issues at stake. That is, c_A reflects state A's costs of war relative to any possible benefits" (J. Fearon, 1995: 387). As c increases, there are an increasing number of outcomes that the state would prefer to going to war. Conversely, as the relative costs of fighting a war decrease, so too does the size of the win set, and thus the probability of conflict increases.

[9] The size of the win set depends on the states' risk-aversion (as well as the costs of fighting). As Fearon explains, "even if the leaders pay no costs for

thus narrowing the bargaining range of peaceful outcomes that are acceptable to both sides. For example, risk-tolerance leads to aggression in international affairs because it increases the perceived pay-off from risky gambles.[10] Risk-tolerance is relevant for international conflicts because militarized conflicts are much less predictable than accepting the status quo or a bargained outcome.

These two conditions, which affect the probability of conflict internationally, are themselves affected by changes at the level of domestic politics or the individual leader. By focusing on such changes, my argument takes seriously the notion that states are continuously involved in a two-level game that involves states on one level, and the individuals and institutions within a state's domestic politics on a second level.[11] For simplicity, I focus on the dynamics of only one state, but these dynamics also apply in the other state(s) involved. The domestic politics *within* each state can influence the relative costs of fighting or the state's risk-aversion, which in turn affects the interactions *between* states in the international game. Consequently, the probability of international conflict can increase due to factors within the domestic politics of one state.

The two conditions just identified stem from a well-established theoretical model for international conflict.[12] My purpose here is not theoretical originality, but rather to articulate some key features of the

war, a set of agreements both sides prefer to a fight will still exist provided both are risk-averse over the issues" (J. Fearon, 1995: 388). Just as the relative costs of fighting create options that the states prefer to conflict, so too does the states' risk-aversion. As risk-aversion increases, a state is willing to accept a less favorable outcome in order to avoid the gamble associated with an international conflict. Conversely, if a state's risk-tolerance increases (i.e., its risk-aversion decreases), the state becomes more demanding, which reduces the size of the win set and increases the probability of conflict.

[10] D. Byman and K. Pollack, 2001; J. Fearon, 1995; H. Goemans and M. Fey, 2008; S. Rosen, 2007. Someone who is risk-neutral derives the same utility from the expected pay-off of a gamble as from a certain pay-off of the same value. A risk-averse person would choose the certain pay-off, whereas a risk-acceptant person would choose the gamble. A leader who has higher risk-tolerance than another leader is less risk-averse (but is not necessarily risk-acceptant; both could be risk-averse). Risk-tolerance does not imply that a leader likes fighting for fighting's sake: that implies that the cost of war is low or negative. Rather, some leaders are more attracted than others to an uncertain outcome.

[11] R. Putnam, 1988.

[12] To clarify, the conditions just identified are not the only ways in which the probability of war can be affected. For instance, power-transition theory

model which are important for the rest of my argument. One additional benefit of considering the bargaining model of conflict is that it helps to conceptually identify the instigator of conflict: namely, the state that seeks to revise the status quo. Note that this may or may not be the same state that fires the first bullet or otherwise initiates military activity.

Revolutionary leadership makes a state more likely to instigate international conflict

The second step in my argument is that revolutionary leadership makes a state more likely to instigate international conflict. This claim is broadly consistent with existing research that domestic revolutions create conditions ripe for international conflict.[13] However, I argue that previous research has under-emphasized the role that revolutions play in selecting leaders with particular characteristics that make their states more prone to instigate international conflict.

Existing work suggests a number of other causal mechanisms that connect revolutions to a high propensity for international conflict. I do not aim to challenge this work; probably multiple causal mechanisms are at work. Also, other scholars emphasize a revolutionary state's propensity to be the target of conflicts, while my theory focuses on a state's propensity to instigate conflicts. With these issues in mind, I first develop my own theoretical argument, before describing the ways in which it differs or is consistent with previous research on revolutions.

Definition of revolutionary government

Following previous scholars, I define a revolutionary government as one that transforms the existing social, political, and economic relationships of the state by overthrowing or rejecting the principal

---

focuses on changes to the parameter "p," the probability of each state's victory in conflict, as well as changes in perceptions of p. The idea that such changes raise the potential for international conflict has a long intellectual tradition in international relations extending all the way back to Thucydides. See G. Blainey, 1988; R. Gilpin, 1981; A. Organski and J. Kugler, 1981; R. Tammen *et al.*, 2000.

[13] J. Goldstone, 1997; T. Gurr, 1988; Z. Maoz, 1996; T. Skocpol, 1988; S. Walt, 1996.

existing institutions of society.[14] A revolution, which brings such a government to power, necessarily implies new leadership. Revolutions are thus a strict subset of the broader category of regime changes, which includes coups, assassinations, revolts, democratization (complete, partial, or incomplete), and foreign occupations or installations. Some of these events (such as a coup) can be a part of a revolution, but on their own, they are not revolutionary. Revolutionary leaders are those who are central to a revolution and who obtain control of the state's post-revolutionary government. A revolutionary state is simply one where a revolutionary government is currently in power. Note that not all scholars define revolution in the same way.[15] Chapters 3 and 4 give further details about the empirical operationalization of these concepts.

Leadership preferences affect state behavior

My argument begins with the premise that leadership matters for state behavior. State intentions are ultimately set by individuals, and while individuals are not the only influence on state intentions, they are important. As Byman and Pollack argue, "At times, the influence

[14] Walt (1996: 12) defines a revolution as "the destruction of an existing state by members of its own society, followed by the creation of a new political order." Huntington (1968: 264) states, "a revolution is a rapid fundamental, and violent domestic change in the dominant values and myths of a society, in its political institutions, social structure, leadership, and government activity and policies." Huntington explicitly distinguishes revolutions from insurrections, rebellions, revolts, coups, and wars of independence. Gurr (1970), Tilly (1978, 1996), and Skocpol (1979) subsequently made similar distinctions, as do I.

[15] Skocpol (1979: 4), for instance, focused on social revolutions, defined as "rapid, basic transformations of society's state and class structures … accompanied and in part carried through by class-based revolts from below." This definition is narrower than what she calls political revolutions, which "transform state structures but not social structures, and they are not necessarily accomplished through class conflict." The definition used in this book lies in between Skocpol's "social" and "political" revolutions, because while revolutionary governments are not necessarily accompanied by a major class conflict, they do necessarily transform social and/or economic structures and practices in addition to political structures and practices. Consequently, the universe of cases under Skocpol's definition of social revolutions is likely to be smaller than Walt or Huntington's definition, or mine. I use a definition closer to the one used by Walt and Huntington because I believe the broader class of revolutions (not only social revolutions) have profound impact on international relations.

of individuals can be so great as to transform a defender of the status quo into its greatest nemesis. Bismarck fought for the status quo in Europe, whereas Wilhelm II fought to overturn it."[16] Leadership matters because not all leaders behave the same way under the same conditions.[17]

Political scientists argue that leaders' preferences are guided by their desire to remain in office.[18] Leaders without such preferences are unlikely to remain in power long, and are thus relatively unimportant to world politics. Yet the goal of staying in power is not determinative of a leader's behavior: there are different strategies for doing so, and survival in office is not the only thing that leaders can want. I follow in a long tradition of scholars who view leaders as having additional goals besides remaining in office.[19] The nature of a leader's goals varies enormously, and can include personal enrichment, social and religious goals, or territorial ambitions. The amount that the leader cares about achieving these goals, relative to his desire to stay in office, can also vary from leader to leader. Without trying to explain the particular policy goals of leaders, I focus on the variation in leaders' desire to change the international status quo, and the degree to which they are willing to accept risks to make such changes.

Existing research on the role of leaders in international politics can be divided roughly into two categories. The first focuses on the state's leadership context and incentives, as generated by domestic institutions and other factors.[20] Within this category of research, the role of the particular individual, and his or her attributes, is not as important as the incentives that the individual faces. By contrast, the second category of research focuses more on the attributes of the individual, arguing that different leaders behave differently even within the same

---

[16] D. Byman and K. Pollack, 2001: 134.
[17] This is true for democratic and non-democratic states. The influence of leaders might be comparatively smaller in democracies, as their actions are constrained by other actors and institutions, but even in democracies leadership is important. See E. Saunders, 2011 for a richly detailed argument about US presidents.
[18] B. Bueno de Mesquita *et al.*, 2004.
[19] D. Byman and K. Pollack, 2001; R. Fenno, 1978; N. Keohane, 2010; E. Saunders, 2011.
[20] B. Bueno de Mesquita *et al.*, 2004; G. Chiozza and H. Goemans, 2011; J. Weeks, 2012.

domestic political context.[21] My argument builds on both of these strands of research. As I describe below, oil politics affects the leadership context and incentives, whereas revolutionary politics affects both the attributes of the leader and the leadership context.

Revolutions select risk-tolerant, ambitious leaders

I theorize that leaders who take office through a revolution are, on average, more risk-tolerant and politically ambitious than non-revolutionary leaders, because individuals without those characteristics are unlikely to initiate or succeed in a revolution. Of course, all leaders require some risk-tolerance and ambition because taking executive office entails personal risks even in the safest of countries. Yet the level of risk-tolerance required to win office is higher when the leader must do so outside of any regularized process. Taking and holding power outside of a regularized process often requires defeating multiple rivals, sometimes violently. George Bush took some risks to gain office; Fidel Castro took considerably more. In order to garner the support that will allow them to take office, many revolutionaries must take actions that break the law and bring them into direct conflict with the incumbent regime. Consequently, many revolutionaries risk injury or death and actually experience exile or imprisonment before they ever reach office. Many would-be revolutionary leaders never succeed precisely because they are discouraged by these risks, either in anticipation or after experiencing some of them. The individuals who succeed, on the other hand, have the risk-tolerance to persevere.

A revolution that is violent will typically raise the level of personal risk associated with obtaining office, thus increasing the selection effect for risk-tolerant leaders, but violence is not necessarily the key factor. What is more important is the degree to which a leader must operate outside of the regularized political processes of the country. For instance, a palace coup might be violent, but the prince who overthrows his father to take the throne is still working within the framework of a hereditary monarchy (as in the case of the present emir of Qatar, Hamad al-Thani). Much of the population outside of

---

[21] M. Horowitz *et al.*, 2005; M. Horowitz and A. Stam, "Leader Background Experiences, Domestic Politics, and International Conflict: A Systematic Approach" (unpublished manuscript); S. Rosen, 2007; E. Saunders, 2011.

the palace might barely notice the change, let alone challenge it. The risk-tolerance required to conduct even a violent palace coup is therefore relatively low compared to leading a major revolution such as Khomeini's in Iran, in which an individual seeks to overturn the entire political apparatus along with the established monarchy, and replace it with a theocratic republic. The latter process throws open the political possibilities for all kinds of rival leadership claims from multiple individuals or parties, and often there are multiple coup attempts in the months and years after the initial revolution as various parties attempt to seize office, sometimes successfully. Only a highly risk-tolerant (as well as politically skilled and lucky) individual will succeed in the race for power in these conditions.

In addition to risk-tolerance, revolutionary politics will select individuals who are ambitious to change the status quo. Virtually all leaders are ambitious in the sense that they seek national office, so revolutionaries are not different in this sense. Yet while some non-revolutionary leaders are satisfied to simply enjoy the spoils of executive office, revolutionaries are different in the sense that they are systematically more likely to come to office with a strong desire to change the status quo within society. That is, they have important additional goals beyond simply staying in office. A true revolution, in the sense of transformational change to the existing political, economic, and social institutions and practices of a country, is much more likely to occur when the leader's preferences support such a transformation. Thus when a revolution occurs, the individual that leads it tends to have strong anti-status quo preferences. Of course leadership preferences are not the only factors that determine the extent to which the status quo is altered: sometimes a revolution is led by a reluctant leader, and sometimes a leader has frustrated revolutionary aspirations. Still, the general tendency of revolutionary leaders towards ambition further distinguishes them from non-revolutionary leaders, even non-revolutionary leaders who have seized office violently.

Risk-tolerant, ambitious leaders are aggressive and conflict-prone

The risk-tolerance and ambition of revolutionary leaders tends to make the states they lead more aggressive and likely to instigate international conflict than non-revolutionary states, for three mutually reinforcing reasons. First, as discussed earlier, risk-tolerance leads to aggression in international affairs because it increases the perceived pay-off of risky gambles.[22] Thus a leader with high risk-tolerance is likely to view armed conflict more favorably as a way to settle a dispute. Revolutionaries tend to have that kind of risk-tolerance.

Second, the ambitious goals of revolutionary leaders also contribute to aggression, in a slightly different way. Often a revolutionary leader's ambition for domestic changes requires or would be facilitated by change at the international level. Even when this is not the case, a desire for profound change at the domestic level is frequently associated with a desire to make further changes at the international level. Consequently, many (though not all) revolutionaries have ambitions that transcend domestic boundaries. Pan-Arabism, Marxist-Leninism, and Islamic Republicanism are examples of revolutionary ideologies that sought changes both inside and outside of the revolutionary state. Thus ambition at the domestic level often spills over to foreign policy.[23] This ambition increases the perceived benefits of conflict relative to its costs. Equivalently, it lowers the relative costs of conflict.

Third, revolutionary leaders are less likely to be constrained by domestic constraints than non-revolutionary leaders. As part of the revolutionary process, the domestic political landscape is overturned and replaced by a new order.[24] This process typically undermines institutional constraints on the executive, providing the leader with more scope to pursue his preferences and eliminate or discount dissent from other political elites. Consequently, a potential obstacle to instigating international conflict is removed, which raises the salience of the leader's preferences and risk-tolerance. The lack of domestic constraints also leads to greater opportunities for strategic miscalculation, for it is unlikely that anyone outside of the revolutionaries' inner circle can provide independent input on decisions and help the government avoid groupthink.[25]

This is not to argue that there is a single "revolutionary personality" or psychology that such leaders always have, but rather that the political dynamics of revolutions select certain leadership characteristics more frequently than a non-revolutionary process. Every revolution

---

[22] D. Byman and K. Pollack, 2001; J. Fearon, 1995; S. Rosen, 2007.
[23] D. Byman and K. Pollack, 2001.
[24] S. Huntington, 1968; T. Skocpol, 1979; S. Walt, 1996.
[25] S. Walt, 1996.

has its own particular political dynamics, and not all of them produce leaders with the characteristics just described. Nor are revolutions the only way in which leaders with these attributes can come to power. Nonetheless, on average there is a tendency in revolutionary politics to select ambitious and risk-tolerant leaders.

Revolutions will vary in the degree to which they increase the state's propensity to instigate international conflict. For instance, revolutions are breeding grounds for personalist dictatorships, and research suggests that personalist dictatorships are especially likely to engage in international conflict.[26] Other revolutionary governments, however, appear to be no more aggressive than non-revolutionary states. For instance, the democratizing revolutions that occurred in Russia and Eastern Europe at the end of the Cold War are at least partial exceptions to the general pattern. Identifying precisely which types of post-revolutionary governments are most conflict-prone is a topic of ongoing research.[27] For the purposes of this book, I simply argue that revolutions increase the state's propensity to instigate conflict on average. This leads to the first hypothesis:

> H1: States led by revolutionary governments are more likely to instigate militarized interstate disputes than comparable non-revolutionary governments.

This hypothesis should be situated in the broader theoretical context. In his seminal book *Revolution and War*, Stephen Walt theorizes the relationship between revolution and international conflict as arising from changes in the "balance of threat" between states. He emphasizes causal mechanisms based on international systemic factors. By contrast, I identify a set of causal mechanisms arising from domestic politics. However, nothing in the theory presented here is inconsistent with the idea that systemic factors also connect revolution and war. In terms of how revolution is linked to *oil* and international conflict, the key point is that domestic politics are an essential cause of revolutionary states' elevated propensity for international conflict. On this point, Walt clearly agrees.[28] Other scholars

---

[26] J. Colgan and J. Weeks, 2011; J. Weeks, 2012.

[27] J. Colgan and J. Weeks, 2011.

[28] Walt dismisses simplistic arguments based on the aggressiveness of revolutionary states (1996: 10–12), but he also argues that domestic politics

are perhaps even more comfortable with the notion that revolutionary states are aggressive, and that this is an outgrowth of their monadic characteristics.[29]

Oil interacts with revolutionary politics to increase state aggression

The third link in the chain of my argument is that the net effect of oil income is to amplify the effect of a domestic revolution, thereby generating petro-aggression.

Oil, the resource curse, and domestic political accountability

To understand the impact of oil on a petrostate's foreign policy, one has to start with the "resource curse" at the domestic level.[30] The symptoms of the resource curse include the prevalence of authoritarianism, widespread clientelism, and increased frequency of civil conflict. One theme that runs through the literature on the resource curse is the idea that oil erodes domestic political accountability. Political accountability is the degree to which domestic audiences can punish a leader or even remove him from office; political autonomy is the degree to which a leader is free from accountability.

Consider first the prevalence of authoritarianism in petrostates. In a seminal article, Michael Ross argued that oil hinders democracy, and many other studies reached a similar conclusion.[31] Inevitably, some scholars disagree,[32] while others argue that oil has an ambiguous effect on democracy.[33] Even among those who agree that oil hinders democracy, there is considerable debate about the causal mechanisms through which oil has its effect. Still, most scholars believe that the resource curse is real, and that it occurs principally because of *rentier*

---

are a key reason that revolutionary states are aggressive and engage in international conflict (see especially, pp. 38, 65–70, 223–225).

[29] A. Enterline, 1998; T. Gurr, 1988; Z. Maoz, 1996; T. Skocpol, 1988; R. Snyder, 1999.

[30] Recall that in Chapter 1, I defined a petrostate as one in which revenues from net oil exports constitute at least 10 percent of gross domestic product.

[31] D. Bearce and J. Laks Hutnick, 2011; E. Bellin, 2004; E. Goldberg *et al.*, 2008; N. Jensen and L. Wantchekon, 2004; M. Ross, 2001, 2012; J. Ulfelder, 2007.

[32] D. Acemoglu *et al.*, 2008; S. Haber and V. Menaldo, 2011.

[33] T. Dunning, 2008; M. Herb, 2004.

politics.[34] Rentier politics occur when resource-rich governments use low tax rates, high public spending, and widespread patronage to relieve pressures for political accountability.

A second, related symptom of the resource curse is widespread patronage or political clientelism. Clientelism is the prevalence of relationships based on political subordination in exchange for material rewards.[35] Like authoritarianism, clientelism reduces the domestic accountability of the leader of the state, by eliminating the incentives and opportunities for political opposition. One especially important expression of clientelism is in the provision of public sector employment by patrons for their clients.[36] These soft public sector jobs frequently require relatively little work in relation to the salary, thus providing a significant material incentive for clients to retain them. Of course clientelism occurs even in non-petrostates, but it is more pervasive when a leader has large oil revenues with which to purchase political support.

The third symptom of the resource curse is an increased frequency of civil wars, or more broadly, domestic armed conflicts. Oil is believed to promote civil war in three ways: by providing finances to warring parties, especially rebels; by increasing the financial value of victory in a civil war, and thus the motivation to fight; and by encouraging corruption and weakening the institutions of the state.[37] A large and growing body of scholarly literature provides evidence that resource-exporting states, especially oil-exporting ones, are more likely to experience civil war than non-resource exporting states.[38] Armed conflicts in Nigeria, Angola, Sudan, Indonesia, Algeria, and elsewhere are consistent with this claim.

---

[34] E. Bellin, 2004; E. Goldberg *et al.*, 2008; K. Morrison, 2009; M. Ross, 2012; J. Ulfelder, 2007. On the development of the concept of the rentier state, see H. Beblawi and G. Luciani, 1987; J. Crystal, 1990; T. Karl, 1997; H. Mahdavy, 1970.

[35] J. Fox, 1994; H. Kitschelt and S. Wilkinson, 2007; S. Stokes in C. Boix and S. Stokes, 2007.

[36] J. Colgan, 2011a; M. Herb, 1999; S. Hertog, 2010; T. Karl, 1997; P. Vicente and L. Wantchekon, 2009.

[37] P. Le Billon, 2007.

[38] P. Collier and A. Hoeffler, 2004; J. Fearon and D. Laitin, 2003; H. Hegre and N. Sambanis, 2006; M. Kaldor *et al.*, 2007; M. Ross, 2006, 2012. But also see B. Smith, 2004.

Despite frequent conflicts, rebels rarely succeed in violently overthrowing a petrostate regime.[39] This is important because it resolves an apparent paradox stemming from the resource curse literature: oil generates stability in one sense (i.e., persistent autocratic regimes) while simultaneously generating instability in another sense (i.e., frequent violent rebellions). One might expect that one form of instability would lead to the other, but this is not so, because the domestic conflicts rarely cost the incumbent leaders their positions. Thus even in the face of frequent domestic conflicts, multiple researchers have found that petrostate leaders tend to have greater domestic political autonomy and longer tenure in office than those in comparable non-petrostates.[40] The fact that rebels rarely succeed in overthrowing petrostate regimes also means revolutions are not necessarily more frequent in petrostates, as discussed later.

In sum, the idea that oil reduces domestic political accountability is backed by a considerable body of evidence. Still, the erosion of political accountability in petrostates should not be mistaken for a complete lack of opposition. Some active opposition can exist even in states with low political accountability; the latter simply means that the opposition is unable to remove the leader from power or significantly affect the constituency that supports the regime. From the leader's perspective, the first step is to secure and maintain a core constituency that is of sufficient size to maintain power (what Bueno de Mesquita *et al.* call a "winning coalition"[41]). If, in addition to being of sufficient size, the core constituency is highly satisfied, then the leader has considerable autonomy in selecting his policies. Under such conditions, the leader can act with relatively little fear of the consequences of his choices, because the high satisfaction within his core constituency creates a cushion of political support. A leader without such a cushion of support constantly fears taking a decision that is politically unpopular, which might cost him the support of his core constituency.

---

[39] J. Colgan, "Oil, Domestic Conflict, and Opportunities for Democratization."
[40] J. Colgan, 2011a; K. Morrison, 2009; M. Ross, 2012; B. Smith, 2004; see also Chapter 4.
[41] B. Bueno de Mesquita *et al.*, 2004.

Effects of oil on the costs of international conflict

I theorize that oil income has two effects on petrostates' foreign policy behavior, with opposite implications for international conflict. On one hand, oil lowers the risks for the leader of domestic punishment for aggressive foreign policy; on the other, oil increases the economic incentives to maintain peaceful, stable trade relationships with the international community.

The first mechanism increases the potential for aggression and thus the probability of international conflict. As just discussed, one of the special properties of oil income is that it is easily centralized and controlled by the state. This gives the leader an independent source of financial resources, which in turn generates political resources.[42] The leader of a petrostate has a greater degree of policy autonomy than a non-petrostate leader, on average, because of his greater ability to redistribute income to buy political support.[43] Political autonomy allows the leader to take decisions that differ from the preferences of the domestic audience. Consequently, the leader of a petrostate faces a lower risk of being removed from office or otherwise punished for potentially unpopular foreign policy adventurism.[44]

The lower risk of leader punishment due to international conflict is evident in a number of petrostates. Saddam Hussein led his country into a costly and bloody war with Iran that ended after eight years in little gain for either side; yet he was not removed from office. Even after he launched another unsuccessful war against Kuwait in 1990, he continued to maintain power for years until he was finally

---

[42] As Robert Dahl (1961) observed more than a generation ago, the question of "who governs?" depends greatly on who has access to resources; the individual's resources tends to be proportional to his political influence, or at least the potential for it.

[43] T. Dunning, 2008; T. Karl, 1997; K. Morrison, 2009; M. Ross, 2001, 2012.

[44] The argument focuses on the level of domestic political risk that a leader faces for seeking to alter the international status quo (i.e., for instigating a questionable international conflict, especially if it results in failure), but some leaders face the opposite risk: i.e., being too conflict-averse and failing to act on the aggressive preferences of the domestic audience. It is true that both of these risks can exist, but my argument assumes that the political risks associated with trying to alter the status quo (e.g., by instigating a war) are typically greater than the risks associated with maintaining the status quo (e.g., by keeping the peace).

removed, not by domestic opposition, but by an external invading force. Ayatollah Khomeini also faced significant opposition to his policy of continued warfare in the Iran–Iraq War, especially after Iraq repeatedly offered to settle the dispute, but he was able to isolate his domestic enemies and continue the war for years, at huge cost to his country. Libya's Muammar Qaddafi faced domestic opposition to his foreign policy aggression, which included an intermittent war with Chad, the support of at least thirty foreign insurgencies around the world, and several major acts of international terrorism. Despite the opposition to his adventurism, Qaddafi maintained power for over four decades. Indeed, in contrast to non-petrostates, there is no evidence that a leader has *ever* lost power in a petrostate due to risks taken or failure in a major international conflict. The theory being developed here suggests that these facts are explained, in part, by the greater political autonomy afforded to the leader by the state's oil resources.

On the other hand, oil income also generates incentives to avoid international conflict and maintain peace and stability. Oil-exporting petrostates face unusually strong economic incentives to maintain stable trade connections with the international community. In the short-term, there are direct financial opportunity costs to interrupting the trade of oil. For example, despite his fiery rhetoric against the United States, Venezuela's President Chávez has not followed through on his threats to cut off oil exports to the United States, most likely because he realizes how valuable those exports are to his government. Another potential cost of conflict is the loss of assets invested overseas that are frozen or seized after the outbreak of conflict, such as when the United States froze Iranian assets in 1980 during the embassy hostage crisis. Given the nature of petrostates' economies, they are likely to hold sizeable overseas assets (recently in the form of sovereign wealth funds). There are also long-term costs to conflict for petrostates: oil-consuming states respond to price volatility with energy diversification (e.g., nuclear, coal) and investment in alternative fuels.[45]

---

[45] A. Cheon and J. Urpelainen, 2012; A. Goldthau and J. Witte, 2011; G. Ikenberry, 1986. Oil must compete with other energy alternatives in the long run, and international conflict drives up the cost of oil relative to its competitors. This was evident in the change in the energy consumption profile of the United States and other Western states in the 1970s, when questions about the cost and reliability of oil supply were being raised: oil lost market

For these reasons, petrostates face significant incentives to maintain international peace and stability, and to prevent the interruption of oil exports.[46]

Oil income therefore creates opposing incentives for petrostate leaders: it makes international conflict both more and less costly than for non-petrostates. The net effect of these incentives is theoretically ambiguous, and depends on the magnitude of the incentives, which in turn depends on the nature of the petrostate's domestic politics. Consequently, sorting out the relative likelihood of petrostates to instigate conflict is an empirical challenge that I take on in subsequent chapters, especially Chapter 4.

We now come to the heart of the argument. Even though the effect of oil on its own is theoretically ambiguous, its interaction with revolutionary politics is not. Thus far, the effects of oil and revolution on a state's level of aggression have been considered separately. I now turn to their interaction, which offers a new insight and a clear testable hypothesis.

The interaction of oil income and revolutionary government is crucial

From a leader's perspective, the costs of state conflict can be divided into two categories: the costs to the state, and the costs to the leader himself.[47] Oil increases one of those costs (to the state), but lowers the other (the risk to the leader). The difference in the type of cost, and who bears it, generates an important asymmetry. One effect of oil is to raise the cost of conflict to the state as a whole, due to the prospect of disrupted oil sales. That increased cost of conflict is present regardless of whether the petrostate is revolutionary. The effect is to make

share to other energy sources, and was essentially eliminated from use for electricity generation. At least for large exporters of oil, interruptions of supply caused by international conflict raise the risk that consuming nations will permanently alter their consumption patterns away from oil.

[46] The expectation that oil exports create incentives for petrostates to avoid international conflict touches on the larger issue of the general relationship between trade and conflict. The argument here is consistent with those scholars (e.g., C. Gelpi and J. Greico, 2008; R. Keohane and J. Nye, 1977; J. O'Neal and B. Russett, 2001; B. Russett, 1994) who argue that trade has a pacifying effect, though this effect is disputed by some (K. Barbieri, 2005).

[47] G. Chiozza and H. Goemans, 2011; H. Goemans, 2000.

fighting less attractive and thereby lower the probability of conflict. Consequently, this effect of oil is independent, and does not interact with the effect of a domestic revolution.

By contrast, the effect that oil has in lowering the risks to the leader, namely by reducing the risk of domestic punishment for instigating a conflict (especially an unsuccessful one), interacts significantly with the domestic politics of the state. In part, the effect of oil depends on the leader's ambition and preferences with regard to the existing status quo, which in turn are systematically affected by whether the leader is a revolutionary. If the leader actively seeks to revise the status quo, the costs of fighting increase in salience. The demand for a revision of the status quo compels both sides (the leader's state and its adversary) to re-evaluate the situation.[48] The process of this re-evaluation generates opportunities for uncertainty and miscalculation, thereby raising the potential for international conflict. Thus the costs of fighting are more important when the old political bargain is no longer acceptable to at least one side. The effect that oil has in reducing those costs has a greater impact on behavior when conflict is a real possibility. Conversely, if the leaders have no interest in revising the status quo, the costs of conflict do not much matter.

There is also a deeper interaction between oil and revolutionary government. Specifically, the effect of oil interacts with the pre-existing risks to the leader's position in power. In general, revolutionary leaders face a higher risk of being unseated from power than non-revolutionary leaders do.[49] Oil income allows the leader to reduce that risk (by funding patronage and repression), and the effect of the leader's oil money depends on the extent of the pre-existing risk. In general, the effect is larger for revolutionaries: when a leader has a high initial risk of being deposed, and thus is surrounded by potential enemies, the marginal utility of being able to purchase the political support of some of those

---

[48] In terms of Fearon's bargaining model, this means each state implicitly or explicitly re-estimates all of the relevant parameters in the bargaining space (e.g., its probability of victory, its estimation of the other side's resolve, its own resolve, etc.).

[49] Revolutionary leaders face a higher risk of being overthrown despite (or perhaps because of) the fact that institutional constraints on the executive have typically been swept away in the revolution. The nature of a revolution means that the leader took power outside of any regularized process, which invites others to do the same.

enemies is higher than when the leader has few significant domestic political enemies.

My claim here is central to the argument. The effect of oil does not simply add to the effect of revolutionary politics; rather, the two effects interact in a non-additive fashion to reduce the leader's costs of conflict. The non-additive effect could take any of several different mathematical forms. I only assume that the marginal benefit of oil to the leader, in terms of reducing his risk of being deposed, increases as the *ex ante* risk of being deposed increases. This seems plausible. A leader who has few significant domestic political enemies and prefers status quo policies is already relatively safe, meaning that the marginal benefit of having oil income is small. By contrast, a revolutionary leader who faces multiple potential challengers to his leadership benefits greatly from having oil income to shore up his political support. Instigating an international conflict magnifies the risk of being deposed, and oil money reduces that risk. Accordingly, the conflict-enhancing effect of oil will be higher in revolutionary petrostates than in non-revolutionary petrostates.

An historical example might help illustrate the interaction between oil and revolutionary politics. When Iran and Iraq went to war in the 1980s, there came a point in 1981–1982 when Khomeini and his fellow revolutionaries had to decide whether to end the war or press the attack by invading Iraqi territory. The revolutionaries decided to press the attack. As I argue in Chapter 7, the revolutionary regime's hold on power in Iran at this point was still contested domestically. If the war with Iraq went badly, the regime might have been toppled. Yet the risk to the regime was greatly reduced by Khomeini's use of the state's oil income to fund patronage and consolidate power, even as Iran fought Iraq. Khomeini acknowledged that the oil industry was the lifeblood of the revolution, and could fail without it.[50] Thus, in Iran, oil facilitated the revolutionaries' ambitions, which led to (further) conflict. By contrast, Saudi leaders reacted very differently in 1990–1991 when Iraq invaded Kuwait and attacked a Saudi port. After the US-led coalition pushed the Iraqi armies back, the Saudi king might have pressed for a counter-attack into Iraqi territory, just as the Iranians did in 1982. Yet the king did not do so. Though the oil income of Saudi Arabia provided the king with significant domestic political autonomy, which

---

[50] R. Ramazani, 1987: 206–207.

would have reduced the domestic risks associated with such a conflict, those reduced risks were simply not relevant because of the Saudi leader's baseline preferences and political context.

Consequently, my theory suggests three implications for the costs of international conflict. First, the economic incentives to maintain stable international economic connections will increase the costs of conflict for petrostates relative to non-petrostates. Second, the reduced risk of domestic punishment will tend to lower the costs of conflict for (the leaders of) petrostates relative to (the leaders of) non-petrostates. And third, the magnitude of this latter effect will be larger for states led by revolutionary leaders than those led by non-revolutionary leaders. This third implication suggests the following hypothesis:[51]

> H2: The difference between revolutionary and non-revolutionary governments, in terms of their propensity to instigate international conflict, will be greater in petrostates than in non-petrostates.

As noted earlier, the net effect of oil is theoretically ambiguous, and thus some additional premise is needed to anchor any hypotheses about the relative propensity of petrostates for instigating international conflict. To supply such a premise, I make an empirical conjecture, one that I subsequently test (and verify) in Chapter 4. The conjecture is the following: in a non-revolutionary petrostate, the effects of oil income on a state's propensity for conflict are of roughly equal magnitude and thus tend to cancel each other out. Given this conjecture, two more predictions can be made. First, among non-revolutionary states, petrostates will instigate international conflict at roughly the same rate as non-petrostates. Second, among revolutionary states, petrostates will instigate international conflict at a higher rate than non-petrostates. In petro-revolutionary states, the combination of aggressive preferences and the reduced risk of domestic punishment makes it especially likely that the leader will decide to instigate an international conflict.

The theory thus generates hypotheses that are testable using empirical evidence. Figure 2.1 illustrates the empirical predictions to be tested.

---

[51] Mathematically, if the conflict propensity of a non-revolutionary non-petrostate is NPNR; the propensity of a revolutionary non-petrostate is NPR; the propensity of a non-revolutionary petrostate is PNR; and the propensity of a revolutionary petrostate is PR; then the theory states that PR − PNR > NPR − NPNR.

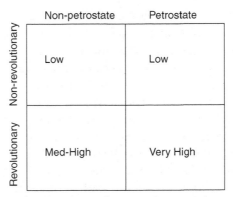

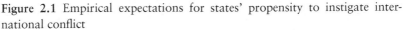

Figure 2.1 Empirical expectations for states' propensity to instigate international conflict

A quantitative example of the different effects of revolution and oil might help illustrate the expectations identified in Figure 2.1. Suppose that a non-revolutionary non-petrostate has a 10 percent chance of instigating international conflict with another state in a given period.[52] First, consider how oil income alone affects that propensity. For a non-revolutionary petrostate, oil increases the propensity by reducing the leader's risk of domestic punishment (thus adding X percent to the state's conflict propensity) but also decreases it by generating economic incentives for peaceful trade (thus decreasing it by Y percent). I find in Chapter 4 that these incentives are roughly offsetting, so X=Y. Thus the non-revolutionary petrostate has the same conflict propensity as the non-revolutionary, non-petrostate, namely 10 percent.

Revolutionary leaders are risk-tolerant and ambitious, so in this example suppose those leaders increase the state's base propensity for international conflict by 15 percentage points. A revolutionary non-petrostate then has a conflict-propensity of 25 percent. For a revolutionary petrostate, its conflict propensity is equal to 10 percent (the base value) + 15 percent (for being revolutionary) + Z (the increase due to the leader's lower risk of domestic punishment) − Y (the decrease due to economic incentives for peaceful trade). The interaction effect between oil and revolutionary government means that Z>X. So while

---

[52] This conflict rate (10 percent) is purely hypothetical.

the two effects of oil cancel each other out for a non-revolutionary petrostate ($X=Y$), that is not true in a revolutionary petrostate ($Z>Y$). The revolutionary petrostate has a conflict propensity equal to 25 percent plus some quantity ($Z-Y$), the exact magnitude of which must be identified empirically. Therefore, revolutionary petrostates have the highest conflict-propensity of any of the four state-types in Figure 2.1.

Questions arising from the theory

How do political constraints, accountability, and autonomy relate to each other?

One point that deserves emphasis is the relationship between political constraints, political accountability, and political autonomy. *Political constraints* have to do with the leader's ability to act on his preferences and execute his decisions. *Political accountability* is the degree to which domestic audiences can punish a leader or even remove him from office in reaction to his decisions. Political constraints are pre-hoc, whereas political accountability is post-hoc. A state's regime structure and institutions will largely determine the level of domestic political constraints on the executive, with autocrats generally facing fewer constraints than democratic leaders. Political accountability, however, can vary even between two states that have identical institutions and structures, as some leaders are more secure in their position due to the depth of political support from their constituencies.

In this book, I use the term *political autonomy* to refer to the degree to which a leader is free from political accountability. In common parlance, political autonomy might be used to refer to a leader's freedom from either constraints or accountability, but I use a more narrow definition focusing only on accountability. This distinction is important because, as discussed above, I theorize that oil income has a significant effect on political accountability (and thus autonomy). This is true even among autocracies: leaders of petrostates typically have less accountability than leaders of non-petrostates – and thus more autonomy.[53] So while a revolutionary leader in a non-petrostate might act

[53] J. Andersen and S. Aslaksen, n.d.; M. Ross, 2012. Research on the resource curse (e.g., M. Ross, 2001, 2012) also suggests that over the long-term, oil hinders democratic transitions, and thus affects the political constraints within a regime. However, I concentrate on the effect that oil has on weakening the

with the same freedom from constraints as a revolutionary leader in a petrostate, the theory states that the petrostate leader is likely to have greater political autonomy.

What other effects does oil have on a state's foreign policy?

The theory developed above focuses on how oil affects the costs of engaging in international conflict, but oil income has other effects that are relevant for foreign policy. For instance, the government's access to oil income makes elevated military spending common among petrostates.[54] This is likely to be especially evident in periods of high oil prices, when petrostates engage in spending sprees on military equipment and personnel.[55] Petrostates also commonly use foreign aid and commercial relationships to accomplish foreign policy objectives (sometimes known as "checkbook diplomacy"). A third common tendency is to use the state's finances to fund foreign insurgencies. All of these tendencies derive from the ease with which oil revenues can be centralized and controlled by the state's leadership, and thus spent on foreign policy.

In subsequent chapters, I pay considerable attention to these behaviors empirically. However, for the sake of theoretical parsimony I choose not to try to include them in my main theoretical argument. I acknowledge that these behaviors could affect the state's propensity for international conflict and further that they might vary depending on whether the state has a revolutionary government. Still, a theory that tries to capture every causal factor quickly becomes unwieldy. I focus on what I judge to be the principal causal factors.

How do oil and revolution affect states as targets of international conflict?

As indicated above, the primary dependent variable in this inquiry is a state's propensity to *instigate* conflicts. However, scholars have found that revolutionary governments are also more likely to be the

political accountability of a leader in order to emphasize that, even among autocracies, leaders of petrostates typically have less accountability than leaders of non-petrostates.
[54] S. Chan, 1980; M. Ross, 2001.   [55] J. Colgan, 2011c.

targets of international conflict than non-revolutionary governments, for two reasons. First, the domestic turmoil of revolutionary states can be perceived as weakness by predatory neighboring states,[56] creating a "window of opportunity" to attack and permanently alter the balance of power.[57] Second, neighboring states could justifiably fear that the revolutionary process would become a catalyst and model for groups in other countries, including their own.[58] Indeed, revolutionary states sometimes actively assist sub-national revolutionary groups in other countries by providing weapons, funding, training, and other assistance. Consequently, the neighboring states might try to limit the perceived success of the revolutionary government by altering the international status quo to the detriment of the revolutionary government. The attempted invasion of revolutionary Cuba by the United States at the Bay of Pigs, the Austrian invasion of revolutionary France, and Iraq's invasion of Iran in 1980 are examples of this type of behavior.

As discussed in Chapter 1, there is also reason to believe that petrostates have a higher propensity to be the target of attacks than non-petrostates. Resource competition could provide the incentive for predatory states to attack petrostates for their oil. One example of this type of aggression is Iraq's attack on Kuwait in 1990, and it is plausible that resource competition was a motivation in other conflicts as well. The empirical tests of this idea to date have not been perfect, but that does not mean that the idea is invalid.

While these considerations are important for the overall behavior of revolutionary states and petrostates, they do not conflict with the core theoretical propositions advanced in this chapter. Instead, they create a methodological challenge. If the analysis were to focus on the correlation between the independent variables and an overall measure of international conflict, the tendency for these states to be targets of attacks would generate "false positives" that do not actually indicate support for the theory proposed above. Consequently, the theory should be tested by examining only the conflicts in which a state acted as the aggressor. In practice, determining which party is the "aggressor" and which is the "target" is sometimes difficult to do.

[56] Note that "neighboring states" implies interaction between the states, not necessarily geographic contiguity.
[57] J. Goldstone, 1997; S. Walt, 1996.
[58] Z. Maoz, 1989, 1996; S. Walt, 1996.

Nonetheless, an appropriate methodology can ensure that even when some measurement error occurs, it does not generate a systematic bias in the analysis. The methodology used for doing so is described in Chapter 4.

Does oil income make a state more susceptible to revolution?

One might reasonably wonder whether oil causes revolutions, making revolutionary governments more likely to occur in petrostates than in non-petrostates. It is an intriguing question, and I explore it in Chapter 10. To preview the results, I find no evidence that this is the case. True, the high frequency of civil wars and domestic conflict in petrostates could plausibly generate opportunities for revolutions to occur. It turns out, however, that incumbent governments in petrostates rarely lose such conflicts, in the sense that they are overthrown by rebels. Moreover, a true revolution is much more than just a coup or rebellion; it requires significant upheaval of the fundamental political, economic, and social institutions of the state. Even if oil creates "greed" incentives for coups or civil wars, it does not necessarily follow that revolutions will be the result. My analysis in Chapter 10 suggests that revolutionary governments occur with more or less the same frequency in petrostates and non-petrostates.

3 | Evidence and research design

Propose theories which can be criticized ... but do not give up your theories too easily – not, at any rate, before you have critically examined your criticism.

– Karl Popper

Chapter 2 set out a theory of how oil and revolutionary governments generate international conflict. I now seek to test the theory against the empirical evidence. My strategy is to subject the hypothesized relationships to multiple tests using different kinds of evidence and methods. Subsequent chapters carry out the various tests.

This type of research design, using multiple empirical methods to test a theory, has produced some of the best research in political science.[1] The key benefit of using both quantitative and qualitative methods is that the strengths of each method tend to compensate for the weaknesses of the other.[2] For instance, the statistical analysis complements the qualitative case studies by revealing the relative importance of multiple variables, something that is nearly impossible to do convincingly using a small number of cases. The rigor of statistical methods also serves to guard against unintentional selection bias that can crop up relatively easily in case studies. The qualitative analyses, on the other hand, are much better at revealing the political processes and causal mechanisms that link the explanatory variables to the state's propensity for international conflict. Historical case studies also allow us to examine the evidence of whether and how decision-makers considered alternative options and "off-the-equilibrium-path" outcomes, other

---

[1] Some examples include C. Davis, 2003; A. Downes, 2008; V. Fortna, 2004, 2008; H. Goemans, 2000; S. Kalyvas, 2006; K. Schultz, 2001; B. Simmons, 1997 [1994]; M. Tomz, 2007. This list is far from comprehensive.
[2] D. Collier and H. Brady, 2004; A. George and A. Bennett, 2005; J. Gerring, 2012; G. Goertz and J. Mahoney, 2012; G. King et al., 1994; E. Lieberman, 2005.

than the ones they actually chose. Overall, a multi-method approach provides a parallax for theory-testing that is difficult to achieve using a single methodology. As Beth Simmons points out, "to choose one method to the exclusion of the other is like closing one eye and trying to make judgments about distance: it is easy to lose perspective."[3]

My method for the qualitative studies in Chapters 5–9 draws heavily upon the structured-focused case study approach described by Alexander George and Andrew Bennett.[4] As I describe below, I use a structured analysis with a standardized set of questions to explore the impact of the variables over time in each country. Wherever possible, my work draws on first-hand interviews and primary documents. I conducted interviews of policymakers, former government officials, ambassadors, academics, and others, especially in Venezuela, where I did field research. I also used primary documents such as the Iraqi files declassified after the fall of Saddam Hussein.[5]

This chapter describes the rationale for my research design choices. I address five issues in turn: operationalizing the dependent variable; identifying revolutions and how long they last; identifying petrostates; case selection for qualitative studies; and testing the causal mechanisms.

Operationalizing the dependent variable

The dependent variable in this inquiry is the state's aggressiveness and propensity to instigate international conflict. Aggression is a remarkably difficult concept to define precisely. The *Oxford English Dictionary* defines aggression as "the act or practice of attacking without provocation, especially beginning a quarrel or war." While this definition is somewhat helpful, it is not clear that an act must be totally unprovoked in order to be considered aggression. I use the term to mean a propensity to try to revise the status quo in ways that are

---

[3] B. Simmons, 1997 [1994]: 14.
[4] "The method is 'structured' in that the researcher writes general questions that reflect the research objective and that these questions are asked of each case under study to guide and standardize data collection ... The method is 'focused' in that it deals with only certain aspects of the historical cases examined." A. George and A. Bennett, 2005: 67.
[5] K. Woods *et al.*, 2011a, 2011b; also see Conflict Records Research Center at the National Defense University www.ndu.edu/inss/index.cfm?secID=101& pageID=4&type=section.

contrary to the preferences of other actors. Yet my meaning is probably made clearer by focusing on the observable indicators I use to measure the concept.

The statistical tests conducted in Chapter 4 focus primarily on the state's propensity to instigate militarized interstate disputes (MIDs). MIDs are a class of international events in which a state threatens, displays, or uses force against another state(s).[6] While there is heterogeneity in these events, from full-fledged wars to relatively minor disputes, they provide considerable information about a state's interstate conflicts. Most of the statistical models analyze all MIDs instigated by the state as the dependent variable, but some tests also focus exclusively on the "high-intensity" MIDs, namely those in which fatalities occurred. Theoretically, I expect the hypotheses developed in Chapter 2 to apply to both high- and low-intensity MIDs. The data sources and methods used to identify which state instigated a MID are described in Chapter 4.

In the qualitative studies in Chapters 5–9, other forms of aggressive foreign policy can be considered in addition to MIDs, thereby broadening our understanding of the dependent variable.[7] For example, states sometimes aid and abet foreign rebel or terrorist groups, by lending political or material support. These actions are typically viewed by foreign governments as a form of aggression. Other instruments of foreign policy aggression include hostile military mobilizations, support for transnational terrorism, nuclear weapons development, antagonistic diplomacy, and efforts to undermine important multilateral international organizations. Some of these factors, such as military mobilizations, are both indicators of foreign policy aggression in their own right, and indicators of the underlying risk of more severe forms of international conflict, such as outright war.

To gain further purchase on the question of a state's propensity for conflict, the qualitative studies also consider the state's bilateral relationships with other key states over time. A bilateral relationship is the product of multiple factors, of which the aggressiveness of the state in question is only one. Bilateral relationships are therefore an imprecise indicator of the aggressiveness of the state under analysis, but they are nonetheless useful. Accordingly, I map a state's

---

[6] F. Ghosn, *et al.* 2004.   [7] A. George and A. Bennett, 2005.

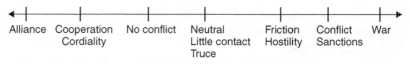

Figure 3.1 A spectrum of hostility in a bilateral relationship

relationships along a continuum, as indicated by Figure 3.1. When looking across a state's portfolio of bilateral relationships, states that have more alliances and generally cooperative relationships can be considered non-aggressive; states that have more hostile relationships, perhaps involving active conflict and war, can be considered aggressive. The continuum in Figure 3.1 is illustrative and necessarily imprecise. For instance, in some cases "friction" (i.e., an active low-level dispute) might indicate a worse bilateral relationship than "hostility" (i.e., a situation of declared animosity without an active dispute), but in other cases hostility might be worse than friction. In Chapters 5–9, I use the terms identified in Figure 3.1 wherever possible, but the task of summarizing bilateral relationships into a single label is rarely easy, and in some cases I use other terms, such as "complex."

Identifying revolutionary governments

In Chapter 2, I defined a revolutionary government as one that transforms the existing social, political, and economic relationships of the state by overthrowing or rejecting the principal existing institutions of society. The variable "revolutionary government" can be conceptualized as either a dichotomous or continuous variable. A continuous conceptualization of the variable allows some governments to be understood as more revolutionary than others, due to the greater upheaval and transformation they enact and experience in the political, economic, and social relationships of their society. However, identifying *how much* a government is revolutionary in comparison with other governments in other societies is a highly difficult task, one that demands deep knowledge of each particular case. For the large-N statistical analysis, which includes hundreds of observations, the practical difficulties involved in addressing the heterogeneity among revolutionary governments is simply too great. Therefore I operationalize revolutionary government as a dichotomous variable for the statistical analysis in Chapter 4. The coding procedures for the dataset that identifies revolutionary governments are discussed in that chapter. The same general coding procedures are used for the small-N historical cases. However, in the qualitative studies a more nuanced approach is possible. In Chapters 5–9, I classify state regimes as either non-, slightly-, moderately-, or highly revolutionary, based on the extent of upheaval and transformation of the society. Theoretically, one can expect that the more revolutionary the state's politics are, the more likely it is to subsequently instigate international conflict.

One important question for empirical analysis is: how long does a government stay revolutionary before it becomes non-revolutionary? A transition clearly occurs eventually: e.g., France obviously should not still be considered revolutionary today because of its revolution in 1789. Unfortunately, theory does not provide a clear, well-defined period of time in which a state is revolutionary.

For practical purposes, and for testing the theory, a revolutionary duration of some sort must be adopted. Walt offers one possible answer, arguing that

Many of the problems caused by a revolution arise from misjudging the balance of power, the intentions of others, and the probability of contagion or counterrevolution. From this perspective, "socialization" [i.e., declining international conflict] is simply the process by which both sides acquire greater information about each of these factors. As evidence accumulates, the uncertainty that permits exaggerated perceptions of threat to flourish declines proportionally.[8]

On this view, the "end" of a revolution's effect on the probability of international conflict is simply a matter of time, as evidence accumulates. In practice, scholars have simply picked an arbitrary duration for a revolution, such as five, ten, or fifteen years.[9] One limitation of this approach, however, is that it fails to explain the apparent variation between cases. For instance, the Khmer Rouge's revolutionary regime lasted just four years in Cambodia, whereas Qaddafi's most dramatic political changes did not start until he had been in power for almost a decade.

[8] S. Walt, 1996: 43.
[9] See A. Enterline, 1998; Z. Maoz, 1996; S. Walt, 1996, respectively.

By contrast, some scholars argue that the effect of a revolution on the state's propensity for conflict can persist for an extended period of time, and ends only when there is a shift in the domestic politics of the state. Halliday, for instance, argues that conflict between a revolutionary state and its neighbors is likely to continue "until or unless their domestic system so changes that the revolution itself, as defined within the country itself, is terminated."[10] Similarly but somewhat distinctly, Terhalle argues that the combination of domestic politics and revolutionary ideas is what explains the persistence of a revolution.[11] While this approach allows for greater variation in the duration of a revolution, it provides little guidance for *ex ante* expectations of that duration. On this view, the revolution ends when the revolution ends.

I take a different approach. For the sake of identifying a consistent rule, I treat the duration of a revolution as equal to the length of time that the original leader or leaders of a revolution control the state's executive office. Some revolutions generate multiple revolutionary leaders: e.g., Lenin and Stalin in Russia, Paz Estenssoro and Siles Zuazo in Bolivia, Saw Maung and Than Shwe in Myanmar, al-Bakr and Saddam Hussein in Iraq. I consider all of these men revolutionary leaders, because they played an important leadership role in their respective revolutions, even if they did not come to power immediately after it. Still, I restrict the term "revolutionary leader" to its senior leadership. Thus both Lenin and Stalin can be considered to have led the Russian Revolution, but not Khrushchev, even though the latter fought at a young age in the Red Army in the revolution.

My approach has two important virtues and at least one drawback. Its first virtue is that it is not based on a rigid and arbitrary length of time, and thus allows the duration to vary across different revolutions. Second, this approach is consistent with my theory's focus on the attributes of the revolutionary leader. Since I theorize revolutions as a selection mechanism for leaders with ambitious, risk-tolerant preferences, it makes sense to match the duration of the revolution to the duration of such leaders' tenure in office. However, the approach is not perfect, in part because it does not capture the speed with which revolutionary fervor cools, new institutions take root, and the politics of the state become normalized. It is possible that a government could

---

[10] F. Halliday, 1999: 139.   [11] M. Terhalle, 2009.

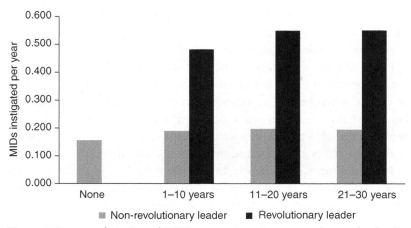

Figure 3.2 Rate of instigated MIDs over time since a revolution, by leader type

be considered revolutionary even after its original leader has left office, or be considered non-revolutionary before that time, especially if the leader is in office for many years.

Empirically, there is considerable justification for taking this leader-centered approach to the duration of a revolution.[12] Consider the number of militarized interstate disputes (MIDs) instigated by a state per year, as indicated in Figure 3.2. (The data underlying this graph are explained in Chapter 4.) Along the x-axis, the time since the state's last revolution is indicated; the y-axis indicates the average rate of MIDs instigated by the state per year. The black bars show the rate of MIDs instigated by revolutionary leaders that are still in office; the grey bars show the rate of MIDs instigated by states in which the original revolutionary leader is no longer in power. Thus as revolutionary leaders exit office, the state is re-classified as non-revolutionary, such that it contributes to the conflict rate represented by the grey bar rather than the black bar. For purposes of comparison, the rate of MIDs instigated by states that have never had a revolution is indicated on the far left-hand side. As the figure indicates, the rate of MIDs is consistently higher among revolutionary leaders than among non-revolutionary leaders. This is true even thirty years after the revolution. By contrast,

[12] J. Colgan, "Domestic Revolutionary Leaders and International Conflict," forthcoming.

after the revolutionary leader(s) have left office, a state returns to a much lower rate of instigated MIDs (as represented by the grey bars), even in the first decade after the revolution.

Figure 3.2 shows that revolutionary states' elevated propensity for conflict exists for as long as the original revolutionary leader(s) is in power, whether for five years or twenty-five years, but disappears once the leader is no longer in power. The evidence thus reveals that much of the effect of revolutions is contingent on the leader, rather than on a temporary disruption in international relationships that fades over time. Consequently, the focus on leaders provides a useful way to address the difficult question of when to consider a revolution "finished" in terms of its effect on aggressive foreign policy.

Identifying petrostates

The second key explanatory variable for my analysis is oil income. As with revolutionary government, one can operationalize this variable either continuously or dichotomously. Principally, I use a dichotomous identification: a state is considered a petrostate if its gross revenues from net oil exports constitute at least 10 percent of annual GDP in a given year. Chapter 4 has a table that identifies the 33 states that met this requirement for at least one year in the period 1945–2001. One benefit of conceptualizing petrostates in terms of their dependence on oil exports is that it is consistent with elements in my theory, such as the incentives that such export sales create for a state to avoid international conflict.

I also use four alternative definitions of petrostate. There are several ways to operationalize the concept; indeed, the best methodology has been the subject of some debate.[13] Two methods to generate a continuous rather than dichotomous variable are to measure the revenue from petroleum exports as a percentage of GDP, or to measure the per-capita revenue associated with oil exports; each has its advantages and disadvantages.[14] One disadvantage to these continuous measures is that they implicitly assume that a state that has a higher measured value is "more of a petrostate" than a state that has a lower value, and it is not

[13] M. Ross 2006.
[14] Variants of these measures have also been used: see K. Ramsay, 2011; M. Ross, 2001, 2012.

always clear this assumption is warranted.[15] Another approach is to focus on total oil production instead of net oil exports; thus I generate a third alternative measure using oil production as a percent of GDP (dichotomously, with a threshold of 10 percent). I generate a fourth measure by raising the threshold for my original measure to 20 percent, thereby excluding some of the more marginal cases. In the statistical analysis in Chapter 4, all of these alternative operationalizations are used to test the robustness of the empirical findings, and the results do not change materially regardless of which measure is used.

Some scholars raise concerns about using a measure of petrostate based on oil exports as a share of GDP. Ross, for instance, argues that such a measure tends to be biased towards poorer countries, which is inappropriate for some studies.[16] I agree that studies of whether oil inhibits democratization probably should not use this type of measure because low GDP per capita (as distinct from oil income) is correlated with autocracy.[17] However, for the analysis in this book, there is value in conceptualizing a petrostate in terms of its dependence on oil exports, and any income-bias is much less likely to be a problem. The correlation between GDP per capita and the onset of MIDs is weak and statistically insignificant (see Chapter 4). Moreover, to the extent that a bias in the measure exists, it would probably run against my argument: if petrostates are generally poor, they might be slightly less likely to instigate MIDs. Analytically, any disadvantage in this respect must be weighed against the benefits of conceptualizing petrostates in terms of export dependence (e.g., theory-consistency). Again, I conduct additional tests in Chapter 4 to ensure that my findings are robust to alternative definitions of petrostate.

One potentially interesting question is how annual changes in a state's oil income might impact the foreign behavior of the state. This is a subject that is considered in the chapters that follow, but is not emphasized in great detail. It is not clear that short-term variations

---

[15] For instance, Nigeria's oil exports are a higher percentage of GDP than in Venezuela, but its revenue per-capita is lower. Whichever measure is used, one state will be considered "more" of a petrostate than the other, but it is not clear either judgment is appropriate.

[16] M. Ross, 2012.

[17] I adopt Ross' measure in my own work on oil, civil conflict, and democratization: see J. Colgan, "Oil, Domestic Conflict, and Opportunities for Democratization."

in oil revenue have a significant causal role in affecting a petrostate's aggression and hence the probability of conflict. More likely, an increase in oil income in one period has effects (e.g., on domestic political dynamics, increased military expenditures) that alter the leader's incentives and state capabilities for many years afterward, even if the oil income subsequently goes down. It is therefore unlikely that there is a tight correlation between changes in oil revenues and the state's propensity for international conflict. Admittedly, variation in oil revenues could matter for petrostates' military expenditures, as petrostates tend to build military capacity during periods of high oil revenue.[18] But the actual outbreak of international conflicts, which after all involve at least two parties, is likely to be determined by many other factors besides one side's current level of oil revenues.

Moreover, even if we did want to study the impact of changes in oil revenue on petrostates' foreign policy, there is a significant endogeneity problem. The difficulty is that the causal arrow probably points at least as much in the reverse direction: wars and other forms of international conflict involving petrostates cause oil prices to react. At the very least, the endogeneity makes it problematic to investigate the extent to which short-term variations in oil revenue affect international conflict. To limit the inferential threat posed by endogeneity, my principal focus is on the medium- to long-term, to determine whether the state has sufficient oil revenues to be considered a petrostate. My aim is to be sensitive to how variations in oil revenues have affected petrostates' and their leaders' behavior, without exploring it in any great depth. The impact of variation in oil income on petrostates' foreign policy represents an intriguing area for future research.

Case selection for qualitative studies

Only a small number of in-depth historical studies of individual countries is feasible, so they must be chosen well. In the qualitative analyses my principal aim is to test the hypothesized causal mechanisms, because case studies have some important advantages in this respect relative to statistical analysis.[19] Consequently, I select "on the regression line" cases – that is, cases in which I expect there to be reasonable

---

[18] S. Chan, 1980; J. Colgan, 2011c.
[19] A. George and A. Bennett, 2005: 11–21.

correlation between the independent variables and the dependent variable – in order to test whether the correlation occurs as a result of a causal process or, alternatively, whether the correlation is spurious.[20] At the same time, I seek to exploit the variation in the independent variables and use congruence methods so as to test the strength of the correlation and reveal potentially falsifying evidence.

I selected country cases according to three criteria: geopolitical importance; geographic coverage; and variation in the revolutionary variable.[21] The first criterion suggests focusing on the petrostates that have large oil reserves and exports. I therefore selected the three revolutionary governments with the largest oil reserves and incomes: Iran (under Khomeini), Iraq (under Saddam), and Libya (under Qaddafi). I then paired each of these cases with a second case: the same state under the non-revolutionary government that preceded the first case. Thus the primary focus of each chapter is longitudinal analysis, comparing the behavior of a revolutionary government to other period(s) in the same state's history in which a non-revolutionary government was in power (e.g., comparing Iran under Khomeini to Iran under the Shah). While no comparison in social science is perfect, longitudinal analysis is highly useful because it holds constant many potentially confounding factors (e.g., regional context, history of border disputes, cultural heritage, geography).

I then selected two more countries. Saudi Arabia is an attractive country to study for three reasons. First, it is the state with the world's largest conventional oil reserves, and thus scores highly on the criterion of geopolitical importance. Second, Saudi Arabia did not have a revolutionary government at any point, and can thus be used as a point of comparison to the neighboring countries that did. Third, and perhaps most importantly, I seek to take advantage of the fact that Saudi Arabia and Libya are very well suited to a matched-pair comparison. As I describe in Chapter 9, the two countries were in many respects similar in the 1960s: each country was an economically underdeveloped, monarchical petrostate, with a small, homogeneously Muslim and Arab population. Analytically, the initial similarity of the two countries is

---

[20] A. George and A. Bennett, 2005: 34–35; E. Lieberman, 2005.
[21] See J. Mahoney and G. Goertz, 2006 on the value of selecting substantively important cases, which is consistent with my "geopolitical importance" criterion.

helpful in that it allows us to consider one country as having a received a "treatment" (a revolutionary government) and another country that did not receive the treatment. Given that controlled experiments are not possible in world politics, this paired-comparison is one of the strongest analytical tools available for social science. Comparing the political and foreign policy behavior of these two states is thus highly informative for my theory.

Finally, to test whether the argument has some portability outside of the Middle East, I selected Venezuela for in-depth study. Venezuela is a very different kind of case than Iraq, Iran, or Libya, because its revolutionary government – the so-called Bolivarian Revolution led by Hugo Chávez – is what I would characterize as moderately revolutionary. Consequently, I do not expect based on my theoretical argument that Venezuela under Chávez would instigate the same degree of international conflict that we see with the Middle Eastern petro-revolutionaries. Nonetheless, I do expect to observe indications of the same kinds of incentives and causal processes leading to aggressive foreign policy. Ideally my argument could be tested on a recent, highly revolutionary government (akin to Khomeini's, for example) in a petrostate outside of the Middle East, but history has not provided us with such a case (there are relatively few unambiguous petrostates outside of the Middle East). Nonetheless, the political dynamics of Venezuela provides a valuable opportunity to test my argument.

This research design emphasizes the variation in one of the key variables, revolutionary government, and places less emphasis on cross-national variation in the other variable, oil income. While ideally one could test both variables in an equally comprehensive fashion in the historical studies, I chose (somewhat reluctantly) not to do so in this project. In the book's conclusion, I suggest how future research could extend my work in this regard. Still, the general behavior of revolutionary states (in non-petrostates) has already been studied extensively by other scholars.[22] In this book, my principal interest is limited to the combination of oil-and-revolutionary politics. The quantitative analysis in Chapter 4 provides multiple tests as to whether and to what extent revolutionary governments have a different propensity for aggression when they emerge in petrostates, as compared to

---

[22] J. Goldstone, 1997; T. Gurr, 1988; Z. Maoz, 1996; T. Skocpol, 1988; R. Snyder, 1999; S. Walt, 1996.

non-petrostates. The historical case studies complement this analysis by illustrating *how* oil income plays a role in the foreign policy of these states, rather than *that* it does. Process-tracing within cases that have both a revolutionary government and oil income is especially valuable in this task. Therefore the qualitative analysis focuses solely on petrostates, and does not give equal weight to non-petrostates.

The other major reason for focusing my historical analyses on petrostates is to addresses one of the two central puzzles of this book: explaining the variation in conflict-propensity among petrostates. In addition to process-tracing, my method allows for some qualitative comparisons between cases. Comparisons between cases are often very challenging in qualitative analysis, because typically many variables change between cases rather than just the variable(s) of interest. My approach is to make comparisons between a revolutionary government and previous, non-revolutionary governments of the same petrostate. This type of within-country longitudinal analysis is highly useful because it holds constant many potentially confounding factors (e.g., regional context, cultural heritage, geography). Cross-national comparisons, by contrast, tend to produce weaker inferences because of the many differences associated with the shift in context. The only exception to this general approach is the cross-national comparison I make between Libya and Saudi Arabia, because of the extraordinarily good match in their characteristics as countries prior to the emergence of a revolutionary government in one of them (Libya). In sum, my historical analyses of petrostates has two goals: an understanding of the interaction between oil and revolutionary politics generated through process-tracing of petro-revolutionary cases; and an understanding of the role of revolutionary governments in contributing to the variation among petrostates. Cases are selected to match those goals.

One petrostate that I could have chosen based on my criteria is Russia. The collapse of the Soviet regime and the subsequent changes under Yeltsin are coded as revolutionary in my large-N statistical dataset. However, Russia's democratizing revolution did not put in power a particularly aggressive leader, and Russia is not well-described by the theory developed in Chapter 2 because of the particular characteristics of its revolution. Russia did have a major militarized conflict with Chechnya and engaged in several MIDs during the 1990s, but on the whole it was not markedly more prone to conflict than it was as the USSR in previous years. The hypothesized causal mechanisms, present in other revolutionary cases, were largely absent in Russia during the 1990s. Rather than empowering a leader with ambitious preferences and dismantling the institutional constraints on the executive, the revolution in Russia moved toward democratization and decentralization of power.[23] In addition, while many revolutionary governments (e.g., Iran) are aggressive in part because the domestic regimes they overthrew were perceived as too conciliatory with the United States and other foreign powers, the opposite was true in Russia. The Soviet Union was a classic Cold War antagonist in the international system, and by opposing it the new revolutionary government was thus disposed to *avoid* international disputes rather than instigate them. It was not until the nationalistic backlash in the late 1990s that Russia became more aggressive, leading to wars with both Chechnya and Georgia under Putin. Russia is thus an example of the heterogeneity among revolutionary states.[24] Consequently, I elected not to conduct an in-depth historical study of Russia. To avoid selection bias that would tilt the evidence in favor of my argument, however, Russia is included in the statistical analysis (along with all states 1945–2001).

Testing the causal mechanisms

An important strength of qualitative analysis is the investigation of causal mechanisms.[25] I adopt a structured-focused case study approach for the qualitative studies, which is designed to discipline the analysis and expose the theory to strong additional empirical tests. Each one of Chapters 5–9 has a standard structure. It begins with a historical narrative of a single country, focused on the key variables. As part of the narrative, I explicitly assess the value of each variable in each time period within the case, along with my predicted value for the dependent variable and its actual value. The systematic mapping of

---

[23] President Yeltsin's regime was quite centralized and even autocratic by Western standards. However, in comparison to the Communist regime that preceded it, Yeltsin's regime was considerably more democratic. Moreover, the personalization of power was considerably less severe under Yeltsin than it has become in Vladimir Putin's regime.

[24] The variation in the propensity of revolutionary states to instigate militarized international conflict is something I investigate elsewhere: see J. Colgan and J. Weeks, 2011.

[25] S. Van Evera, 1997; A. George and A. Bennett, 2005: 21.

the key variables over time allows for rigorous congruence testing.[26] I do not expect to see perfect congruence between predicted and actual values, given the general nature of the theory being tested, but there should be a high degree of correlation. The second part of each chapter then asks and tries to answer three standardized questions: (1) did the revolutionary government make the state more aggressive; (2) did oil generate incentives for aggression and conflict; and (3) did oil generate incentives to avoid aggression and conflict? These questions are designed to test whether there is evidence in support of the hypothesized causal mechanisms.

In Chapter 2, I theorized that revolutionary politics tends to select for risk-tolerant, ambitious leaders. I test this causal mechanism against the historical evidence by examining the process by which the leader rose to office and consolidated power. The leader's tendency to take risks, particularly prior to coming to power, is observed to gauge the leader's risk-tolerance. Attention is also paid to the leader's rivals, to investigate whether other leaders could have been selected and why they were not.

I also theorized that revolutionary government led to the removal of institutional and political constraints on the executive. The extent of domestic constraints is therefore investigated systematically. Two types of domestic constraints can exist to inhibit an executive from engaging in international conflict, even in autocracies: political "influencers" and procedural constraints. Political influencers are other actors within the society that have an impact on the scope and tenure of the leader's power, such as the royal family in Saudi Arabia. Conceptually, these actors are similar to "veto players," defined by George Tsebelis as "actors whose agreement is required for a change of the status quo."[27] The key difference is that influencers do not need to have a formal veto, only influence. Procedural constraints are those features of the institutional setting of the state that the leader needs to navigate in order to implement a desired foreign policy or action. The removal of these constraints enhances the leader's ability to make aggressive foreign policy decisions.

To test the role of domestic constraints, the historical evidence is examined for both procedural constraints and political influencers.

---

[26] S. Van Evera, 1997: 58–64; A. George and A. Bennett, 2005: Chapter 8.
[27] G. Tsebelis, 2002.

Various procedural constraints potentially affect the leader's ability to implement foreign policy decisions, including formal approval of major foreign policy decisions; military operations and oversight; budgetary and financial control; and executive oversight (i.e., procedures to evaluate the leader and/or limit his tenure). Table 3.1 illustrates the kind of questions that are used to evaluate the evidence with regard to these constraints.

The method for identifying political influencers is more difficult to specify in a standardized fashion. Still, the principal criteria for identifying an influencer is whether an actor (1) has the ability to impact the leader's abilities and tenure and (2) is independent in the sense that the leader cannot lightly remove the actor from political influence. Potential influencers include: legislative bodies (in democracies); the leader's family (in autocracies, especially monarchies); the senior military command; a deputy or vice-president; other members of a military junta; the cabinet or royal council; and political parties. To the extent that the leader requires approval or cooperation from other political actors and institutions to implement his preferences, his foreign policy is partially constrained.

Finally, the hypothesized causal mechanisms linking oil to foreign policy are tested qualitatively. The analysis focuses on the manner in which oil income was spent by petrostates. Domestically, to what extent was the oil money used to build political support and increase the leader's autonomy for taking foreign policy risks? Internationally, to what extent was oil money used to finance foreign aid, support foreign insurgents, and build alliances with the aim of revising the international status quo? Militarily, was oil money used to finance above-normal expenditure? To what extent was the military expenditure supportive of actual military capacity, and how much was it used for other purposes such as patronage, personal enrichment, and alliance-building? By answering these questions, the analysis tests the extent to which oil generates incentives for foreign policy aggression.

The conflict-reducing effect of oil is also tested against the historical evidence. Oil exports are hypothesized to provide a significant financial incentive to petrostates to avoid international conflict which interrupts export sales and other economic links. This hypothesis is tested by observing the extent to which the opportunity costs of international conflict associated with the oil exports are present in

Table 3.1 *Types of domestic procedural constraints on foreign policy*

Decision approval	Subject
Does the legislative body have to approve a declaration of war?	*War vote – parliament*
Does the cabinet or council have to approve a declaration of war?	*War vote – cabinet*
Military cooperation and oversight	
Does the leader have the ability to unilaterally appoint the senior military command?	*Appointment*
Does the leader have the ability to unilaterally dismiss the senior military command?	*Dismissal*
Does the leader have direct command over the military without intermediation by another political actor?	*Command*
Does any other body have oversight authority on the conduct of military operations?	*Oversight*
Budgetary and financial control	
Does the leader have principal responsibility for proposing the budget?	*Bud. Proposal*
By what mechanism does the leader's budget receive approval?	*Bud. Approval*
Do sub-national units such as states control much of the budget?	*Federalism*
Are the central bank and national financial reserves independently controlled?	*Central Bank*
Executive oversight	
Is the leader elected by popular vote?	*Election*
Is the leader subject to term limits?	*Term limits*
Can the leader be removed or impeached by another political body?	*Impeachment*
Can the leader be recalled through popular election?	*Popular Recall*

the leaders' calculations and dialogue. Although there are significant methodological challenges associated with determining leaders' beliefs and thoughts (as these are inherently unobservable, and public statements may not reflect them accurately), the cases nonetheless probe the plausibility of this mechanism empirically. This is done by identifying the incentives facing the leader, the extent to which those incentives were recognized, the information considered, the options available, and the actions taken.

Conclusion

The stage is now set to test the theory. The chapters that follow combine large-N statistical analysis with in-depth historical analysis of individual petrostates. This multi-pronged empirical strategy, combining both quantitative and qualitative methods, offers a stronger series of tests, and contributes more to theory development, than any one of them would have done alone.

4 | *Quantitative impact of oil and revolution on conflict*

Aside from military defense, there is no project of more central importance to national security and indeed independence as a sovereign nation
than energy security.

– Henry Kissinger

Chapter 2 argues that the combination of oil income and revolutionary politics generates systematic political incentives that increase a
state's aggressiveness and propensity to initiate international conflict,
a phenomenon I call *petro-aggression*. This chapter tests the argument
using statistical evidence. Specifically, the theoretical hypotheses to be
tested are:

H1: States led by revolutionary governments are more likely
to instigate militarized interstate disputes than comparable
non-revolutionary governments.

H2: The difference between revolutionary and non-revolutionary
governments, in terms of their propensity to instigate international
conflict, will be greater in petrostates than in non-petrostates.

To preview the findings, the empirical evidence supports both
hypotheses. Among non-petrostates, revolutionary governments are
about 50 percent more likely to instigate militarized interstate disputes
(MIDs) than non-revolutionary ones. And among petrostates, the difference is even more dramatic: petro-revolutionary governments are
about 250 percent more likely to instigate MIDs than non-revolutionary
ones.

This chapter is based primarily on an article I published in
International Organization.[1] While there are some new details and
additional robustness checks not published in that article, readers who
are familiar with that article might like to focus on the new material,

[1] J. Colgan, 2010.

most of which begins in the section called "Further evidence of a petrostate leader's political autonomy." Other readers, however, should
begin with the first section, which describes the methodology and data
sources used for the empirical testing. The second section provides the
core results. It also examines the role of non-oil natural resources in
international conflict, and finds a very different result. The third section presents the new evidence, which suggests that petro-revolutionary states have a lower probability of victory in international crises,
and an elevated propensity to be targeted for economic sanctions. A
short final section concludes.

Methodology

Dependent variable

As discussed in Chapter 3, the dependent variable is the onset of a
militarized interstate dispute (MID), with a special focus on whether
the state's role in a dispute was as an aggressive (revisionist) power
or a defensive (non-revisionist) power. These events have been coded
in the Correlates of War (COW) dataset (v.3.02), and the data are
widely used by scholars for studying international peace and conflict.[2]
(All data including the COW datasets have their limitations, so the
International Crisis Behavior data were used as a robustness check;
the results are broadly similar.) This analysis focuses on the onset of
MIDs, since the factors leading to dispute onset are not necessarily the
same as those that lead to dispute continuation or duration. The analysis begins by focusing on a monadic property – the state's propensity
for instigating MIDs – and then moves to a dyadic analysis.

Operationally, the main dependent variable is *Aggressor-MIDs*,
which is a count of the MID onsets in each year in which the state has
been coded as the aggressive state. This follows from the fact that one
of the major theoretical claims being tested is that revolutionary governments, especially petro-revolutionary governments, are aggressive
rather than simply being the targets of disputes. The term "aggressor"
is used in the same way that the terms "dissatisfied" or "revisionist"

---

[2] Dataset: F. Ghosn *et al.*, 2004. Data used by, e.g., B. Bueno de Mesquita *et al.*,
2004; K. Gleditsch *et al.*, 2008; E. Mansfield and J. Snyder, 2005; J. Weeks,
2008, 2012.

are used in the international relations literature.[3] As the codebook for the COW dataset explains:

Within the data, the revisionist variable attempts to indicate which states are dissatisfied with the existing status quo prior to the onset of a militarized interstate dispute. Both sides of a dispute can be considered revisionist if they both are dissatisfied with the status quo, but the state that openly attempts to challenge the pre-dispute condition by 1) making claims to territory, 2) attempting to overthrow a regime, or 3) declaring the intention not to abide by another state's policy, was coded as revisionist.[4]

Some variants of this dependent variable are also used, including *MIDs* (all MID onsets involving the state), and *Defender-MIDs* (MID onsets in which the state is coded as non-revisionist). The analysis uses the "revisionist" variable rather than the "side A" initiator, as the creators of the COW dataset specifically warn against this latter practice.[5] The time period of the analysis is 1946–2001, based on the availability of data.

My use of the COW revisionist variable to identifying the conflict instigator is consistent with my theoretical argument in Chapter 2, which defines the instigator as the state which seeks to revise the status quo. Nonetheless, other scholars sometimes use the "side A" indicator in the COW dataset, which indicates which state took the first military action, as a way of identifying the instigator. To ensure the robustness of my analysis, the "side A" indicator was used as an alternative to the principal dependent variable, and it did not materially change the results obtained below.

Explanatory variables

One problem that has plagued the research on revolution and war is that there is no widely-accepted universe of cases of revolution or revolutionary governments. Indeed, variations on the universe of cases are almost as numerous as the number of scholars who have examined the question.[6] This difficulty can lead to selection bias in the empirical

[3] R. Powell, 1999.
[4] From the Correlates of War data project, D. Jones *et al.*, 1996: 178.
[5] D. Jones *et al.*, 1996.
[6] Walt focuses his (1996) research on revolution and war on ten cases of "unambiguous" revolutions, though he suggests in later work (1997) that

testing of theoretical hypotheses, particularly if the analysis focuses on cases that are supportive of the theory. Avoiding this bias is facilitated by using a comprehensive domain of cases, subject to a well-specified identification procedure. Accordingly, a unique dataset was constructed to operationalize the variable, *Revolutionary Government*. Each state-year is given a dichotomous 1/0 coding, based on two principal criteria plus two exclusions. "Governments" and "leaders" are used interchangeably: for the purpose of this dataset, a government is equivalent to the period of time that a leader was continuously in power (e.g., four or eight years for a US president). Each observation in the dataset was coded independently at least twice, by different coders.[7] The dataset created new variables, but its basic structure was built on the Archigos database (v.2.8.1) of state leaders developed by Goemans *et al*. Greater detail on all of the coding rules is given elsewhere.[8]

The first criterion for the coding is whether the leader came to power through use of armed force, widespread popular demonstrations, or similar uprising (henceforth called an "irregular transition"). Two questions were used for this coding. First, has the individual leader used armed force against his own state at any time prior to coming to office as an integral part of his coming to national influence, and ultimately, state leadership? Second, were there mass demonstrations or uprisings, violent or non-violent, which were instrumental in deciding the outcome of the transition? If the answer to either of those questions was yes, the transition was coded as irregular. This specification implies that the rise of a leader such as Adolf Hitler, who led an attempted (but failed) coup to rise to national influence, and subsequently came to power through an election, is considered as an irregular transition and thus potentially revolutionary. The term "used armed force" requires leadership in the act; an individual who is a relatively low-level functionary of a revolution or coup is not considered to have led it. As discussed in Chapter 3, it is possible for more

---

many other cases exist. Skocpol focuses on only the "great" revolutions, which appears to limit the universe of cases to fewer than ten in the last 500 years. Snyder (1999) identifies twenty-four revolutions for his research. Maoz (1996) identifies even more.

[7] I am grateful to Summer Lopez, Thomas Scherer, and Lamis Abdel-Aziz for their assistance in this effort.

[8] See J. Colgan, 2012. A codebook is also available.

than one leader to have "led" an irregular transition, but the term is restricted to its senior leaders.

The second criterion is that once in power, the government must have implemented radical domestic changes for the purpose of transforming the organization of society, including its social, economic, and political institutions and practices. In all cases, the focus is on domestic policy, rather than foreign policy. Seven possible areas of change have been identified: the selection and power of the national executive; the structure of property ownership; the relationship between state and religion; the state's political ideology and party structure; the official state name; the institutionalized status of ethnicity and gender; and the presence of a governing revolutionary council or committee. These areas were identified by studying the distinguishing characteristics of well-known revolutions.[9] Dramatic changes in policy in at least three of the seven categories are required for the government's policy to be considered revolutionary. For example, the Iranian Revolution in 1979 changed the relationship between state and religion (political dominance by clerics), the power and selection of the national executive (replacement of the monarchy by a clerical Supreme Leader), the status of women (inequality in inheritance law and segregation of the sexes), and the official name of the country (changed to the Islamic Republic of Iran), as well as many other changes. From a social science perspective, some of these categories are easier to objectively measure (e.g., changes in the official name of the state), others are more directly connected to the substantive changes of interest (e.g., a major change in the nature of the executive), but all of them provide information about the degree to which the state is transformed by the government. In all cases, changes are measured relative to the relevant prior government, rather than some external standard. Thus a change from monarchy to theocracy is equally revolutionary as a change from theocracy to monarchy.

Two types of governments are excluded from the revolutionary category even though they represent significant changes from the status quo. First, leaders who are installed by foreign powers after a major international war are not coded as revolutionary. States with foreign-installed leaders do not always have a free hand to control

---

[9] The revolutions used to determine these categories were: Iran (1979); Cuba (1959); China (1949); Ethiopia (1974); and Nicaragua (1979).

their state's policy, especially in the realm of foreign affairs; indeed, the behavior of such states has been shown to be considerably different from other states.[10] Second, the founding government of a state is not coded as revolutionary, simply because it is often difficult or impossible to judge the degree to which a founding government changes the institutions relative to a "prior government," because of changes in the territory's status, population, and/or geography.[11] When the two principal criteria are met, and neither of the exclusions applies, the state-year is coded as being a revolutionary government. All state-years are also coded with a dichotomous variable called *Ambiguous* to indicate borderline cases or cases where information was missing; this variable is used for robustness testing.

Table 4.1 provides a complete list of the domestic revolutions and their associated governments/leaders in the period 1946–2001. Note that readers are encouraged to see my more recent work for an updated list.[12]

The second key explanatory variable is whether the state is a petrostate. For this analysis, the state's gross revenues from net oil exports must constitute at least 10 percent of annual GDP to be classified as a petrostate in a given year. There are thirty-three states that met this requirement for at least one year, as listed in Table 4.2. Bahrain and Brunei are excluded due to their small size and lack of quality data, leaving thirty-one petrostates. This definition is used as the principal operationalization of the variables.

As discussed in Chapter 3, there are several alternative ways to operationalize the concept of "petrostate," including a variety of continuous measures. Four additional measures are used as well as the principal measure to test the robustness of the empirical findings, and the results do not change materially regardless of which measure is used.

The third and most important explanatory variable is the interaction between petrostate and the revolutionary government, called *Petro Revolution*. This is also a dichotomous variable, which takes the

[10] N. Lo *et al.*, 2008.

[11] Some colonies did have prior governments with similar territorial boundaries as the states that replaced them, but this is frequently not the case.

[12] J. Colgan, 2012. The principal difference in the updated list is that some leaders from "divided" countries (e.g., Czechoslovakia, Yemen) are included, even though they were omitted in my initial analysis (and hence Table 4.1).

Table 4.1 *List of revolutions and associated governments/leaders*

Country	Leader	Year	Country	Leader	Year
Afghanistan	Taraki	1978	Costa Rica	Figueres Ferrer	1953
Afghanistan	B. Rabbani	1992	Cuba	Castro	1959
Afghanistan	Mullah Omar	1996	DR Congo	Mobutu	1965
Albania	Berisha	1992	Egypt	Naguib (Nasser, Sadat)	1952
Algeria	Boumedienne	1965	El Salvador	Majano Ramos (Duarte)	1979
Argentina	Peron	1946	Ethiopia	Banti (Marriam)	1974
Bangladesh	Ziaur Rahman	1977	Ethiopia	Meles Zenawi	1991
Benin	Kerekou	1972	Ghana	Rawlings	1981
Bolivia	Paz Estenssoro (Zuazo)	1952	Greece	Papadopoulos	1967
Bolivia	Torres	1970	Guinea	Conte	1984
Brazil	Costa de Silva	1967	Guinea-Bissau	Vieira	1980
Bulgaria	Mladenov (Popov)	1989	Hungary	Szuros (Antall)	1989
Burkina Faso	Sankara	1983	Iran	Khomeini (Rafsanjani)	1979
Burkina Faso	Campaore	1987	Iraq	Karrim Kassem	1958
Burundi	Micombero	1966	Iraq	Salem Aref	1963
Burundi	Bagaza	1976	Iraq	Al-Bakr (Saddam)	1968
Burundi	Buyoya	1987	Laos	Phomivan	1975
Cambodia	Pol Pot	1975	Liberia	Doe	1980
Chile	Pinochet	1973	Libya	Qaddafi	1969
China	Chiang Kai-shek	1946	Madagascar	Ratsiraka	1975
China	Mao Tse-Tung	1949	Madagascar	Zafy	1993
Comoros	Soilih	1975	Mali	Traore	1968
Comoros	Abdallah	1978	Mauritania	Ould Haidalla	1980
Congo	Ngouabi	1969	Myanmar	Ne Win	1962
Costa Rica	Leon Herrera	1948	Nicaragua	Daniel Ortega	1979

Table 4.1 (*cont.*)

Country	Leader	Year	Country	Leader	Year
Pakistan	Ayub Khan	1958	Sudan	Nimeiri	1969
Pakistan	Zia	1977	Sudan	Al-Bashir	1989
Panama	Torrijos Herrera	1968	Syria	Al-Hafiz (El-Atassi)	1963
Peru	Velasco Alvarado	1968	Thailand	Pibulsongkram	1946
Poland	Walesa	1990	Thailand	Sarit (Kittakachorn)	1958
Romania	Roman (Ion Iliescu)	1989	Uganda	Amin	1971
Russia	Yeltsin	1991	Uganda	Museveni	1986
Somalia	Siad Barre	1969	Venezuela	Hugo Chávez	1999
South Africa	Mandela	1994	Yugoslavia	Milosevic	1989
South Korea	Hee Park	1961	Zimbabwe	Mugabe	1980

Note: Some revolutionary governments that came to power prior to 1946 (e.g., those led by Franco and Hoxha) are included in the dataset but not shown in this list.

value of 1 when both *Petrostate* and *Revolutionary Government* are equal to 1; otherwise it is 0. The effect of introducing this variable into the regression is to isolate the specific political dynamics of revolutionary petrostates. The variable *Petrostate* thus focuses on the effect of oil politics in non-revolutionary petrostates.

In the data, there are 804 state-years in which *Petrostate* has a value of 1; of these, *Petro Revolution* has a value of 1 in 125 state-years and 0 in the remainder.[13] These observations are based on thirty-one petrostates over the time period 1946–2001. While there are five states that are classified as petrostates during the entire period under analysis, many states are classified as petrostates only for part of the time period under analysis, as oil is discovered or runs dry. This is an advantage, because it allows the variation over time within a state to be exploited for the purpose of analysis.

[13] Consequently, there are 679 non-revolutionary petrostate observations; 125 revolutionary petrostate observations; 4,844 non-revolutionary non-petrostate observations; and 759 revolutionary non-petrostate observations in the dataset.

Table 4.2 *List of petrostates*

State	Period as petrostate	Petro-revolutionary period
1 Qatar	1971–2001	
2 UAE	1971–2001	
3 Kuwait	1961–2001	
4 Bahrain	1971–2001**	
5 Saudi	1945–2001	
6 Oman	1971–2001	
7 Libya	1961–2001	1969–2001
8 Iran	1945–2001	1979–1996
9 Iraq	1945–2001	1958–2001
10 Syria	1974–1981, 1989–2001	****
11 Algeria	1962–2001	1966–1977
12 Yemen	1990–2001	
13 Russia	1991–2001*	1991–1999
14 Turkmenistan	1991–2001*	
15 Kazakhstan	1996–2001*	
16 Azerbaijan	1991–2001*	
17 Indonesia	1949–1990***	
18 Venezuela	1945–2001	1999–2001
19 Ecuador	1973–2001	
20 Trinidad and Tobago	1962–2001	
21 Nigeria	1961–2001	
22 Angola	1975–2001	
23 Gabon	1967–2001	
24 Equatorial Guinea	1993–2001	
25 Congo	1973–2001	1973–1976
26 Sudan	2000–2001	2000–2001****
27 Cameroon	1980–1998	
28 Brunei	1984–2001**	
29 Egypt	1977–1985	*1977–1980* ****
30 Malaysia	1979–1990***	
31 Norway	1980–2001***	
32 Mexico	1980–1983	
33 Tunisia	1974–1985***	

Notes: Time period of analysis is 1945–2001.

Italics indicate periods of revolutionary leadership that are classified as ambiguous.

* The USSR was initially excluded in the analysis (e.g., in Table 4.3), but was included in subsequent robustness checks, and the results did not materially change. ** State excluded from analysis due to missing data. *** The state did not qualify as a petrostate for all years in this period. **** Revolutionary periods when the state is not classified as a petrostate are not listed (e.g., Syria 1963–1969).

Control variables

The regression controls for a set of other variables that could affect a state's propensity to engage in MIDs, and have been used by previous work in the literature. The analysis includes (logged) population size, (logged) GDP per capita, and the number of contiguous territorial borders with other states, as basic characteristics of a state's likelihood to engage in international conflict. These variables proxy for the degree to which the state is capable of waging war (population, GDP) and the geographical likelihood of contact and thus friction with its neighbors (borders).[14]

Democratic peace theory suggests that democracies may be less inclined to engage in revisionist MIDs than other kinds of governments.[15] Modern theorists of the democratic peace argue that this tendency is strongest (and perhaps only present) in a dyad of two democracies.[16] However, the basic argument by Immanuel Kant is that, in a republican regime, "those who would have to decide to undergo all the deprivations of war will very much hesitate to start such an evil game."[17] This suggests that democracies will be less likely to engage in war in general, regardless of their opponent. To address this possibility, the state's composite Polity IV score is included as a control variable. (As a robustness check, a dichotomous variable for democracy was also used.[18]) In the dyadic analysis, a dichotomous variable is used that is positive only when the dyad contains two democracies.

Major powers in the international system tend to take a much more active role than other kinds of states, even accounting for their large GDP and population sizes. This is addressed by introducing a dichotomous variable, *Major Power*, following the COW dataset's specification. A dummy variable was also included for the Cold War period (pre-1990), which may have altered the environment for international disputes.

[14] P. Diehl, 1985; A. Enterline, 1998; K. Gleditsch *et al.*, 2008; B. Lai and D. Slater, 2006.
[15] M. Doyle, 1986; E. Gartzke, 2000, 2007; J. O'Neal and B. Russett, 2001.
[16] B. Bueno de Mesquita *et al.*, 2004; C. Lipson, 2003; Z. Maoz and B. Russett, 1993.
[17] I. Kant, quoted in J. Levy, 1988: 658.
[18] For the dichotomous measure, the state is coded as a democracy if its composite Polity IV score is above +6 on the –10 to +10 scale; otherwise it is a non-democracy.

Some cultural dimensions are included. Huntington contends that religious and cultural factors shape the fault lines and disputes in the international system, and that Islamic countries in particular have "bloody borders" and "bloody innards" because they have cultural and demographic features that make them violence-prone.[19] I do not seek to pass judgment on this claim, but to account for its possible effect, the Muslim percentage of the population is used as a control variable. I emphasize that the inclusion of this variable does not mean that I assume Islam is inherently violent; the point of inserting the variable in the regression model is to simply control for potential correlation. Each analysis also includes dummy variables for each geographical region. Eight regions were used, similar to the World Bank's classification: North America; Latin America; Western Europe; Eurasia and Central Asia; Middle East and North Africa; South Asia; Sub-Saharan Africa; East Asia and Pacific.

Finally, it has become standard practice in the literature to include a statistical control for temporal dependence, whereby some countries engage in multiple disputes over time: "war begets war." Following Beck *et al.*, this analysis includes a natural spline function (with three knots) of the number of years that have elapsed since the country last experienced a MID.[20] This spline function is included in all of the regression models, although the estimates of these parameters are not shown in the tables.

Data sources

Data on states' borders, population, and major power status come from the COW dataset.[21] Fearon and Laitin's (2003) dataset provides the GDP per capita data. The World Bank's World Development Indicators was used to provide GDP per capita data where they are missing from the Fearon and Laitin data. Data on states' religious make-up are based on the World Christian Database. The measure of government type is based on the Polity IV dataset, as is the initial year as a polity.[22] Data on oil revenues, prices, and export volumes

---

[19] S. Huntington, 1996.
[20] N. Beck *et al.*, 1998; E. Mansfield and J. Snyder, 2005.
[21] F. Ghosn *et al.*, 2004.
[22] This score is a proxy for the regime's "degree of democracy"; it ranges from −10 to 10.

are drawn from the BP Statistical Review of World Energy and the US Energy Information Agency.

Considerable effort went into addressing missing data and ensuring that the dataset was as complete as possible. Reasonably high-quality data exist for most of the variables over this time period, such as population and state borders. However, other variables are more difficult. Only a single observation is available for the religious demographics of each country, but since this proportion is thought to change relatively slowly over time, this value is used for all years. The GDP per capita data from Fearon and Laitin are complete for 87 percent of the observations of interest, but are missing for some of the key states such as Iraq. Consequently the World Bank data were used as a complement, bringing the total completion rate to 94 percent. The two data sources are generally consistent: for state-years where observations exist from both sources, the two datasets are correlated at the 0.96 level. With regard to oil income, the data for years prior to 1965 are generally unavailable to the public. However, a special request was made for BP data for 1946–1964 to complement the public reports, and these additional data allowed the analysis to be extended through the full time period.[23]

The dataset on revolutionary governments contains 1,076 governments/leaders, containing data on all governments/leaders from 1946–2001 for 170 countries, for a total of 6,407 state-years.[24] As indicated, each observation was coded twice, by different coders, and reconciled so as to improve the accuracy and concept validity of the data. Of this total set, eighty-four governments/leaders or about 7 percent are coded as revolutionary.[25]

Empirical results

Table 4.3 shows the results of the analysis of states' propensities for international military conflict (MIDs). A random-effects Poisson

[23] I thank Peter Nolan for his assistance in obtaining these data.
[24] Countries that do not have a Polity score are not coded. The "number of leaders" reported counts leaders who have come to office at two distinct times (with at least a year out of office) as two leaders; the number of unique leaders is slightly smaller.
[25] Under a highly restrictive secondary definition, less than 1 percent of leaders are coded as unambiguously revolutionary. See the discussion under "Robustness Checks" for use of this definition.

Table 4.3 *International disputes by state type – monadic regression analysis*

	Model 1	Model 2	Model 3	Model 4	Model 5
DV: Aggressor-MIDs	No Revol	Base	Base FE	Petro Base	Petro FE
Revolutionary Govt		**0.443**	**0.432**	**0.286**	**0.289**
		0.089	0.094	0.099	0.104
Petrostate				**–0.433**	**–0.328**
				0.158	0.179
Petro Revolution				**0.707**	**0.660**
				0.203	0.212
GDP / cap, log	–0.072	–0.022	0.059	–0.025	0.052
	0.059	0.060	0.075	0.060	0.075
Population, log	**0.237**	**0.236**	–0.063	**0.244**	–0.070
	0.067	0.067	0.135	0.066	0.137
Polity IV	**–0.016**	–0.008	–0.004	–0.010	–0.006
	0.007	0.007	0.008	0.007	0.008
Contiguous borders	**0.141**	**0.121**	**0.193**	**0.112**	**0.180**
	0.022	0.022	0.028	0.022	0.029
Coldwar	0.148	0.123	0.101	**0.135**	0.100
	0.078	0.078	0.095	0.078	0.095
Muslim, %pop.	0.099	0.140		0.182	
	0.299	0.292		0.287	
Major power	0.320	0.311		0.330	
	0.439	0.421		0.413	
Fixed Effects	No	No	Yes	No	Yes
N	6,272	6,244	5,377	6,244	5,377
log-likelihood	–2,780	–2,755	–2,349	–2,747	–2,344

Notes: All models use Poisson regression analysis for time-series panel data. Panel-adjusted standard errors are given below the coefficients; bold indicates p<0.05. *Regional dummies and a spline of peace years are included but not shown.*

regression analysis was used, adjusted for time-series panel data. Poisson regression is used because the dependent variable is a count variable, in which the variance is proportional to the mean; this follows the practice of previous work.[26] The unit of analysis is the state-year. The base models use random effects for greater statistical efficiency in estimating the coefficients, but fixed effects models are also used in order to control for state-specific variables that do not vary over time.

The results provide significant support for the theory. States with revolutionary governments are associated with considerably more militarized interstate disputes than states without revolutionary governments, especially when they occur in petrostates. The dependent variable for all models in Table 4.3 is *Aggressor-MIDs*. Model 1 is a basic model without the new dataset on revolutionary governments, used as a baseline for comparability to other scholarly studies. Model 2 shows the changes when the new data are added; model 3 is specified with panel fixed effects instead of random effects.[27] As expected by hypothesis H1, the coefficient for *Revolutionary Government* is positive and strongly significant, with confidence levels above 99 percent. This is true in all models, regardless of the specification used, suggesting a very strong relationship between revolutionary governments and MIDs.

Models 4 and 5 introduce the second key variable, *Petrostate*, and the interaction variable *Petro Revolution*. As expected, the interaction variable *Petro Revolution* is positive and strongly significant, indicating that revolutionary governments in petrostates are even more warlike than revolutionary governments in non-petrostates. This finding holds in model 4, which replicates the specification structure of model 2. The finding also holds in model 5, which uses fixed effects to control for all state-specific variables that do not vary over time. The

---

[26] L. Martin, 1993. Negative binomial models were also used to test for possible over-dispersion in the data, and the results were consistent. However, the Poisson models are preferred because they are more efficient (possibly much more efficient) in estimating the coefficients. See J. Wooldridge, 2002: 657, 672–674, for more details.

[27] Approximately 900 observations are dropped when switching from the random-effects models (2 and 4) to the fixed-effects models (3 and 5). The dropped observations are ones where there is no within-country variation on the dependent variable: i.e., states that did not engage in any MIDs during the period of analysis.

striking finding in model 5 is that, even when the analysis focuses only on within-state variation over time, the interaction variable is found to be strongly associated with *Aggressor-MIDs*. As expected by the theory, the coefficient for *Petro Revolution* is positive and strongly significant, again with confidence levels above 99 percent. Note also that this result is obtained even though the models include regional dummy variables, and thus controlling for variation in the amount of international conflict between regions (e.g., controlling for the high levels of conflict within the Middle East). Thus there is considerable evidence to support the most important hypothesis, H2.

Perhaps surprisingly, the coefficient on the variable *Petrostate* is negative, indicating an inverse correlation between non-revolutionary petrostates and *Aggressor-MIDs*. This finding is statistically significant in model 4, but not significant in model 5 once fixed effects are introduced. Thus these results are not conclusive, but they suggest that non-revolutionary petrostates are no more likely to launch MIDs than comparable non-petrostates, and possibly significantly less likely. This finding is striking because overall, the opposite trend holds: petrostates launch more MIDs on average than non-petrostates. The implication is that the overall above-average rate of international disputes is driven almost entirely by the small subset of revolutionary petrostates, which are extremely aggressive; the rest of the non-petrostates do not launch many MIDs. This finding provides further support for the claim that *Revolutionary Government* is an essential variable in explaining the behavior of petrostates, and suggests that the conventional explanation for the relationship between oil and international conflict is not satisfactory.

The results also provide insight into the importance of the control variables in determining the conflict propensity of a state. Consistent with earlier findings in the literature, the number of territorial borders is an important factor: the more contiguous neighbors a state has, the more opportunities it has for international disputes.[28] Population size is associated with increased conflict-proneness cross-nationally, but this effect becomes statistically insignificant when state fixed-effects are added (models 3 and 5). The Muslim percentage of the population, income per-capita, Cold War years (pre-1990), and the state's status as a major power are not associated with propensity for *Aggressor-MIDs*

[28] P. Diehl, 1985.

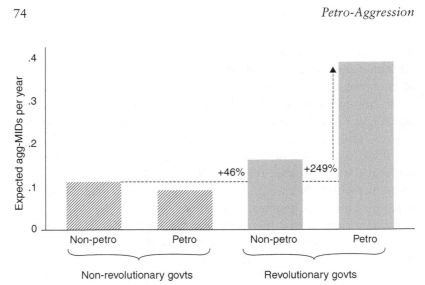

Figure 4.1 Effect of the combination of oil and revolutionary governments on MIDs

Note: Error bars are not shown, but differences between the revolutionary governments (solid bars) and the non-revolutionary governments (striped bars) are statistically significant, as are the differences between petro-revolutionaries and non-petrostate revolutionaries. The 95 percent confidence intervals associated with the estimated annual rate of aggressor-MIDs are: for revolutionary petrostates (0.22, 0.67); for revolutionary non-petrostates (0.13, 0.21); for non-revolutionary petrostates (0.06, 0.13); and for non-revolutionary non-petrostates (0.09, 0.13).

in any of the models. Finally, the state's Polity score (from −10 to +10) is inversely associated with MIDs in model 1, consistent with the hypothesis that democracies engage in fewer aggressive disputes. However, this relationship disappears (i.e., is not statistically significant) in models 2 to 5, when the data on revolutionary governments are used. This latter result suggests that it may be worth investigating the extent to which revolutionary governments are related to the democratic peace thesis.

The magnitude of these statistical effects is worth considering. Figure 4.1 shows the effect of the variables *Petrostate*, *Revolutionary Government*, and *Petro Revolution* on the onset of aggressive MIDs for a typical state. In this comparison, a "typical state" is considered, in which population, GDP per capita, Polity score, Muslim percentage of the population, and the number of state borders are all set to the average of the data sample.[29] The behavior of four types of this "typical state" is considered. The first type is a state which has no oil and is led by a non-revolutionary government. As indicated by the bar on the left of Figure 4.1, such a state could be expected to aggressively engage in 0.11 MIDs per year, or about one every decade. The second type is a petrostate but is still led by a non-revolutionary government; Figure 4.1 shows that such a state will aggressively engage in 0.09 MIDs per year. Thus, as discussed previously, non-revolutionary petrostates appear no more aggressive (and perhaps slightly less aggressive) than comparable non-petrostates.

The most important findings are shown in the two bars on the right-hand side of Figure 4.1. As expected, non-petrostates with revolutionary governments aggressively engage in MIDs more than comparable states with non-revolutionary governments; they do this at a rate of 0.16 per year, or 46 percent more per year than comparable states with non-revolutionary governments. However, this difference pales in comparison to the effect of revolutionary governments in petrostates. Such states aggressively engage in MIDs at a rate of 0.39 per year, which is more than three times the rate of comparable non-petrostates. As Figure 4.1 makes clear, the combination of a revolutionary government and an oil-exporting economy is a toxic mix for international peace and security.

These results suggest that the theory under investigation provides powerful insight into the behavior of petrostates. Indeed, when one moves past the quantitative results and considers a broader view of foreign policy behavior, the relationship between petro-revolutionaries and aggressive conflict becomes even more evident. This topic will be taken up in case studies, but some examples can be highlighted here. Saddam Hussein seized power by force, revolutionized his country's domestic politics, and then used his country's oil income to centralize power and build a powerful military apparatus. Under his leadership, Iraq invaded both Iran (1980) and Kuwait (1990). Moreover,

[29] The model used for Figure 4.1 is model 4. For the "typical state" being compared in Figure 4.1, the GDP per capita is $2,110, population is 8.3 million, Polity score is –0.6, the state has 5.5 external borders, and Muslims make up 24 percent of the population. Other values, such as the geographic location of the state, the presence of the Cold War, and the state's status as a major power are not adjusted in this analysis, meaning that they vary according to the data within each category of Figure 4.1.

Iraq engaged in a number of lower-level militarized disputes with other states, including the Tanker Wars of the 1980s and violations of UN sanctions throughout the 1990s. In Libya, Muammar Qaddafi's revolutionary government aggressively engaged in four separate border wars with neighboring Chad, and a variety of militarized disputes with other countries such as Uganda, Sudan, and the United States. In addition, Qaddafi's government supported terrorists and insurgencies in at least thirty countries around the world, though this dimension of conflict activity is not captured in the MIDs dataset. In Iran, the revolutionary government under Khomeini did not initiate the Iran–Iraq War, but it did decide to continue the war for many years after Saddam Hussein declared his willingness to negotiate for peace in 1982. Further, Iran's continuing aggressiveness and pursuit of nuclear weapons in the twenty-first century can be partially attributed to the revolutionary hardcore members of its regime. In Venezuela, President Hugo Chávez's Bolivarian Revolution started when he came to power in 1999, largely too late to be captured in this dataset (which ends in 2001). However, Chávez's multiple aggressive foreign policy actions, such as the Venezuela–Colombia military crisis in 2008, is very much consistent with the expectations of the theory being tested here.

In sum, the theoretical hypotheses being tested are strongly supported by the empirical evidence. It is worth noting that the number of petrostates in the world is relatively small, and so the number of petro-revolutionary governments under analysis is also small. This should make us cautious in reaching conclusions. Still, the data include 125 observations of petro-revolutionary state-years. This analysis benefits from variation across countries as well as variation across time within countries, in which both the nature of the government and the state's oil income can change. The analysis of both cross-national and cross-temporal variation suggests that petro-revolutionary governments have a dramatically higher propensity for international conflict than comparable non-petrostates.

Dyadic analysis

International conflict is commonly modeled by political scientists as a dyadic interaction. The theory being tested is primarily about the unit-level characteristics of states, and therefore the monadic analysis used above is an appropriate initial testing method. However, the analysis can also be extended to dyadic tests. This sequential research design – first monadic, then dyadic – follows the practice of other scholars.[30] There are two principal benefits to the dyadic analysis. First, dyadic tests are able to control for dyadic attributes that might be omitted variables in a monadic analysis. Second, these tests allow the work presented here on oil and revolutionary states to be connected and compared easily to the large existing literature that is cast at the dyadic level of analysis.

This analysis uses data and methodology similar to that used by Gleditsch *et al.* (2008) in their work linking civil wars and MIDs. Building on their model serves to increase the comparability between the results presented here and those already published. A logit regression model is used to conduct the analysis, with directed dyads as the unit of analysis.[31] Consistent with much of the literature on international conflict, the data sample is restricted to politically-relevant dyads: that is, only dyads in which the states are geographically contiguous or at least one of the states is a major power. The use of directed dyads allows the analysis to capture which state is the aggressor or revisionist party in the conflict.

Table 4.4 provides the results of the analysis, which are quite consistent with those from the monadic analysis. The table shows three models, each with a different dependent variable: Model A focuses on MIDs in which state A was the aggressor; Model B focuses on MIDs in which state A was the defender; and Model C uses all MID onsets. The results are most informative when the three models are interpreted together. Model A generates positive and significant coefficients for both *Revolutionary Government* and *Petro Revolution* for state A, as expected. Similarly in Model B, these coefficients are significant for state B, which is typically the aggressor in these MIDs. In Model C, the results are symmetric for states A and B, and again show the positive and significant coefficients for *Revolutionary Government* and *Petro Revolution* as expected. Model B shows that revolutionary states are also more prone to *Defender-MIDs*, as can be seen from the positive coefficient in the first row. (Somewhat curiously, the results in Model

---

[30] E. Mansfield and J. Snyder, 2005.
[31] The monadic analysis used a Poisson regression because a significant number of observations have multiple MIDs in a given year. In the dyadic analysis, values greater than one are very rare, so a logit model is used instead. A rare events logit model was used as a robustness check; the results were consistent.

Table 4.4 *International disputes by state type – dyadic regression analysis*

	A: Agg-MID		B: Def-MID		C: All MID	
	Coeff	Std Err	Coeff	Std Err	Coeff	Std Err
Revolutionary Govt – State A	**0.625**	0.145	**0.323**	0.135	**0.483**	0.106
Petrostate – State A	–0.183	0.210	–0.089	0.164	–0.154	0.139
Petro Revolution – State A	**0.891**	0.276	0.102	0.272	**0.617**	0.216
Revolutionary Govt – State B	–0.021	0.155	**0.799**	0.123	**0.483**	0.106
Petrostate – State B	–0.154	0.185	–0.168	0.172	–0.154	0.139
Petro Revolution – State B	0.510	0.317	**0.681**	0.237	**0.617**	0.216
Civil War – State A	0.202	0.143	**0.402**	0.110	**0.334**	0.099
Civil War – State B	0.287	0.135	**0.333**	0.122	**0.334**	0.099
Democracy-Democracy	**–0.863**	0.197	**–0.663**	0.153	**–0.792**	0.138
Contiguous Border	**1.628**	0.192	**1.512**	0.133	**1.623**	0.112
Former Colony	–0.524	0.279	**–0.593**	0.226	**–0.547**	0.202
Colonial Contiguity	**0.698**	0.212	**0.750**	0.180	**0.737**	0.144
Alliance S-score	**–0.512**	0.225	**–0.523**	0.178	**–0.543**	0.160
Low Trade Dependence	–11.637	9.793	**–12.217**	5.902	**–11.954**	5.922
Shared IGOs	**0.016**	0.007	0.008	0.004	**0.013**	0.004
Major Power – State A	–0.150	0.201	**0.398**	0.156	0.173	0.130
Major Power – State B	0.258	0.182	0.071	0.156	0.173	0.130
N	71,836		71,836		71,836	
Pseudo-R2	0.196		0.189		0.215	

Notes: All models use logit regression analysis; rare-events logit used also for robustness.

Standard errors are clustered by directed dyad; bold indicates $p < 0.05$.

A spline (three knots) of peace years is included in the regression but not shown.

A for state B do not suggest that revolutionary states are more likely to
be the targets of *Aggressor-MIDs*; however, this appears to be an arti-
fact of the COW data.[32]) The variable *Petrostate* is generally negative
but not statistically significant; this is also consistent with the results
of the monadic analysis.[33] In sum, the results support the hypotheses
that oil interacts with the effect of revolutionary governments, and
together they generate a strong propensity for states to launch international conflicts.

Robustness checks

These analyses were subjected to a battery of robustness checks.
Table 4.5 shows six additional models, each of which is a variation of
model 4 in Table 4.3. Model 6 introduces a lagged dependent variable,
to control for any ongoing disputes perpetuated through a process of
"war begets war."[34] (Note that this is in addition to the spline function on the number of peace years which is included but not shown
in all of the regression models, as discussed above.) This variable is
positive and highly significant, but reduces the significance of the three
key explanatory variables only slightly. Given the tendency of lagged
dependent variables to absorb the significance of all other variables, it is
striking that the principal findings of the analysis are sustained. Model
7 introduces a dummy variable for each year, to take into account any
possible system-wide temporal effects on conflict. Model 8 uses a variation of the dependent variable, focusing only on *Aggressor-MIDs* in
which international force was used (as opposed to including displays
and threats of force).[35] In model 9, the COW measure of National

---

[32] Recall that *Aggressor-MIDs* are identified using the *revisionist* variable from
the COW dataset. There are some MIDs in which neither party is coded
as revisionist. The results appear to suggest that although revolutionary
governments are significantly prone to (non-revisionist) *Defender-MIDs*
as expected, the other state(s) in these MIDs also tends to be coded as a
non-revisionist party. This leads to the non-significant coefficient in Model A.
[33] This analysis was also expanded to include permutations of the three key
independent variables for *both* states in the dyad (for a total of sixteen
variables); the results were consistent.
[34] D. Stinnett and P. Diehl, 2001.
[35] As an additional robustness check, the analysis was re-tested using only
MIDs with hostility level of 2 or above on the five-point scale; the results are
consistent. I thank Jessica Weeks for suggesting this check.

Table 4.5 *International disputes of revolutionary petrostates – robustness checks*

DV: Aggressor-MIDs	Model 6 Lag DV	Model 7 Year vars	Model 8 Force only	Model 9 CINC	Model 10 Alt IV	Model 11 Alt IV
Revolutionary Govt	0.230	0.270	0.308	0.245		
	0.106	0.107	0.142	0.106		
Petrostate	−0.362	−0.434	−0.478	−0.454	−0.430	−0.372
	0.163	0.164	0.204	0.163	0.190	0.156
Petro Revolution	0.569	0.849	0.750	0.848		
	0.218	0.210	0.278	0.208		
Revol Regime – Alt					0.055	0.502
					0.094	0.169
Petro-Revolution – Alt					0.262	1.146
					0.190	0.292
Lagged DV	0.117					
	0.013					
Military Capability				−6.259		
				2.449		
GDP / cap, log	−0.093	−0.087	−0.169	−0.082	−0.110	−0.087
	0.063	0.076	0.080	0.062	0.062	0.063
Population, log	0.225	0.267	0.341	0.294	0.296	0.271
	0.073	0.078	0.090	0.074	0.075	0.076
Polity IV	−0.010	−0.011	−0.020	−0.008	−0.010	−0.017
	0.008	0.008	0.010	0.008	0.008	0.007
Contiguous Borders	0.138	0.120	0.146	0.140	0.168	0.164
	0.024	0.024	0.031	0.023	0.023	0.024
Coldwar	0.083	−20.970	0.306	0.169	0.190	0.104
	0.080	15482	0.108	0.079	0.080	0.081
Muslim, %pop.	0.141	0.178	0.192	0.143	0.162	0.148
	0.321	0.319	0.386	0.325	0.336	0.338
Major Power	0.532	0.613	−0.629	0.817	0.513	0.553
	0.474	0.484	0.575	0.498	0.511	0.509
Fixed Effects	No	No	No	No	No	No
N	6,131	6,244	6,244	6,244	6,244	6,244
log-likelihood	−2,743	−2,741	−1,975	−2,792	−2,815	−2,791

Notes: All models use Poisson regression analysis for time-series panel data. Panel-adjusted standard errors are given below the coefficients; bold indicates $p<0.05$. *Regional dummies and a spline of peace years are included but not shown.*

Capabilities was added to the regression.[36] As Table 4.5 illustrates, the correlation between revolutionary governments in petrostates and *Aggressor-MIDs* is remarkably robust.[37]

To further probe the robustness of the results, the definition of "revolutionary government" was made broader and then narrower. It was broadened to test whether the transformative domestic policy of a revolutionary government is actually important as an indicator of foreign policy behavior; one could imagine that all governments that have come to power through an irregular transition are similarly inclined to behave aggressively in their foreign policy. Thus model 10 replaces the key explanatory variable, *Revolutionary Government*, with a variable indicating any irregular transition. (*Revolutionary Governments* are a subset of this group.) The *Petro Revolution* variable is also replaced by the appropriate interaction term. It is clear from the lack of statistical significance on these two variables that *Revolutionary Governments* are indeed a special set of governments. Conversely, if one narrows the definition of revolutionary government to include just eleven "unambiguous" cases of revolutionary governments, the effect on MIDs grows even stronger in size and significance, as shown in model 11.[38]

In addition to the analyses presented in Table 4.5, the results were probed to ensure that no single country case was driving the result. All of the state-years associated with each important country case (e.g., Iraq, Iran) were dropped, one country at a time, and the regressions

---

[36] This was done in an attempt to determine whether the impact of oil was solely acting through an increase in military capability. However, as I have argued elsewhere (J. Colgan, 2011c), the cross-national time-series datasets on military expenditure and capability are prone to significant measurement error. The inclusion here is for purposes of comparison to existing scholarly work; in the event, the results are robust with or without including this variable.

[37] Only in model 8 did the significance of the coefficient for *Petro Revolution* dip below 95 percent confidence, and this is due to an increase in the standard error due to the relatively small number of events in this specification. Even so, the significance remains with confidence above 90 percent in all models.

[38] The eleven "unambiguous" revolutionary leaders/regimes are: Mao (China), Castro (Cuba), Khomeini (Iran), Pol Pot (Cambodia), Ortega (Nicaragua), Banti (Ethiopia), Qaddafi (Libya), Kerekou (Benin), Ngouabi (Congo), Al-Bashir (Sudan), and Ne Win (Myanmar). These regimes are selected based on the frequency with which they have been identified as revolutions by other major scholars (e.g., Walt, Huntington, etc.). Each of the regimes also had revolutionary societal transformation under at least four of the seven categories identified above.

re-tested. The results did not materially change, and the key findings remained robust. Moreover, to ensure that the Iran–Iraq War was not driving the results by itself, all of the observations involving either Iran or Iraq during the period 1980–1988 inclusive were dropped from the analysis. In this latter specification, the results were somewhat weaker, but remained significant at the 90 percent level.

A series of further robustness tests were conducted. First, all of the tests conducted in Table 4.5 were repeated using country fixed-effects models. Second, the definition of revolutionary governments was modified in various ways using the coding for *Ambiguous* cases. For instance, in one specification, all governments coded as ambiguous were temporarily coded as revolutionary governments; in another specification, they were all temporarily coded as non-revolutionary governments. Third, the four variants of the definition of petrostate described above were each substituted for the dichotomous measure *Petrostate*, and the regressions re-tested. Fourth, the models were re-tested when the sample was restricted to the developing countries only (i.e., non-OECD). Fifth, all of the independent variables were lagged by one year, to avoid any possible endogeneity. Sixth, a dummy variable for the "Tanker Wars" that make up a large number of MIDs involving Iraq or Iran in the mid 1980s was included; this dummy variable was set to 1 for Iraq and Iran during the years 1984–1988 inclusive, and 0 otherwise. Seventh, the few long-serving revolutionary governments, which had been in power for at least twenty-five years, were excluded after their twenty-fourth year to account for the possibility that they were no longer truly revolutionary. In none of these robustness tests did any of the results change materially.

As a final robustness check, the specification of the model was changed from a panel Poisson count model to a logit model, in which the dependent variable is set to 1 if the state engaged in any *Aggressor-MIDs* in a given year and 0 otherwise. This specification focuses the analysis on the onset of any international dispute rather than on the number of them, to ensure that the results obtained are not driven solely by the observations in which states engaged in multiple *Aggressor-MIDs*. Under this specification, none of the results changed materially, again supporting the robustness of the principal findings in Table 4.3.

The empirical evidence is strongest in the Middle East. It is a simple fact that most petrostates are in the Middle East, and thus the region has the greatest concentration of data points by which this argument can be evaluated. There are fewer data points outside of the Middle East, and it is therefore appropriate to be cautious about the argument's generalizability. However, there are three reasons to believe that the findings are broadly applicable. First, and perhaps most importantly, it is not obvious why we should expect theoretically that the political dynamics of oil should be different in the Middle East than they are elsewhere. In the absence of a well-articulated theory of Middle East exceptionalism, it is reasonable to expect to see similar dynamics in other regions. Second, there are statistical controls in the analysis that ought to isolate a "Middle East effect" for international conflict, to the extent that this exists. Third, the political dynamics described here appear to apply to revolutionary governments outside the Middle East, such as in Venezuela, the Congo, and Sudan. For instance, while Venezuela's Chávez has not (yet) initiated a major war, his foreign policy is aggressive and Venezuela has initiated lower-level militarized conflicts, particularly with neighboring Colombia, as expected by the theory.

Other natural resources

Given these findings regarding the impact of oil and revolution on international conflict, it is ordinary to wonder whether other natural resources have a similar effect on the relationship between revolutionary governments and international conflict. Testing this possibility empirically is not as straightforward as it might appear. The data on oil are better developed than data on other natural resources. Moreover, at least in the case of natural gas, there is a considerable problem of coincidence: most of the major producers of natural gas, such as Russia, Iran, and Qatar, are also producers of oil, making it difficult to isolate the impact of natural gas alone. Nonetheless, a preliminary investigation was conducted and is presented here. The role of non-oil natural resources is tested using data on the amount of mineral revenue generated by the production of bauxite, copper, iron, lead, nickel, phosphate, tin, zinc, gold, and silver.[39] Using these data, a dichotomous variable analogous to *Petrostate* was constructed: *MineralState* is

---

[39] This was done using the World Development Indicator data on "adjusted net savings: mineral depletion."

equal to 1 for all state-years in which income from minerals is at least 10 percent of GNI, and 0 otherwise. *MineralState* was equal to 1 for 129 state-years in the dataset, seven of which were in conjunction with revolutionary governments.

Regression analysis suggests that the null hypothesis cannot be rejected: that is, there is no evidence that non-oil natural resources have the same effect as oil on international conflict.[40] Oil income appears to be genuinely special, potentially because it is more easily controlled and centralized by the state leader. Most of the oil industry has been organized into state-owned enterprises, whereas the same is not generally true of other minerals. Ghana's recent experience is telling: although its gold exports accounted for 40 percent of exports in 2008, the government received just 5.3 percent of the associated revenue in taxes and royalties; by contrast, oil production which began in 2011 is expected to bring in far more tax revenue.[41] However, this "non-result" should be treated very cautiously, as the sample size is small: just seven state-years have both a revolutionary government and a large source of mineral revenues. In addition, the quality of the data is suspect, and its range extends only back to 1970. This topic awaits further investigation.

Further evidence of petrostate leaders' political autonomy

The results discussed thus far already demonstrate significant support for my theory. However, identifying and testing further empirical implications of the theory increases the confidence which can be placed in it. One place to start is by looking at the hypothesized causal mechanisms, especially the argument that oil grants more political autonomy to leaders of petrostates. This hypothesis already finds considerable support from the existing literature. Many qualitative studies of the domestic politics of petrostates support such a claim.[42] Additionally, recent quantitative work provided by Michael Ross, Kevin Morrison, and Benjamin Smith also supports the hypothesis.[43]

---

[40] The regression analysis follows the pattern of model 4 above, with *MineralState* and the interaction between *MineralState* and *RevolutionaryGovt* added to the existing set of independent variables.

[41] *The Economist*, 2010: 68.

[42] K. Chaudhry, 1997; J. Crystal, 1990; T. Karl, 1997.

[43] K. Morrison, 2009; M. Ross, 2012; B. Smith, 2004.

Table 4.6 *Leader tenure in petrostates and non-petrostates*

State type	Tenure (years) All states	Tenure (years) Non-democracies
Non-petrostates	5.22	6.85
Petrostates	8.82	11.09

Source: Archigos dataset v.2.8.1, 1945–2001.

One additional implication is that a leader with greater political autonomy is less likely to be forced out of office, and thus can be expected to have a longer tenure, on average. If the theory is correct, the leaders of petrostates should have a longer tenure in office than those in non-petrostates. And indeed that is exactly what is observed.

Table 4.6 shows that leaders of petrostates are in office about 70 percent longer, on average, than those in non-petrostates.[44] The second column in the table restricts the comparison only to the non-democratic states, where leadership tenure is generally longer in part because term limits in autocracies are either non-existent or more easily flouted. Again, petrostate leaders have far longer tenure than those in non-petrostates. Thus the data on leader tenure provide additional support for the theory.

A second empirical implication of the argument is that leaders of petrostates can be expected to spend public money to build patronage networks and political support, in order to increase their political autonomy. Consequently, petrostates should be expected to have larger public expenditures as a proportion of GDP. Figure 4.2 confirms that this is true, on average. The data are drawn from the IMF's International Financial Statistics, and the graph shows the proportional size of the public sector (y-axis) as a function of GDP per capita (the x-axis).[45] Petrostates typically have considerably higher public expenditure as a percentage of GDP than do non-petrostates (about ten percentage points higher, on average). This graphical conclusion

[44] The data on leader tenure were drawn from the Archigos dataset collected by H. Goemans *et al.*, 2009.
[45] Public expenditure is calculated by subtracting the private consumption in the state from the total GDP, and then dividing by GDP. The initial values are measured in current local currency units for each state-year. Due to availability of the data, the time period for this analysis is 1960–2001.

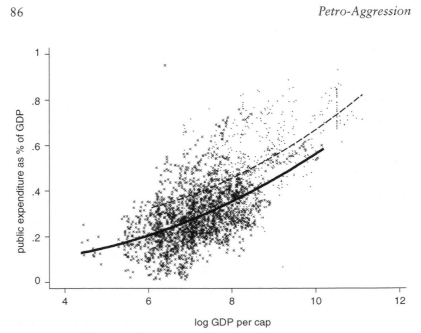

Figure 4.2 Public expenditure in petrostates and non-petrostates
Note: The dashed line and dot-markers represent petrostates; the solid line
and x-markers represent non-petrostates. The dashed line, being higher on
the y-axis than the solid line, indicates that public expenditure is significantly
higher in petrostates than in non-petrostates. This difference is statistically
significant ($p<0.05$).

is supported by regression analyses (not shown) that include control
variables such as GDP per capita, population size, Polity scores of
regime type, economic openness (exports as a percentage of GDP), and
regional and year dummies. Thus the theory is again supported.

A third empirical implication of the theory is that leaders of petrostates ought to engage in riskier international conflicts, on average,
and therefore lose more often than non-petrostates. This implication is
derived from the idea that petrostate leaders have more autonomy, so
the costs of losing are lower for them than they are for non-petrostate
leaders, who would be more likely to be thrown out of office after
defeat. For instance, although Iraq and Libya both suffered a number
of military defeats in the 1980s and 1990s, their leaders managed to
resist domestic challenges to their power and remain in office.

Figure 4.3 provides evidence in support of this empirical implication. The graph shows the average rate of victory in international

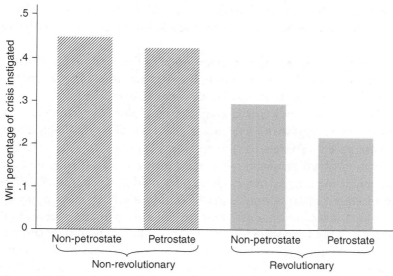

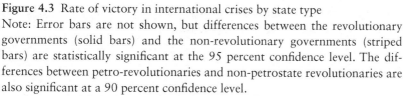

Figure 4.3 Rate of victory in international crises by state type
Note: Error bars are not shown, but differences between the revolutionary governments (solid bars) and the non-revolutionary governments (striped bars) are statistically significant at the 95 percent confidence level. The differences between petro-revolutionaries and non-petrostate revolutionaries are also significant at a 90 percent confidence level.

crises instigated by each type of state, according to the four types of states described in Figure 4.1. The rate of victory was calculated using the International Crisis Behavior dataset, coding 1 for a victory, 0 for a defeat, and 0.5 for a compromise or stalemate.[46] As expected, the revolutionary states engage in riskier behavior, resulting in a lower rate of victory than non-revolutionary states; moreover, the effect of oil is conditional on the presence of a revolutionary government. Petro-revolutionary states have the lowest rate of victory (21.3%), followed by revolutionary non-petrostates (29.1%). The differences between these states and the comparable non-revolutionary states (which have victory rates of 42.2% and 44.7%, respectively) are statistically

---

[46] The ICB dataset was chosen because of the limitations in the MIDs dataset in regards to conflict outcomes (e.g., the vast majority of MIDs are coded as compromises, rendering the data nearly useless). The "instigator" of a crisis was identified in the ICB dataset using the variable "Source of Perceived Threat."

significant. This empirical finding is especially compelling evidence supporting the theory, as it was not tested until well after the theory was derived.

A fourth and final empirical implication of the theory relates to economic sanctions. Petro-revolutionary states are more likely to be targeted for economic sanctions for the same reason that they are more likely to instigate militarized conflicts: they often have leaders with risk-tolerant, aggressive preferences, high levels of political autonomy, and enhanced resources for foreign policy adventurism. The effect of revolutionary governments once again plays a crucial role, because one might expect that on its own, oil would create a rather different incentive: oil-importing states face an incentive to avoid applying economic sanctions on a petrostate in order to maintain access to oil supplies.[47] As I have shown elsewhere, the evidence is entirely consistent with the theory: revolutionary non-petrostates and revolutionary petrostates are targeted for economic sanctions 160 percent and 580 percent, respectively, more frequently than "typical states" (e.g., comparable non-revolutionary non-petrostates).[48]

Conclusion

This chapter provides new evidence on the relationship between oil and international conflict. Petro-revolutionary governments constitute a special threat to international peace and security. The evidence reveals that petrostates led by revolutionary leaders are dramatically more aggressive and instigate more MIDs than other kinds of states, even compared to non-petrostates that are led by revolutionary leaders. The interaction of oil and revolution often leads to a state with an unrestrained, warlike government capable of harnessing a significant portion of the state's resources toward international conflict. The implications for the global political economy are significant.

---

[47] This incentive is not necessarily very strong: the United States has not hesitated to sanction oil producers such as Iraq, Iran, and Libya in the past, knowing that it could obtain imported oil from other sources, such as Saudi Arabia, Norway, or Canada. Nonetheless, there is some reason to believe that major oil-importers hesitate to cut off their trade access to petrostates by the use of sanctions. China's reluctance to sanction Sudan and Iran are possible examples of this incentive.

[48] J. Colgan, 2011b.

Petrostates were involved in 22 percent of all MIDs since 1970, even though they are just thirty-one states and account for a small fraction of the world's population.[49] In short, the combination of oil and revolutionary governments is explosive.

These findings are especially significant in light of Middle East politics. Observing the correlation between oil and international conflict, one might be tempted to believe that this is because much of the world's oil is found in the Middle East, and the Middle East is a violent and conflict-prone region. On that view, the correlation might be spurious. However, this chapter shows that when the analysis controls and adjusts for regional effects, the effect of petro-revolutionary governments remains strong. That is, even relative to other Middle East states, the petro-revolutionary governments in states like Iraq, Libya, and Iran are especially prone to aggressively engage in MIDs. Moreover, the toxic interaction between oil income and revolutionary governments can be seen in the behavior of states outside of the Middle East, such as Venezuela. On the whole, the evidence suggests that oil contributes significantly to the violence in the Middle East.

Perhaps surprisingly, the evidence shows that petrostates with nonrevolutionary governments have a propensity to instigate conflict that is no higher, and perhaps somewhat lower, than comparable nonpetrostates. This is consistent with the theory developed in Chapter 2. The implication is that the above-average rate of MIDs for petrostates overall is driven largely by the small subset of petro-revolutionary governments, which have an extremely high propensity for international conflict.

[49] Correlates of War database, based on F. Ghosn *et al.*, 2004. Author's analysis.

5 | Iraq

The Revolution chooses its enemies.
— Saddam Hussein[1]

In a double coup in July 1968, Saddam Hussein came to power at the right hand of Hasan al-Bakr, the secretary-general of the Baathist Party and new president of Iraq. The events of July 1968 were only the latest in a period of extraordinary political tumult in Iraq, beginning with the overthrow of the monarchy and establishment of a republic in 1958. Still more political changes were to come. By the end of the 1970s, Saddam Hussein had displaced al-Bakr and transformed his country politically, economically, and socially using an enormous influx of oil revenues. Saddam's strategy, based on the twin forces of patronage and fear, was in its essence as simple as it was ruthlessly effective. With Saddam in power, Iraq was to become one of the most aggressive states of the twentieth century.

The principal aim of this chapter is to evaluate the extent to which Iraq's behavior is explained by the theory described in Chapter 2. The first step in testing the theory is to consider the value of the key variables for each time period under analysis, exploiting the variation over time. If my theory is correct, the actual behavior of Iraq should match the theory's predictions based on the explanatory variables. Table 5.1 below provides a brief summary of the key variables: the aggressiveness of the state's foreign policy, the presence of revolutionary government, and the presence of oil income.

Iraq was a petrostate for the entire period under analysis. By 1958, 80 percent of government revenues were based on oil income.[2] Three major international wars left Iraq with an unusually volatile oil production profile from the 1970s onward. Yet while the total amount of

[1] Quoted in E. Sciolino, 1991: 88.
[2] C. Tripp, 2002.

Table 5.1 *Summary of key variables in Iraq, 1945–2010*

Iraq	1945–1958	1959–1968	1969–1978	1979–1990	1991–2003	2003–2010
IV: Revolutionary regime	Non-	Turmoil	Highly	Highly	Highly	Transition
IV: Petrostate	Yes	Yes	Yes	Yes	Yes	Yes
DV: Foreign policy:						
with Iran	Cooperation	Friction	Truce	War	Friction	Complex
with Kuwait	No conflict	Friction	No conflict	Alliance	War/Sanctions	n.a.
with United States	Little contact	Hostility	Warming	Alliance	War/Sanctions	Occupation
with Israel	Hostility	Conflict	Conflict	Hostility	Hostility	n.a.
Aggressiveness						
Expected value	Low	Unclear	High	High	High	n.a.
Actual value	Low	Moderate	Low-Moderate	High	High	Low

Note: For more information about the labels used in this table, see Figure 3.1.

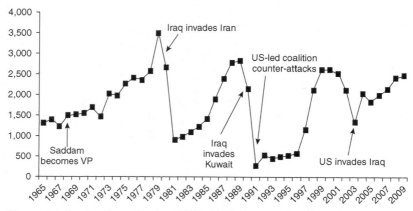

Figure 5.1 Iraq's oil production 1965–2009, thousands of barrels per day
Note: reliable data for Iraq's oil pricing and revenue are unavailable. Data on
production volume are from BP Statistical Review of World Energy, 2010.

revenue fluctuated considerably, the high degree of economic dependence on the oil sector in Iraq did not. The oil industry was the largest
single sector in the Iraqi economy and the dominant source of export
revenue throughout the period under analysis.[3] Figure 5.1 shows Iraq's
oil production over time.

Once in power, Saddam revolutionized Iraq. Emerging from the political turmoil in the 1960s, Saddam was determined to promote Baath
Party unity and ensure social stability. He also sought to change and
modernize his country. Saddam helped enact a new constitution for
Iraq, overhaul the government's structure, make the Baathists the sole
official party of Iraq, and install a puppet National Assembly. Saddam
vastly increased the power of various organs of the secret police, which
enabled the government to suppress dissent and opposition. He nationalized the Iraqi oil industry, eliminated all taxes on income and sales,
and championed a socialist political and economic vision. Socially, he
banned the use of personal last names, increased the rights of women,
and permitted the sale of alcohol in Shi'a mosques for the first time.
He feigned reconciliation with the Kurds by granting them greater
autonomy in 1970, and then revoked it in 1974. Throughout this
period, Saddam solidified his own personal power by using the government's resources to hand out choice jobs and government contracts

[3] P. Marr, 2003: 265.

in exchange for political support. Occasionally he flew from town to town in a helicopter and handed out cash directly to individuals who came to see him.[4]

Saddam's leadership was not the only force stimulating change in Iraq. The country's oil income made things possible that would have been inconceivable otherwise. In the 1970s, the nationalization of the oil industry, the four-fold increase in global prices, and Iraq's rapidly expanding production capacity was flooding the country with petroleum export revenues. By 1980, Iraq had become one of OPEC's largest producers, earning $26 billion in oil export revenues annually.[5] This laid the foundations for the political outcomes of the next twenty-five years by warping the political and military structures of Iraq. Oil money allowed Saddam to purchase political support, create a loyal (and intimidated) coterie of followers, and build a highly repressive domestic security apparatus. He was therefore insulated to a large degree from the risk of being overthrown, even after he led his country into disastrous foreign adventures.

As expected by the theory, Iraq's foreign policy was highly aggressive under Saddam Hussein. The combination of oil income and revolutionary politics created conditions for a sharp increase in the state's aggressiveness, leading to two major wars (with Iran in 1980 and Kuwait in 1990), as well as a host of smaller military conflicts with other powers, including Syria, Saudi Arabia, Israel, the United States, and the United Kingdom. The principal exception to the expectations of the theory is the period 1968–1979, in which a revolutionary government was in place but Iraq's foreign policy was only moderately aggressive. As this chapter demonstrates, however, this was a period in which Saddam was biding his time and laying the groundwork for future aggression.

Therefore the theory passes the first test. As suggested by Table 5.1, there is considerable correlation between the actual foreign policy behavior of Iraq and the behavior expected by the theory on the basis of the independent variables. The rest of this chapter explores the hypothesized causal mechanisms in the context of the historical evidence. It is organized in five parts. The first section focuses on Iraq politics prior to Saddam's ascension to power in 1968. The second

---

[4] G. Packer, 2005: 337–339.
[5] M. El-Gamal and A. Jaffe, 2010: 90.

section focuses on Iraq domestic politics 1968–1991, with particular attention to how revolutionary politics and oil income affected the regime. The third section maps Iraqi foreign policy 1968–1991, which was highly aggressive. Fourth, Saddam's final days of defiance and aggression, 1991–2003, are discussed. Finally, the fifth section revisits Iraq's political history in the context of three specific analytical questions to highlight the role of the key causal mechanisms.

Iraqi politics to 1968

The modern state of Iraq was born out of the collapse of the Ottoman Empire at the end of World War II. In a meeting at San Remo in 1920, the British were given the Mandate to govern the territory, and the following year the British appointed Faisal al-Hashemi as king of Iraq. The Hashemite family, to which the kings of both Iraq and Jordan belonged, had roots that could be traced back to the days of the Prophet Mohammad, lending Faisal a certain amount of legitimacy. Nonetheless, the monarchy was contested by Arab nationalists, leading to a period of instability following Faisal's death in 1933. Still, a regent for the infant Faisal II was installed in 1941, and the new king was enthroned in 1953.

By the time World War II ended, the government of Iraq was already quite dependent on the income from the oil industry. In 1925, Iraq granted a concession to the Turkish Petroleum Company, later to become the Iraq Petroleum Company (IPC). Two years later, the first major oil discoveries near Kirkuk were made. A consortium of French, British, and American oil companies owned and controlled the IPC. Under the agreement that created the IPC, none of the companies could explore or produce oil anywhere inside the area demarcated by a Red Line – an area that included most of modern-day Saudi Arabia, Iraq, Yemen, and the Gulf monarchies – except through their participation in the IPC.[6] Consequently, the agreement gave the companies a significant incentive to explore and produce oil in Iraq.

In foreign affairs, the Iraqi monarchy generally sought to protect and increase Iraqi sovereignty even as it maintained positive relations with the West and its neighbors Iran and Turkey. Faisal II's prime minister, Nuri al-Said, occasionally gave voice to rhetorical pan-Arabism

---

[6] D. Yergin, 2008 [1991].

but in practice his chief concerns were for Iraqi nationalism.[7] In 1955, Nuri signed the Baghdad Pact, a defensive alliance between Iraq and Turkey designed to repel aggression in the region. Iran, Pakistan, and Great Britain quickly joined the Pact, and although the United States remained formally outside of it, it was nonetheless supportive. By contrast, the Soviet Union and Egypt under Nasser denounced the Pact. Playing on Iraqis' historical animosity to Turkey and Western powers, Nasser maintained a relentless propaganda campaign against the Pact.

In 1956, Nasser nationalized the Suez Canal, and became a hero to Arabs everywhere. In Iraq as in other Arab countries, a group of disgruntled military officers formed the "Free Officers," modeled after Nasser's own revolutionary organization. Other than their dislike of the status quo and their resentment of the monarchy, the Iraqi Free Officers had little in common. The members of this group had links to various opposition groups, such as the Iraq Communist Party (ICP), the Baath Party, the National Democratic Party, and the Istiqlal Party. Although these groups cobbled together a United National Front, subsequent events would demonstrate that their unity was shallow. Still, the United Front and the Free Officers appointed Brigadier Abd al-Karim Qasim as their leader in 1957. Qasim was the chairman of the Supreme Committee, and quickly began laying plans for the overthrow of the monarchy.

Their opportunity came in July 1958. Alarmed by a political crisis in Lebanon and the increasing aggressiveness of Egypt and Syria (which at this time were merged in the United Arab Republic), Nuri ordered units of the Iraqi army to the western border. These units were stationed in the east. Qasim and his protégé, Abd al-Salam Arif, conspired to divert the troops to pass through Baghdad. At the appointed time, the troops occupied all of the strategic buildings in Baghdad, including the radio station where Arif announced the formation of the Iraqi republic.

The Qasim government, 1958–1963

Qasim's government quickly declared itself revolutionary, and the overthrow of the monarchy was followed by mass demonstrations of

[7] C. Tripp, 2002.

support and celebration in Baghdad. Qasim fits both of the criteria for a revolutionary leader identified in Chapter 4: he came to power through use of armed force, and he led the implementation of radical policies that transformed Iraqi society. Major change occurred in three of the seven categories used to code revolutionary policy: the monarchy was replaced by a republic; the name of the country was changed; and a Revolutionary Command Council was put in place to preside over the government. There was also significant change in a fourth category, property ownership, although here the magnitude of the changes is nuanced.

Qasim made economic changes primarily in two areas, land reform and oil policy. He passed legislation aimed at redistributing much of the land from the country's largest estates to the smaller and middle-tier landowners. Oil revenues were redirected toward the immediate needs of the poorer sections of society, including housing and education, resulting in significantly more public services. Qasim's Law 80 took back a vast portion of the Iraq Petroleum Company's concessionary area, thereby confining it to the oil fields in which it already operated. And Iraq joined OPEC as a founding member in 1960.

Although significant on paper, the economic reforms under Qasim were not as important as those that occurred in the 1970s under the Baathists. In practice, Qasim's land reform transferred relatively little land away from the powerful elite. Even after a decade of land reform, almost a third of the country's fertile land was owned by less than 3 percent of the owners.[8] Similarly, changes in the oil sector were less substantial than they appeared. The IPC continued to produce all of Iraq's oil through the 1960s, as the government was unable to develop the oil fields in the territory that it had reclaimed from the IPC's concession. Further, Iraq had no more sovereignty over its oil production policy under Qasim than it did under the monarchy: the foreign companies that controlled the IPC responded to the creation of OPEC by slowing down production in Iraq, thereby punitively reducing the payments it generated for the Iraqi government. Thus while Qasim's economic reforms were important politically and as building blocks for future changes, they had a relatively modest impact in terms of redistributing income and property.

[8] R. Gabbay, 1978.

Qasim was moderately aggressive in foreign policy. Distracted by an ongoing power struggle at home, Qasim had limited time and energy for foreign policy.[9] Still, he rejected the unpopular Baghdad Pact and distanced himself from the Western powers and their allies. This led to a number of hostile incidents with Iraq's neighbors Iran and Kuwait. For instance, foreshadowing a much larger dispute under Saddam's leadership, Qasim abrogated an old treaty demarcating the Iraq–Iran border in the area of the Shatt al-Arab. This led to military confrontations between Iran and Iraq, including shots being fired over the waterway in 1960. Moreover, when Kuwait declared its independence in 1961, Qasim revived an ancient Iraqi claim to the Kuwaiti territory, again foreshadowing a future conflict. However, at the time both of these disputes were settled relatively quickly. Iran and Iraq signed a new peace agreement in 1961, settling the dispute over the Shatt al-Arab for a time. And while British military forces were sent to Kuwait to defend against possible Iraqi aggression, Qasim did not pursue his claim by force. The Arab League quickly admitted Kuwait as a member state, and thereafter Iraq was no longer in a position to pursue its claim any further.

Political turmoil, 1963–1968

In 1963, the loose political coalition that Qasim had managed to hold together for five years fell apart. The Baath Party could count only a small core membership at this time, but it was radical and well-connected within the armed forces. On February 8, a group of conspirators assassinated the commander of the air force and launched an armed rebellion against Qasim's regime. The next day Qasim was captured, brought before a Baathist tribunal, and summarily executed. Abd al-Salam Arif, Qasim's former protégé, became president of the new regime. Arif was not a Baathist but commanded support among the senior ranks of the military.

The next five years were a period of intense political turmoil in Iraq. The Baathists fell prey to factionalism and internal confusion. Although Arif had come to power with the backing of the Baathists, he soon fell out with them, and in November of the same year (1963), he ejected

---

[9] M. Farouk-Sluglett and P. Sluglett, 1987.

them from power. This led to a number of important Baathists being imprisoned, including both Hasan al-Bakr and Saddam Hussein.

In April 1966, Abd al-Salam Arif was killed in a helicopter accident, though suspicions remain about whether the incident was truly accidental. His brother Abd al-Rahman Arif replaced him as president. For a short time, the prime minister al-Bazzaz was primarily in control of the government, but Rahman Arif dismissed him in August of the same year. The next two years of Iraqi politics were dominated by conspiracy and intrigue.

Saddam Hussein at home: 1968–1991

Between 1958 and 1967, Iraq saw no less than eight coup attempts, two rebellions, and a civil war (with the Kurds).[10] The Baathist Party participated in two successful coups, only to have the leader that they supported turn on them, forcing them out of power and into hiding. In July 1968, history seemed to be repeating itself once more. Hasan al-Bakr and his kinsman Saddam Hussein, on behalf of the Baathists, joined forces with a number of key military commanders: Colonel al-Nayif, head of military intelligence, Colonel al-Daud, commander of the Republican Guard, and Colonel Sadun Ghaidan, commander of the Republican Guard's tank regiment. Together, this group sought to take advantage of a political crisis occasioned by the resignation of the Prime Minister Tahir Yahya on July 12. Five days later, the Baathists and their co-conspirators seized control of the government and exiled President Arif. On July 18, Hasan al-Bakr was proclaimed the new president.

Having been down this road twice before, the Baathists acted swiftly to ensure that they would not be toppled by their erstwhile allies. The Baathists felt they had to act quickly, because even with al-Bakr as president, a majority of positions went to non-Baathists, including the three key military commanders (al-Nayif, prime minister; al-Daud, minister of defense; and Sadun Ghaidan, commander of the Republican Guard) and their protégés. Persuading Sadun Ghaidan to join them, the Baathists waited until al-Daud was out of the country to launch a second coup. On July 30, al-Nayif was permanently exiled; al-Daud was ordered not to return to Iraq and was given various

[10] S. Khalil, 1990.

ambassadorial positions until he was retired in 1970 (and later assassinated). The elimination of these leaders is important for my argument because, as discussed below, revolutionary politics acts as a selection mechanism for a particular type of leader.

Thus in July 1968, a double coup brought Hasan al-Bakr and his associate Saddam Hussein to the pinnacle of Iraqi politics. Al-Bakr was president, chairman of the Revolutionary Command Council (RCC), and secretary-general of the Baath Party; Saddam was his deputy secretary-general in the party and was soon made vice-chair of the RCC. From the beginning, the new regime declared itself a revolutionary government that was a natural extension of the 1958 revolt against the monarchy.[11] Indeed, the new regime would eventually transform their country in profound ways. Under Saddam's leadership, the political and economic institutions of the country, especially in the crucial oil industry, would be overturned and reconstituted. Yet in the late 1960s, the struggle for power was still far from over.

Emergence of Saddam Hussein as leader

Saddam's gradual transformation from al-Bakr's loyal right hand to the undisputed leader of Iraq unfolded in three stages. In the first stage, 1968–1973, Saddam worked with al-Bakr to consolidate their power as leaders of the Baathist Party. The Party's core constituency was the Sunni Arab tribes from the provincial northwest of Iraq. Saddam and al-Bakr placed members of this constituency in key posts in the government, both as a form of patronage and to ensure control of the regime. Still, they did not yet have full control of the Baathist Party. Some, like Abd al-Khaliq al-Samarrai, believed in the ideological tenets of Baathism; others, like Minister of Defense Hardan al-Tikriti and Interior Minister Salih Mahdi Ammash, had significant constituencies of their own. These men needed to be eliminated. Saddam and al-Bakr first moved against al-Tikriti and Ammash, making them both vice-presidents in 1970 – a ceremonial role with little real power – while stripping them of their ministries. Within eighteen months, al-Tikriti was stripped of all his posts and assassinated in Kuwait. Ammash was dropped from the RCC and never again played a significant role in Iraqi politics.[12]

---

[11] M. Farouk-Sluglett and P. Sluglett, 1987.
[12] P. Marr, 2003.

The leadership's hold on power was also threatened by non-Baathists. In 1968–1969, a factional leader of a Communist Party led a "popular revolutionary war" against the regime. The revolt was quickly squashed and its leader, Aziz al-Hajj, forced to publicly recant. Still, the Baathists greatly feared the Communists and decided to publicly extend a hand of friendship to the Iraqi Communist Party (ICP) in order to expose its members. In 1972, two ICP members were appointed to the cabinet, and in 1973 al-Bakr and the secretary-general of the ICP signed the National Action Charter of supposedly common social goals. Similarly, the Baathists initially extended the olive branch of peace to the Kurds. Three Kurdish members were appointed to al-Bakr's Cabinet in 1968. They resigned within a month, but it opened up opportunities for negotiations, and the Baathists appeared to offer in a manifesto of March 1970 increased regional autonomy and recognition of Kurdish rights. Both the Communists and the Kurds would soon be disappointed by Baathist promises.

The relative fragility of the Baathist regime during this first stage was punctuated by the final serious coup attempt in June 1973 by Nadhim Kazzar. Kazzar, one of Saddam's former protégés, was the head of General Security (*Amn*). His plan to seize control of the country misfired, leading swiftly to his capture and execution. Saddam Hussein used the incident to eliminate other potential opponents, including over thirty senior officials. Others, like al-Samarrai, were imprisoned, shattering the last vestiges of Baathist ideological purity, and leaving instead a party that believed, as Saddam would later say, in whatever the leadership said it believed.

In the second stage, 1974–1976, Saddam increasingly asserted his personal claim to leadership of the country, slowly separating himself from al-Bakr. Oil prices skyrocketed following the 1973 embargo, which created numerous new opportunities for patronage by the state and the Baathist Party, and these opportunities were not lost on Saddam. In order to disrupt potential opposition within the Shi'a population, he offered resources and employment to groups based on their demonstrated loyalty to the regime. Populist economic policies were put in place, including subsidies of basic commodities and public provision of welfare services. At the same time, the government took on an increasingly totalitarian character. In the autumn of 1974, the Baathist relationship with the Communists deteriorated, and the ICP was forced to go underground. By 1976, all non-Baath political activity was outlawed and made a capital offense. Thus the Baathist government followed a familiar pattern of rentier clientelism observed in many petrostates around the world, offering economic patronage in exchange for political quiescence.[13] Increasingly, the man at the center of these patronage networks was Saddam Hussein, not Hasan al-Bakr. In 1976, Saddam also asked al-Bakr to make him a general of the armed forces, despite Saddam's complete lack of military experience. Al-Bakr complied, thereby bolstering Saddam's personal legitimacy and status. Still, Saddam continued to work as al-Bakr's deputy, wanting to ensure that he laid the foundations to secure his eventual leadership.

Finally, in the period 1977–1979, Saddam was in command of Iraq in all but name. In the autumn of 1977, he took two key steps. First, and perhaps most importantly, he seized total control over Iraq's oil policy, giving him exclusive access to the key resource of the state. Saddam personally determined levels of production and controlled the disbursements of oil revenues, and only he knew the exact levels of income and expenditure.[14] Second, all of the members of the Regional Command, a party committee that Saddam had led since 1968 and had enlarged in 1977, were made members of the Revolutionary Command Council (RCC), the highest governing body in Iraq. Consequently, Saddam loyalists were now a majority on the RCC. Together, these steps gave Saddam control over the two central elements of his regime: patronage and fear. In Iraq, these were known by the alliterative moniker *tarhib* and *targhib*: terror and enticement.[15]

To further solidify his leadership, Saddam took additional steps. One was to pay increased lip service to Islam and to encourage the official adoption of more overtly Islamic postures. This gave Saddam a way of building relationships within the *ulema* (Islamic clergy) and identifying individuals who would receive his patronage. Another step was to begin to erode al-Bakr's hold on the official levers of power, by persuading him to relinquish control of the Ministry of Defense to Adnan Khairallah Tulfah, the brother-in-law and first cousin of Saddam Hussein. Tulfah promptly set out to build client networks among the armed forces to support Saddam Hussein. Still another

---

[13] J. Colgan, 2011a; J. Crystal, 1990; S. Hertog, 2010; T. Karl, 1997; M. Ross, 2012; D. Vandewalle, 2006.
[14] C. Tripp, 2002.   [15] E. Sciolino, 1991.

step was to circulate rumors of al-Bakr's unspecified health problems, allowing people to believe that his days as president were numbered.

And indeed they were. In July 1979, al-Bakr was compelled to give up the presidency, and Saddam was sworn in. In the same month, a special convention of the Baath Party was held, which Saddam used as an opportunity to violently eliminate suspected opponents of his regime. One-third of the members of the RCC were executed, along with perhaps 500 top-ranking Baathists.[16] Saddam compelled many of the remaining party members to be personally involved in these executions as part of the firing squad.[17] Saddam used these incidents not only to inspire fear in potential opponents, but also to create a sense of collective responsibility and guilt in the installation of Saddam as president.

Transformation of Iraq under Saddam

In some ways, the revolutionary rhetoric that supported the Baathists' seizure of power in July 1968 was a convenient façade for the leadership. Yet in a number of important ways, the Baathist regime did lead a revolutionary transformation of Iraqi political and economic society. These changes can be measured in relation to the monarchy in place until 1958, and to the tumultuous decade 1958–1968. In the 1970s, Iraq was transformed in four key areas.

First, the structures of the Iraqi government were transformed. A new constitution was put in place in 1970. It was the latest in a series of constitutional revisions in the tumult of 1958–1968, but it far outlived its predecessors, remaining in place until 2003. The Revolutionary Command Council was established as the supreme executive council. The Baathists overhauled the internal security services of the Iraqi state. The new system included four major organizations: the *Amn al-Amm* (general security), the *mukhabarat* (Baathist security), the *istikhbarat* (military security), and the *Amn al-Khas* (special security). Each organization had layers upon layers, each spying upon the others and on the general population. While previous Iraqi governments had also relied on security services, the hydra-headed nature of such services took on a new and grotesque form under the leadership of Saddam Hussein.

[16] S. Khalil, 1990.   [17] E. Sciolino, 1991.

Second, Iraq's economy was transformed. Unlike Qasim's regime, the Baathists were serious about nationalizing the oil sector. In March 1969, the Baathists began negotiations with the Soviet Union to help develop the Iraqi oil sector. In June and July, they signed agreements for Soviet technical assistance to develop oil fields and construct a 70-mile pipeline linking North Rumaila with the port of Fao on the Shatt al-Arab.[18] The agreements marked a significant step away from the IPC, which until this time still controlled all Iraqi commercial oil production. In December 1971, negotiations began between the Iraqi government and the IPC to provide the government with equity in the company.[19] Finally, in June 1972, the IPC was nationalized. From the government's perspective, the timing could scarcely have been better. By the time of the oil embargo of 1973, Iraq was in position to reap the full benefits of increased revenues.

The Baathists also transformed the Iraqi economy in other ways, moving it toward socialism. All taxes on income and sales were eliminated. Most major firms, especially in the iron, steel, petrochemical, and construction industries, were wholly owned and operated by the government.[20] Half of the economically active urban labor force was employed by the state.[21] The public sector's share of the economy rose from 31 percent in 1968 to 80 percent in 1977.[22] Nor was state intervention limited to urban areas. While Qasim's land reform had been moderately successful at best, the Baathists were more aggressive. In 1969, they cancelled all compensation for sequestered lands. With this single act, they greatly benefited the lower classes and removed a major government expense. They extended land reform in the 1970s, and increased investment in agriculture. State-owned cooperatives were established and made mandatory for farmers if they wished to benefit from the subsidized seed, fertilizer, and other benefits of the regime. Food was heavily subsidized, significantly redistributing wealth in Iraq while simultaneously providing more opportunities for patronage by the regime.

The 1973 oil embargo led to an eightfold increase in Iraq's oil revenues. This led to a wave of development projects and new opportunities for patronage. The state added new housing projects and invested

[18] M. Farouk-Sluglett and P. Sluglett, 1987.
[19] C. Tripp, 2002.   [20] P. Marr, 2003.
[21] S. Khalil, 1990: 41.   [22] P. Marr, 2003: 242.

in health and education. It also tried to develop new industries, particularly for export. The boom meant that in sectors like construction and banking, patron–client relationships and access to key government officials became vital business assets. Of course, oil revenues impacted all of the oil-exporting countries in the 1970s, but the path of that development in Iraq was profoundly shaped by the degree of state control and intervention that characterized the Baathist regime. Indeed, scholars suggest that the Baathist government controlled the economy to "an infinitely greater extent than any of its predecessors."[23] Nearly 40 percent of the oil income was spent on military purchases,[24] and by 1980, 20 percent of the labor force was employed by the police, the military, or the militia.[25] Thus the revolutionary character of the Baathist regime significantly affected the flow and direction of the oil income in Iraqi society.

Third, to a certain degree the Baathists transformed social relations in Iraqi society. Women's rights and empowerment increased in the 1970s (though Iraqi women were later to lose some of these rights). Article 19 of the 1970 Constitution guaranteed the equality of the sexes. Women drove cars, dressed as they pleased, went to college, voted, and held more than 10 percent of the seats in the National Assembly.[26] Between 1976 and 1986, the number of female students at the primary-school level increased by 60 percent, and from 35 to 45 percent of the total student body. At the secondary level, the number of female students more than doubled.[27] Female literacy and opportunities for employment outside of the agricultural sector also greatly increased. In 1978, legal reforms gave women greater standing in the courts.[28]

The Baathists also intervened in Iraqi society in other ways, often less positive. The party was an omnipresent component of public life, eventually reaching down to the smallest village and neighborhood. Its membership grew from a few hundred in 1968 to 500,000 by 1976,

[23] M. Farouk-Sluglett and P. Sluglett, 1987: 173.
[24] C. Tripp, 2002: 214.   [25] S. Khalil, 1990: 38.
[26] C. Coughlin, 2002.
[27] Library of Congress, 1990: Appendix Table 4.
[28] Note that while there were substantial changes in Iraq in the 1970s, that does not mean that Iraqi women had the same rights as Western women. Indeed, in 1988 "honor killings" were legalized, permitting men to kill their wives or female relatives if they were judged to have committed adultery.

and 1.5 million by 1984.[29] Universal military conscription was insti-
tuted. The *ulema* increasingly fell under the patronage of the Baathist
regime. The party banned the use of personal last names, and permitted the sale of alcohol in Shi'a mosques. The government even offered
large financial incentives for men to divorce their wives if they came
from families suspected of "Iranian" connections.[30] (These "Iranian"
links were often tenuous, and merely a cover for disempowering and
punishing potential opponents of the regime.) After a Kurdish revolt
had been put down in 1975, Saddam financed a massive operation to
strategically re-transplant key populations into the interior of Iraq.
Half a million Kurds were moved away from their home villages in
these operations.[31] Simultaneously, the government offered financial
incentives for Arab families to move into Kurdish areas, thereby dilut-
ing the Kurdish claims for regional autonomy.

Fourth and finally, the Baathists changed the nature of the Iraqi
military. For decades, the Iraqi military had been home to a range
of independent political thought. After 1968, however, the Baathists
established a new system of accountability in which party men could
thwart the orders of senior non-Baathist officers.[32] This was a significant shift: under the monarchy before 1958, and during the republican
period before 1968, military officers saw themselves as surrogates and
guardians of a national identity that was often distinct from the identity of their political masters. Eliminating this culture of independent
thought was a crucial part of the Baathists' effort to consolidate their
power and prevent additional coups. The implication for foreign policy was that one of the most important mechanisms of accountability on the leader of Iraq was eliminated. As interviews with Saddam's
generals after the fall of his regime later attested, Saddam could take
the risks of instigating a war knowing that the threat of the military
officers rising up against him had been minimized.[33]

Thus compared to the traditional Arab society ruled by a British-
installed monarchy in the 1950s, and the political chaos of the 1960s,
life in Iraq changed dramatically along multiple dimensions under the

[29] S. Khalil, 1990: 39.   [30] C. Tripp, 2002.
[31] C. Tripp, 2002: 214.   [32] S. Khalil, 1990.
[33] For instance, when Lieutenant General Ra'ad Majid Rashid al-Hamdani was
asked whether any military officers verbalized their dismay over Saddam's
decision to invade Iran in 1980, he said "the dissent did not last for long after
the political decision had been made." Quoted in K. Woods *et al.*, 2011a: 56.

leadership of Saddam and the Baathists. Many Iraqis were content: thanks to abundant oil revenues, GDP per capita had more than doubled in the 1970s, and the government's populist policies appeared to be distributing the wealth to the people.

Oil patronage in Saddam's Iraq

Al-Bakr and Hussein were certainly not the first autocratic leaders to ride to power on revolutionary rhetoric. Yet what made the Baathist regime distinctive was the way in which its leaders, especially Saddam, were able to use oil income to fund vast networks of patronage. To seize power in Iraq, the Baathists needed the support of – or at least, to avoid resistance from – a large number of overlapping constituencies: the Sunni tribes, the military corps, key parts of the *ulema*, various business groups, and Communist supporters. In the late 1960s and early 1970s, the direction of support flowed from these groups to the Baathists. Over time, however, the direction of support reversed. At the core of this important reversal of power was the patronage made possible by Iraq's oil income.

Resources were spread widely. The largest beneficiaries of patronage were the Sunni tribes from the northwest of the country, along with senior military officers. Military spending increased dramatically under the Baathists, providing plenty of opportunities for officers to obtain "commissions" and kickbacks on weapons purchases and other military contracts. Resources were also channeled toward favored elements within the Shi'a community, while others were left without, thereby signaling to all the rewards for political loyalty. The *ulema*, who had previously been independent of the state, gradually became direct beneficiaries of government largesse. Hundreds of thousands of displaced Kurds were re-housed at government expense and given government jobs. The Popular Army, a militia-reserve group under the command of Saddam's protégé Taha Ramadhan al-Jazrawi, employed thousands of young men trained to be Baathist loyalists in exchange for their stipend.[34] This "Army," drawn largely from lower-class Iraqis, was doubled in size in 1976, again thanks to the influx of oil revenues.[35]

---

[34] S. Khalil, 1990.   [35] C. Tripp, 2002: 216.

The importance of oil to the structure of the Iraqi economy went far beyond its direct impact in terms of government revenues. The centralized flows of oil income meant that the economy was guided by government planning rather than by market forces.[36] In the agricultural sector, oil income paid for the seed and fertilizer subsidies, which were incentives for farmers to join state-organized cooperatives and collective farms. In business, the economy revolved around various public construction projects, government contracts, regulatory approvals, and state-mandated monopolies, all of which relied on patron–client relationships shaped by oil rentierism. Moreover, oil income paid the salaries of Saddam's various organizations of secret police and security services. These security forces in turn shaped the economy by dispossessing thousands of suspected enemies of the regime and then redistributing or auctioning off the property of the dispossessed.[37]

The patronage system necessarily involved corruption and waste of public expenditure. It was therefore crucial for Saddam's political position that information about the state's finances be kept from the public. Accordingly, only Saddam knew how Iraq's oil money was being spent. After the surge of oil revenues in late 1973, publication of economic statistics relating to "strategic areas" was made a criminal offence.[38] Not surprisingly, it was (and still is) impossible to obtain full, transparent accounting of Iraq's government expenditures during the 1970s. This was another way in which the oil industry weakened domestic accountability in Iraq.

By 1980, Saddam was at the center of the most powerful government in Iraq's modern history. He "had become an institution unto himself, one virtually without checks."[39] Saddam's networks of patronage and overlapping security services gave him total political control over his country. With Iraq firmly under his thumb, it was time to conquer new territories.

Saddam as revolutionary

Unlike some of the other revolutionaries studied in this book, Saddam did not rise from rebel to national leader in one swift act. His path to power covered two decades of activities, from his early acts of violence

[36] P. Marr, 2003.   [37] C. Tripp, 2002.
[38] C. Tripp, 2002.   [39] S. Khalil, 1990: 271.

in 1958 to the presidency in 1979. Still, Saddam fits both of the criteria for a revolutionary leader identified in Chapter 4: he came to power through use of armed force (in 1968), and during the 1970s he led the implementation of radical policies that transformed Iraqi society. Compared to the governments prior to 1968, change occurred in four of the seven categories used to code revolutionary policy: the political institutions and constitution were overhauled; a new Revolutionary Command Council was installed; economic changes were implemented; and the Baathist Party structure excluded all other political activity. The changes in Iraq were even greater when compared to the 1950s. Because the Baathists had been involved in the regime changes of 1958–1967, there is some ambiguity about which regime one should regard as the "prior regime." If one considers the Iraqi monarchy as the "prior regime," there were changes under Saddam in five of the seven categories (executive institutions; property ownership; party structure; state name; revolutionary council). In either case, Saddam can be considered a revolutionary leader.

Saddam's Iraq abroad: 1968–1991

The first priority of any successful revolutionary regime is to secure and consolidate its domestic power. This sometimes means that the regime is compelled to act in a conciliatory manner to its neighbors to bide its time while distracted by power struggles at home. This was Saddam's approach while he slowly secured his own position at home during the 1970s. Once securely installed as president of Iraq, however, Saddam's foreign policy was arguably the most aggressive on earth. After arming his state to the teeth, he started two major wars, first against Iran (1980–1988) and then Kuwait and its allies (1990–1991).

Saddam bides his time

Until he became president, Saddam's primary goals were to secure his own position at home and gradually strengthen Iraq's geopolitical position. This had three implications. First, Iraq had to find ways to placate Iran. The Shah feared and disliked the Baathist regime for its pan-Arab ideology, its revolutionary socialism, and its anti-Western stance.[40]

---

[40] P. Marr, 2003.

Consequently, Iran initiated a confrontation over the Shatt al-Arab, and subsequently occupied the islands of Abu Musa and the Tunbs. Numerous border incidents and low-level military clashes ensued. Still, the Shah did not have the appetite to mount a major invasion of Iraq. Moreover, the Baathists' approach to Iran was pragmatic because their principal concern was the domestic threat posed by the Kurds. When the Baathists first came to power, they were able to split the Kurds by making false promises of regional autonomy. As the Kurds slowly realized they could not trust the Baathists, they renewed their violent campaign against the Baathist regime with Iranian assistance. In 1974, the Iraqi government signaled to Tehran that it sought an end to Iranian aid to the Kurds. Negotiating on behalf of Iraq, Saddam reached a comprehensive settlement with the Shah in March 1975, known as the Algiers Pact. The Pact divided the Shatt al-Arab between Iraq and Iran, specifying the *thalweg* (median line) of the waterway as the border. This satisfied Iran; in exchange, the Shah agreed to desist from aiding the Kurds. Consequently, Iraqi forces crushed the Kurdish revolt and forced one of its principal leaders, Mustafa Barzani, to flee into exile. Although there would be another Kurdish uprising in 1977 (swiftly put down by Iraqi forces), the Algiers Pact allowed Saddam to control the Kurdish region until the 1990s. Iraq and Iran maintained cordial relations until the Shah was deposed.

Second, Saddam swiftly built up the military capacity of Iraq. Iraq's treaty of friendship with the Soviet Union in 1972 paved the way for massive arms purchases after the influx of oil revenues starting in 1973. Russia was far from Iraq's only supplier, however; by the late 1970s, many Western countries, especially France, were selling weapons to Iraq. In the period 1973–1980, Iraq's military expenditure was an estimated 18 percent of GDP, one of the highest rates in the world.[41] In addition to foreign weapons purchases, the Baathists greatly increased the personnel of Iraq's armed forces. Just prior to the Baathist coup, the Iraqi military consisted of 82,000 men; by 1980, just prior to the war with Iran, this had tripled to 242,000. As a percentage of the population, Iraq's military was twice the size of Iran's and Egypt's, and about twelve times that of Brazil, which had the largest army in Latin America. These numbers grew even more rapidly after the outbreak of

[41] M. El-Gamal and A. Jaffe, 2010: 90.

war. By 1984, the Iraqi regular armed forces counted 607,000 men, as well as 450,000 members of the Popular Army (reservists).[42]

Third, Saddam's attention on Iraq's western front was dominated by the issues of Israel and pan-Arabism. Although ideologically the Baathist Party was initially committed to pan-Arabism, in practice there was little desire by its leaders to pursue state unification plans. By the time the Baathists came to power in July 1968, Nasser's legitimacy had already suffered a massive blow from the Six-Day War in 1967. Iraq was scarcely a participant in the 1973 Arab–Israeli War, as Iraq's leaders were not involved in its planning and initiation.[43] Iraq did send an armored division to help Syria on the Golan Heights, but too late for it to participate meaningfully in the combat.

Nonetheless, in the late 1970s Saddam increased his international standing. With Nasser's death in 1970 and Sadat's willingness to make peace with Israel after the Yom Kippur War, Egypt was no longer the center of gravity in the Arab world. As Iraq's oil income increased, Saddam gave money to Palestinian families of those who died in the ongoing fight against Israel, a practice that would ensure his life-long popularity in Jordan and Palestine. During the 1970s, terrorist groups such as Abu Nidal and the Popular Front for the Liberation of Palestine set up shop in Baghdad with the support of the Iraqi government. Further, Saddam maneuvered to position himself as the leader of the Arabs at the 1978 Arab League Summit, held in Baghdad. At this meeting, Egypt was (temporarily) expelled from the League in the aftermath of Sadat's peace treaty with Israel. Saddam took advantage of this opening by sponsoring the Arab Charter, a statement of common Arab goals, which was published in Baghdad in 1980.

Thus Saddam spent most of the 1970s biding his time and putting the pieces in place for his later aggression. However, in the latter half of the 1970s, Iraq's rivalry with Syria foreshadowed the aggression that was to characterize Saddam's presidency. With the dispute with Iran settled in 1975, Iraq was in a better position to act aggressively on its western border. Saddam used Syria's invasion of Lebanon and military action against Palestinian forces to cast doubt on the pan-Arab credentials of Syria's president. Iraq then instigated direct military action

---

[42] S. Khalil, 1990: 32–35.

[43] Indeed, the Syrian government accused Iraqi leaders of refusing any such participation (C. Tripp, 2002).

by moving troops to the border, stopping all oil exports through the Iraq–Syrian pipeline, and initiating an assassination campaign against Syrian officials, including bomb attacks on government buildings. While these attacks never became a full-fledged war, they are evidence of Iraq's aggressive foreign policy behavior under the Baathists.

The war with Iran

In 1979, Khomeini led a revolution in Iran. Saddam viewed these events with a combination of trepidation and opportunism. On one hand, he feared Khomeini. Khomeini had lived in Iraq for many years while in exile, but in 1978 Saddam ordered him to leave because Khomeini was encouraging the Shi'a to revolt and establish an Islamic form of government. Saddam feared that Iraq's Shi'a population, which formed a majority, would seek to follow Khomeini's revolutionary lead. Indeed, Iranian leaders explicitly stated that their goal was to export the Islamic Revolution, and a number of border violations in 1980 appeared to substantiate Iraqi fears.[44]

On the other hand, Saddam also saw an opportunity for conquest. Iran was in turmoil, as a civil war broke out between the various revolutionary factions and the chain of command for the Iranian military was in doubt. Saddam sought to take back the Shatt al-Arab waterway and seize the oil-rich province of Khuzestan. Saddam also wanted to increase his international stature and to seize Nasser's mantle as the leader of the Arabs.[45] Indeed, the unstated reasons for going to war were at least as important as the stated ones. The decision to make war stemmed largely from the character of Saddam's government, which was brimming with self-confidence and had armed itself to the teeth.[46] Even the name of the war, the *Qadisiyyat Saddam* (a reference to a seventh-century Arab triumph over Persian forces), suggested that the war was about establishing Saddam as a great leader in the Mesopotamian tradition.

[44] K. Woods *et al.*, 2011a.
[45] "Since at least 1978, Saddam [Hussein] had been manoeuvring to position Iraq under his leadership as the pivotal Arab state" (C. Tripp, 2002: 230). For instance, Iraq hosted international summits in 1978 and 1979, followed in February 1980 by the publication in Baghdad of the Arab Charter.
[46] S. Khalil, 1990; P. Marr, 2003; C. Tripp, 2002.

Saddam told his senior advisors, in private meetings that were recorded on tapes later captured by the US military, about his calculations on war.[47] He recognized various risks to an attack on Iran but calculated that the benefits outweighed them. Accordingly, he publicly abrogated the 1975 Algiers Pact before a meeting of the National Assembly and asserted Iraqi sovereignty over the whole of the Shatt al-Arab. On September 22, 1980, Iraq invaded Iran.

The war itself was exceptionally costly for both sides.[48] Precise casualty figures are unknown, but the total has been estimated at over 600,000.[49] After it became apparent that Saddam's initial ambitions were going to be thwarted and that Iraq was under serious threat from the Iranian counter-attack, Saddam sued for peace. By 1982, however, it was revolutionary Iran's turn to be aggressive, and it rejected all offers for peace. Desperate to inflict pain on Iran, Saddam launched the so-called Tanker War in 1984. Starting with its initial attack on the Iranian oil terminal on Kharg Island, Iraq sought to reduce Iran's oil revenues and thereby slow down its war machine. Iran counter-attacked, ultimately leading in 1987 to intervention by the United States. Oil tankers were re-flagged and US warships began patrolling the Persian Gulf. Despite continued attacks, both Iraq and Iran shipped oil throughout the war. Only when it became clear that both countries were exhausted by the war effort did they relent and agree to a truce in 1988. The Iran–Iraq War is often called the longest conventional war of the twentieth century; it was certainly one of its bloodiest.

The war with Kuwait

Saddam declared himself the victor of the Iraq–Iran War, but this was a sham. This war had only losers. None of Saddam's territorial objectives had been accomplished, thousands of Iraqis had been killed, and the country's economy was devastated. Although the United States, Saudi Arabia, Kuwait, and other countries had been supportive during the war, their support turned shallow at its conclusion. Particularly

---

[47] NDU Conflict Records Research Center Document SH-SHTP-A-000–835: 6–13.
[48] S. Chubin and C. Tripp, 1988.
[49] E. Sciolino, 1991: 105.

vexing was the issue of Iraq's enormous war debt, amounting to at least $130 billion, which set the stage for its next international war.

The causes of the Iraq–Kuwait War of 1990 were multiple. The war has been the subject of considerable research by scholars,[50] and only the briefest account is offered here. At least three major factors contributed to Saddam's decision to invade. First, unlike some of Iraq's other Arab creditors, Kuwait refused to forgive Iraq's massive war debt. Iraq also accused Kuwait of over-producing oil (relative to its OPEC quota), thereby depressing world oil prices and further damaging Iraq's economy. Second, Kuwait had rich oil fields and massive gold reserves that Iraq could loot. If Saddam could conquer Kuwait, he would control more oil reserves than any other country in the world, including Saudi Arabia. Third, Saddam still craved international influence.[51] The conquest of Kuwait would give him an unprecedented position of influence in OPEC. Moreover, a victory against Kuwait, if Arab leaders accepted it, would eventually bolster his claim as leader of the Arabs.

The decision to invade was complicated by Saddam's political position at home. In one sense, Saddam faced significant domestic political tensions. An open revolt among the Kurds compelled Saddam to take military action against them in the late 1980s, which included the use of chemical weapons. Saddam also feared opposition within the Shi'a population and even his own military officer corps. However, two decades of Saddam's patronage and totalitarian repression had left Iraq without anyone with a real chance of overthrowing the regime. Although Saddam continued to use fear and repression to hold onto power, he could view the risks of a war with Kuwait with some confidence. If he won, his domestic opponents would be discredited and his political position strengthened. If he lost, he would of course face significant political opposition, but he already faced opposition in the Kurdish and Shi'a populations. Moreover, even a loss would provide a scapegoat for the country's mounting economic troubles, and Iraq could plausibly escape from some of its foreign debt. This is not to suggest that Saddam faced no risks or consequences to a military loss, and a less risk-tolerant leader – e.g., most non-revolutionary

---

[50] C. Alfonsi, 2006; J. Bulloch and H. Morris, 1991; C. Tripp, 2002; K. Woods *et al.*, 2011b.
[51] C. Coughlin, 2002: 242; C. Tripp, 2002: 252–253.

leaders – might have found those risks unacceptable. Still, the weak political accountability in Iraq reduced the risks associated with a war, thereby altering the incentives and perhaps tipping the balance for a risk-tolerant leader like Saddam.

Thus on August 2, 1990, Iraq invaded Kuwait. After two days of combat, the Kuwaiti armed forces were overwhelmed and the ruling al-Sabah family had fled. Saddam installed his cousin Ali Hassan al-Majid ("Chemical Ali") as governor of Kuwait. The reaction from the international community was swift. On August 6, the United Nations passed a resolution condemning the invasion and imposing sanctions on Iraq. Attempting to gather Arab allies and deflect diplomatic criticism, Saddam responded by calling for an agreement in which all "occupations" would be resolved simultaneously: i.e., Israel would be required to withdraw from Palestine, Syria, and Lebanon before he would withdraw from Kuwait. This issue linkage meant that, when armed conflict came, Iraq would respond by firing Scud missiles at Israel.

In the remainder of 1990, the United States put together a broad coalition, including many Arab countries, to remove Iraqi forces from Kuwait. First, Operation Desert Shield was put in place to guard Saudi Arabia against a potential invasion from Iraq. Iraqi tank divisions were within easy striking distance of Saudi Arabia's largest oil fields, causing King Fahd to invite US soldiers into Saudi Arabia as a defensive force. The next phase, Operation Desert Storm, liberated Kuwait. On January 17, 1991, the US-led coalition began an aerial bombing campaign against Iraq. On January 29, Iraqi forces attacked and temporarily occupied the port city of Khafji in Saudi Arabia. Two days later, they were driven back by US and Saudi forces. Finally, in late February, hundreds of thousands of ground troops attacked and occupied Kuwait. Although coalition forces initially entered into Iraq (and could have continued with little resistance), they halted their advance.

The postwar domestic political reaction in Iraq and the United States was an important part of the way Saddam viewed the war. In private conversations, Saddam expressed satisfaction that Bush lost the 1992 election.[52] From Saddam's perspective, the fact that he remained in

----

[52] NDU Conflict Records Research Center Document SH-SHTP-A-000–838.

office after the war while Bush was removed was demonstrative proof that Iraq actually won the Gulf War.[53] This line of reasoning probably reflects post-hoc rationalization, at least in part. Nonetheless, it is consistent with the hypothesis that a leader's postwar fate was an integral part of Saddam's calculus about war.

Defiance and aggression: 1991–2003

In March 1991, uprisings broke out across southern Iraq, principally among the Shi'a population. These uprisings were verbally encouraged, but not militarily supported, by the US government. While the protests represented a serious threat to Saddam's government, the protesters faced two serious and ultimately fatal obstacles. First, the uprisings had no effective leadership. Saddam had calculated correctly: years of repression had left Iraq without any significant opposition leadership. One senior cleric, Ayatollah Abu al-Qasim al-Khoi, did give public approval for the formation of a committee to preserve order and security in Iraq, but this was hardly enough to direct a revolution. Within weeks, the authorities forced the Ayatollah to reverse his position and declare his support for Saddam Hussein.

Second, Saddam was ready for the uprisings. The Iraqi military units that held Kuwait at the end of February were crushed by allied forces, but that was a loss that Saddam could do little to prevent. The elite units of the Iraqi Republican Guard had been held in "reserve" in Baghdad, rather than fighting in Kuwait. They were now fully capable of squashing the Shi'a uprising, which they did, inflicting numerous civilian casualties. Over 50,000 refugees poured into Saudi Arabia, and thousands more fled into Iran or the uninhabited marshes of southern Iraq.[54]

Having crushed the Shi'a uprisings, Saddam then turned his forces against the rebellions that broke out in the Kurdish north. The Kurdish rebels enjoyed some brief successes while the government's troops were focused on the south, including the capture of Kirkuk on March 19, but they were soon routed by the Republican Guard. More than two million people were displaced in the resulting chaos. However, the UN

[53] K. Woods *et al.*, 2011b: 168.   [54] C. Tripp, 2002: 256.

Security Council acted in April to create a "no-fly zone" north of the 36th parallel, which halted the Iraqi military.

Saddam was soon up to his old tricks. He appointed a Shi'a member of the RCC, Sadun Hammadi, as prime minister, and hinted that further accommodations to the Shi'a were possible. He also re-opened the dialogue with the leaders of the Kurdish Front and convinced one of the key Kurdish leaders to visit Baghdad and publicly embrace Saddam. As in the past, Saddam used these overtures to buy time, divide the opposition, and re-establish his old networks of patronage and fear.

Military conflicts between Iraq and its enemies, primarily the United States, continued throughout the 1990s. The UN sanctioned Iraq, and the United States enforced a "no-fly zone" over Iraqi airspace. Saddam remained aggressive in the face of international isolation. Iraq allegedly sponsored an attempt to assassinate former President Bush in 1993.[55] Then, in an oft-forgotten incident, 80,000 Iraqi troops moved toward the Kuwaiti border in October 1994, causing international alarm and forcing the United States to redeploy its military in the area.[56] Two years later, Iraqi military units attacked a Kurdish faction supported by Iran in an area beneath the no-fly zone in northern Iraq. This violated UN Resolution 688, and the United States responded by firing missiles on Iraqi military targets and expanding the no-fly zone. By the end of the 1990s, it was clear that the international sanctions regime had been undermined by corruption and that it did little to weaken Saddam's hold on power (and perhaps just the opposite). Iraq's growing defiance of the international community led to repeated military engagements during 2000 and 2001, in which Iraqi anti-aircraft batteries shot at US air patrols. In sum, Iraq participated in a high-stakes game of cat-and-mouse until the United States invaded Iraq in 2003 and removed Saddam Hussein from power.

Operation of causal mechanisms

The preceding discussion has attempted to offer the reader a historical account, necessarily brief and incomplete, of Iraq and its foreign policy in recent decades. Drawing upon this material, the hypothesized causal mechanisms can be probed further through three distinct questions.

---

[55] D. Von Drehle and R. Smith, 1993.
[56] S. Yetiv, 1997.

Did the revolutionary government make Iraq more aggressive?

The revolutionary period in Iraq, beginning with the tumultuous decade 1958–1968, and culminating in Saddam's leadership, resulted in a state with highly aggressive foreign policy behavior. Evidence of the causal factors hypothesized in Chapter 2 can be identified. First, Saddam was a risk-tolerant, ambitious individual. He came to his position of leadership through violence and cunning. Saddam went to jail for the first time at the age of 21 in 1958, having already become a militant nationalist.[57] Almost as soon as he was released, Saddam was active in an attempt to assassinate President Qasim in 1959. Although the attempt failed, Saddam was rewarded for his loyalty and daring, and subsequently became secretary of the Baath Party. He continued to thrive in a highly risky political environment, and though he was sentenced to prison in 1964, he escaped in 1967 and continued to exert leadership in the Baath Party. He served as al-Bakr's right hand during the double coup of 1968 which propelled the Baathists to power. In the 1970s he sought to undermine his former patron, al-Bakr. Saddam's nationalization of the IPC is often described as a major political gamble.[58] Over time, he survived coup attempts, large-scale protests, and multiple assassination attempts. Thus he showed himself to be a shrewd leader willing to take risks in order to achieve political gains.

Many of Saddam's biographers noted his daring and aggression. This is only indirect evidence, as Saddam's mental characteristics are not directly observable. Still, those who have studied intensely his patterns of behavior characterize Saddam as a "daring and aggressive knight," a "gambler," and "risk-taking."[59] His close friends describe Saddam's ambitions even in childhood to rule the Arab world.[60] Seeking to explain Saddam's seemingly irrational degree of risk-tolerance, one Western security service even floated the possibility that the drugs he was taking for angina might be giving him a sense of invulnerability.[61]

---

[57] P. Marr, 2003.   [58] C. Coughlin, 2002: 108.

[59] J. Bulloch and H. Morris, 1991: 26; E. Karsh and I. Rautsi, 2003: 78; L. Yahia and K. Wendl, 1997: 266. See also S. Aburish, 2001; C. Coughlin, 2002; and the chapter by J. Post in S. Renshon, 1993.

[60] General Hamdani noted "Both Saddam and the Ayatollah Khomeini were dictators with grand ambitions … [In childhood, Saddam told a friend] 'I have great ambitions. I want to rule the Arab world and be like Salah ad-Din.'" Quoted in K. Woods *et al.*, 2011a: 53.

[61] Described in J. Bulloch and H. Morris, 1991: 26–27.

Yet Saddam's behavior over a period of decades suggests that ambition and risk-tolerance were ingrained character traits. Byman and Pollack conclude simply, "to say that Saddam is risk tolerant would be a gross understatement."[62]

Second, the revolutionary turmoil in Iraq facilitated the emergence of a leader with Saddam's ambition and risk-tolerance. Politics in Iraq was clearly not for the faint of heart, as leaders were frequently overthrown, assassinated, or executed. Only a leader with a combination of ambition, ruthlessness, risk-tolerance, and luck could succeed in such an environment. Many other contenders for the leadership of Iraq existed. During the tumultuous 1960s, Qasim, the Arif brothers, erstwhile prime ministers Abd al-Rahman al-Bazzaz, Arif Abd ar-Razzaq, and Tahir Yahya, and possibly a dozen other military officers or senior leaders could plausibly have seized power prior to al-Bakr and Saddam. After 1968, there continued to be a host of potential leaders besides Saddam, including the Baathists' three key allies in the coup (al-Nayif, al-Daud, and Ghaidan), the Baathist leader al-Samarrai, senior military leaders such as Hardan al-Tikriti and Salih Ammash, Saddam's protégé Nadhim Kazzar, and of course Hasan al-Bakr, who was formally president. Yet for various reasons, Saddam succeeded in seizing power where they did not. The fluid, ruthless nature of Iraqi politics created a breeding ground for such a leader.

Third, the revolutionary period eliminated all effective institutional and political checks and balances to Saddam Hussein's power. Consider the various formal institutions and procedures identified in Chapter 3. Formal institutional constraints on the chief executive of the state have never been a strong feature of Iraqi government. Nonetheless, some constraints on the monarchy did exist. For instance, the Iraqi Constitution of 1925 stipulates that the king could declare war only with approval of the Council of Ministers, and ratify peace treaties only with the approval of parliament. Moreover, the constitution required that no taxes would be imposed without parliamentary approval, thereby affecting the state's ability to finance a military campaign. Additional provisions stipulated that government budgets were to be drafted by the minister of finance and approved by parliament. Of course, in Iraq's constitutional monarchy, the king had considerable executive powers, including the ability to dismiss parliament

---

[62] D. Byman and K. Pollack, 2001: 129.

or the Cabinet. Nonetheless, the existence of formal institutions that were more than a mere rubber-stamp of the leader's wishes created opportunities for political opposition and leadership constraint. Under Saddam, there were no real institutions that fostered political debate. The National Assembly was a symbolic rubber-stamp. The Revolutionary Command Council, Iraq's highest legislative and executive body, was dominated by Saddam loyalists. Saddam had complete control of the entire governmental apparatus, and was therefore free to pursue his foreign policy preferences at will.

Perhaps just as importantly, there were far fewer voices of independent political thought under Saddam. In all of the previous governments, independent political views existed. Under the monarchy, various ministers contended with one another. Independent political parties also operated, espousing viable political alternatives to those offered by the government. For instance, the Iraqi Communist Party (ICP), created in 1934, was an important locus of political opposition and activity for decades. The ICP led many of the most important national uprisings and protests throughout the 1940s and 1950s. After the 1958 revolution, it continued to be a major player in Iraqi politics, a status which it only lost when it was eventually crushed by Saddam Hussein in the 1970s. Also during the 1960s, other political actors such as the National Democratic Party and the remnants of the Free Officers offered political alternatives to the principal leadership. Such pluralism was effectively squashed in 1976, when all non-Baathist activity was outlawed.

In sum, the evidence from Iraqi politics shows considerable support for the hypothesis that revolutionary politics increase the state's aggressiveness. This is principally due to the emergence of a leader with ambitious, risk-tolerance preferences who was not limited by domestic political constraints.

Did oil generate incentives for aggression and conflict?

Oil income is hypothesized to increase the state's propensity for international conflict, principally by reducing the leader's risk of domestic punishment for foreign policy adventurism. Oil income could also be used to increase the state's military capabilities. There is evidence that both of these effects were present in Iraq.

Saddam used the country's oil income to create a system of patronage and fear that permeated Iraqi society and weakened political accountability. Oil income financed the patronage networks that created government supporters among military officers, businessmen, the *ulema*, the Sunni tribes, the Shi'a population, and even the Kurds. Oil money was used directly to prop up support for military activities. For instance, at the beginning of the Iran–Iraq War, the government paid families of dead soldiers 10,000 dinars (equal to $30,000 at the official exchange rate), though as casualties mounted it had to stop this practice. The government also used oil funds to replace lost wages for the reservists serving in the Popular Army. In addition, the state's abundant resources financed the system of overlapping security services that spied on each other and on the population at large. This combination of clientelism and repression enabled Saddam to gamble with foreign policy adventures, correctly calculating that even if his armies lost, he would be able to maintain power domestically. This lack of domestic accountability, either through political representation or the threat of overthrow, gave Saddam a free hand in foreign policy.

Not surprisingly, oil income also proved instrumental in funding Iraq's military expenditures. From at least the time of the 1972 treaty with the USSR, which explicitly linked oil production with foreign arms purchases, oil income has served as the basis for Iraq's military muscle. There was a steep increase in both the armed forces personnel and expenditures following the flood of oil revenues in late 1973: Iraq spent at least $65 billion in purchases of foreign arms and equipment alone during the period 1975–1990.[63] By the 1980s, total military expenditures averaged $15 billion per year.[64] Iraq's expenditures were so large that in the five years leading up to the invasion of Kuwait, Iraq accounted for around 10 percent of the entire international arms market.[65]

Did oil generate incentives to avoid aggression and conflict?

Oil is also posited to decrease the state's propensity for international conflict by increasing the incentives for peaceful international economic links. In Iraq's case, these incentives are not easily observed, as the dominant incentives were in the opposite direction: to create aggression and conflict. Nonetheless, it is possible that oil still provided

[63] E. Sciolino, 1991: 140.   [64] C. Tripp, 2002: 238.
[65] E. Sciolino, 1991: 141.

conflict-reducing *incentives*, even if these incentives were overshadowed by other factors.

These incentives were present in both of Iraq's major wars. Iraqi records later captured by the US military show that Saddam and his senior advisors were aware of the potential for disruptions in Iraqi oil exports in a conflict with Iran.[66] Predictably, war hurt Iraq's oil production, as Figure 5.1 illustrates. After the invasion of Iran, Iraqi oil production fell to an average of 0.9 million barrels per day in 1981, compared to 3.5 million barrels per day in 1979. Even after oil production recovered somewhat, the Tanker War showed another way in which war could disrupt export revenues. As it turned out, neither Iraq nor Iran was terribly effective at disrupting the flow of oil exports, due to the intervention of outside parties including the United States. Yet the Tanker War illustrates each side's awareness of the vital importance of oil revenues, and the impact that their loss could have on a state. Overall, the Iran–Iraq War represented a loss of approximately 4.1 billion barrels of Iraqi oil production over the course of the war, equal to roughly $230 billion.[67] Even for a leader with highly aggressive foreign policy preferences, the potential for such a loss might give one pause before initiating a war. Indeed, Iraq was only able to carry on the war with Iran because of the huge loans and subsidies that it was receiving from other countries, including the United States, Kuwait, and Saudi Arabia.

Second, the UN sanctions following Iraq's invasion of Kuwait provided another illustration of how a country's oil income could be risked by its aggressive foreign policy. Iraq's oil exports began to shrink almost immediately upon invading Kuwait. While the fighting was over quickly, the damage to Iraq's oil industry was more lasting. In 1991, Iraq produced just 0.3 million barrels per day, compared to 2.8 million barrels per day in 1989. In an effort to reduce the harm that the sanctions imposed on the Iraqi people, the UN gradually allowed Saddam's government to sell increasing amounts of oil: up to $1.6 billion worth in 1992, $4 billion in 1996, $11 billion in 1998, and $16.6

---

[66] NDU Conflict Records Research Center Document SH-SHTP-A-000–835: 12–13.

[67] Calculations based on the assumption that, absent the war, Iraq would have produced approximately three million barrels per day (roughly its pre- and postwar production levels) and that it would have sold that oil at world prices.

billion in 1999.[68] Even so, twenty years later Iraq still had not returned to its 1989 pre-war level of oil production. Again, such a significant loss in the state's finances, the risk of which was entirely foreseeable based on the experience of the 1980s, created an incentive to avoid international conflict. While present, this incentive ultimately proved too weak to stop the actual conflict.

Conclusion

Iraq's foreign policy behavior is in many ways an exemplar of the theory developed in Chapter 2. The tumultuous revolutionary period of 1958 to 1968 created an environment in which a leader of Saddam's qualities – ambitious, risk-taking, and ruthless – was likely to emerge. Saddam used the enormous influx of oil revenues in the 1970s to put in place a political system based on patronage and fear that proved remarkably resilient to popular discontent and opposition. The totalitarian nature of his government allowed him to gamble, correctly, that he could engage in multiple wars of aggression and remain in power even if his war aims were thwarted. In this manner, oil and revolutionary politics combined to create one of the most aggressive, war-prone governments in modern times.

[68] C. Tripp, 2002: 261–262.

6 | *Libya and the Arab Jamahiriyya*

There is no state with a democracy except Libya on the whole planet.

        – Muammar Qaddafi

Libya's short history since its independence in 1951 is a turbulent one. The former Italian colony was initially ruled by a monarch, King Idris, until he was overthrown by a young pan-Arab nationalist named Muammar Qaddafi in 1969. Qaddafi became the de facto ruler of Libya for over four decades, during which he transformed the country with a socialist revolution from above. Geopolitically, Libya moved away from the West and allied itself with the Soviet Union, then switched its orientation to reach a rapprochement with the West, only to become a pariah state once more in 2011. Libya is a fascinating, complex country. This chapter focuses on its history prior to Qaddafi's fall in 2011, both to test my argument and to provide background for understanding contemporary events.

Libya was remarkably aggressive in its foreign policy. At the height of its revolutionary period, 1969–1991, Libya engaged in a multitude of international conflicts and violent struggles, while at the same time seeking pan-Arab unification and solidarity. It engaged in a series of overlapping and violent conflicts with Chad. It also had militarized disputes with Egypt and the United States, and deployed troops to fight against Tanzania in the war in Uganda. Libya supported a wide range of foreign insurgencies and rebel groups, from Abu Nidal to the Irish Republican Army to the Black Panthers. It sustained a nuclear weapons program for more than three decades before reversing course in 2003 as part of its reconciliation with the West. Perhaps most famously, it sponsored several acts of international terrorism in the 1980s, including the Lockerbie airline bombing. Few countries of Libya's size have a history of such intense and violent international affairs.

To evaluate the extent to which Libya's behavior is explained by the theory posited in Chapter 2, the first step is to consider the value of the key variables in each time period under analysis. If the theory is correct, the actual behavior of Libya should match the theory's predictions based on the explanatory variables. Table 6.1 provides a brief summary of the values of the key variables for Libya 1951–2010.

Libya was a petrostate for most of this period. Beginning in late 1961, oil was exported in commercial quantities and, in 1963, petroleum constituted 98.7 percent of the country's exports. Libya's oil revenue vastly increased during the 1970s and hit its peak in the early 1980s. While its revenue fell after that point, due to price changes, economic sanctions, and lower production volume, Libya continued to rely on oil for the majority of its GDP and virtually all of its export revenue through 2010. Figure 6.1 shows the changes in Libya's oil production over time.

There is more variance in the revolutionary quality of Libya's government over this period. In the period 1951–1969, King Idris ruled reluctantly over a non-revolutionary government. By contrast, the first two decades of Qaddafi's rule after 1969 were highly revolutionary. Qaddafi's government met at least five of the seven categories of transformation identified in Chapter 4 to operationalize the concept of "revolutionary": the old monarchy was replaced by a new form of government called a Jamahiriyya; the state's official ideology was a socialist variant described by *The Green Book*, and all other political activity declared illegal; the state's role in the economy changed dramatically, as the oil industry was nationalized, wages and rents were outlawed, and state-owned enterprises distributed much of the economy's goods; the official name and symbols of the country were changed (twice); and a Revolutionary Command Council operated independently from the state's nominal governing institutions. Women's rights also increased, though perhaps only slightly. The revolution hit its peak in the late 1970s, but starting in the late 1980s and early 1990s, revolutionary policies were rolled back and redirected. As described below, political and economic reforms significantly altered the state's role in society.

Libya's foreign policy behavior follows a similar pattern. The country engaged in essentially no international conflicts under King Idris.

Table 6.1 *Summary of key variables in Libya, 1958–2010*

Libya	1951–1961	1962–1968	1969–1973	1974–1979	1980–1989	1990–2000	2001–2010
IV: Revolutionary regime	Non-	Non-	Increasingly	Highly	Highly	Partial retreat	Partial retreat
IV: Petrostate	No	Yes	Yes	Yes	Yes	Yes	Yes
Foreign policy:							
with Chad	No conflict	No conflict	No conflict	Conflict	War	Friction	No conflict
with United States	No conflict	No conflict	Friction	Friction	Conflict	Sanctions	Warming
with Egypt	No conflict	No conflict	Alliance	War	Hostility	Hostility	Neutral
use of terrorism	None	None	None	Some	Extreme	Little	Little
against Israel	Little contact	Little contact	High activity	High activity	High activity	Low activity	Low activity
DV: Aggressiveness							
Expected value	Low	Low	Increasingly	High	High	Decreasingly	Decreasingly
Actual value	Low	Low	Increasingly	High	High	Moderate	Low

Note: For more information about the labels used in this table, see Figure 3.1.

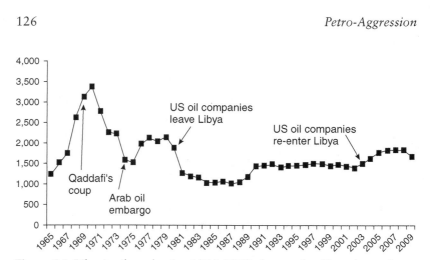

Figure 6.1 Libya's oil production 1965–2009, thousands of barrels per day
Note: Reliable data for Libya's oil pricing and revenue are unavailable. Data on production volume come from BP Statistical Review of World Energy, 2010.

In the period from 1969–1989, when Libya's oil revenues were at their highest and its government at its most revolutionary, it engaged in multiple international disputes, terrorist attacks, and foreign military adventures, against an array of adversaries. After 1990, Libya's foreign policy became considerably less conflict-oriented, particularly with the West. While it did continue to develop nuclear weapons, Libya did not engage in any major interstate disputes. Moreover, in the decade 2000–2010, it was increasingly integrated in – or at least less reviled by – the international community.

Therefore the theory passes the first test. As suggested by Table 6.1, there is considerable correlation between the actual foreign policy behavior of Libya and the behavior expected by the theory on the basis of the independent variables. The rest of this chapter is organized in five parts. The first section focuses on Libyan politics prior to Qaddafi seizing power in 1969, to set a baseline for comparison to the subsequent revolutionary politics. The second and third sections focus on the Libyan domestic and foreign politics, respectively, in the period 1969–1991. Fourth, the politics of the receding revolution in Libya 1991–2010 are discussed. Finally, the fifth section revisits Libya's political history in the context of three specific analytical questions to highlight the role of the key causal mechanisms.

Libyan politics to 1969

After World War II, the Allied powers forced Italy to relinquish its colonial claim over Libya.[1] The three provinces of Cyrenaica, Tripolitania, and Fazzan were initially ruled by British and French military administrations, but on December 24, 1951 the United Kingdom of Libya received its independence. Sayyid Idris al-Sanusi became king, somewhat reluctantly. He faced a difficult task of nation-building. Libya was divided internally, with each of the three provinces distrustful of the others and little sense of national identity among the people. Libya's economic challenges were also significant: an average annual income of $25 per capita, an infrastructure largely destroyed by the war, high unemployment, 94 percent illiteracy, and an infant mortality rate of 40 percent.[2] It was hardly an auspicious beginning.

Libya's economic fortunes soon changed. In the 1950s, King Idris granted the United States and the UK access to strategically valuable military bases on Libyan soil. In exchange, the West offered economic advice, technical assistance, and foreign aid. By the end of 1959, the United States had spent more than $100 million, making Libya the biggest per capita recipient of American aid in the world.[3] This aid had a considerable impact in the 1950s, but in the next decade it became irrelevant and then disappeared, as Libya had a new source of income: oil.

Libya experienced in the 1960s an oil boom of extraordinary proportions. The Libyan Petroleum Law issued in 1955 allowed nine foreign companies to explore, and oil was quickly found and developed. In 1960, the country's total oil production was 20,000 barrels per day; less than a decade later, it was over three million barrels per day. Libya's first crude oil export shipment departed from harbor in 1961; two years later, petroleum exports constituted 98.7 percent of the country's exports. Oil had a comparable effect in Saudi Arabia on per-capita income, but in Libya the increase was far more rapid: in Saudi Arabia, production rose gradually from 1945 to the 1970s, whereas in Libya production increased from zero to its peak in less than a decade. Libya's national income rose from $25 per capita at the time of independence to $2,000 per capita in 1969, an eighty-fold

---

[1] R. St. John, 2008.   [2] D. Vandewalle, 2006: 42.
[3] D. Vandewalle, 2006: 45.

increase in less than a generation.[4] Never in economic history has a single commodity so completely taken over a country's national economy as swiftly as the oil boom in Libya in the 1960s.

The surging oil industry brought with it political consequences.[5] At the time of independence, the three provinces had insisted on a federal structure that sharply limited the power of the national government, including its power of taxation. Aware of these limitations, in 1955 Prime Minister Mustafa Ben Halim sought to transform the monarchy into a republic and to increase the power of the national government over the provinces. The king initially supported the proposal, but it swiftly lost steam. In contrast, a constitutional reform to centralize power in the national government in 1963 succeeded, principally due to the oil industry. By then it was apparent that the federal structures inhibited the industry's economic development. Consequently, the constitutional reform abolished the provincial legislatures and judiciaries, and gave the national government control of economic development and taxation.[6] Thus the oil industry contributed to the centralization of power in Libya, consistent with my argument in Chapter 2.

In August 1969, King Idris issued a letter of abdication, to be made effective September 2, naming his nephew as his successor.[7] He then traveled to Turkey to see his doctors; he would never return to Libya. With Idris away, a group of junior army officers launched a coup one day before his abdication. The coup was perpetrated by the self-styled Free Officers, led by Muammar Qaddafi. Yet in the volatile summer of 1969, Qaddafi and his Free Officers were not the only ones plotting a coup attempt. Daniel Yergin describes the scene:

On the night of August 31-September 1, 1969, a senior Libyan military officer, finding himself unexpectedly awakened in his own bedroom by a junior officer, told the insistent young man that he was too early; the coup was scheduled for a few days later. Alas, for the senior officer, this was a different coup. For months, the whole Libyan military had been seething with conspiracies, as various groups of officers and politicians prepared to topple the ailing regime of King Idris. A group of radical young officers led by the charismatic Muammar al-Qaddafi, beat all the others to the punch, including their military superiors, who had scheduled their own coup for just three or

[4] D. Vandewalle, 2006: 58–63.
[5] L. Anderson, 1986; D. Vandewalle, 1998.
[6] D. Vandewalle, 2006.   [7] E. Clouston, 1992.

four days later. Indeed, many military men participated in the September 1 coup without knowing who was in charge or even which coup it was.[8]

As is so often the case in unstable political environments, it was not predetermined who would be the eventual victor. Yet the incentives of revolutionary political contexts favor those who are sufficiently radical, risk-tolerant, and organized to act decisively. Once Qaddafi made his move, thousands took to the streets to demonstrate their support for the new regime. Though he still needed to shore up support for his position, Qaddafi's boldness and radical ideology gave him a decisive advantage over his rivals.

The Arab Jamahiriyya at home: 1969–1991

In the chaos of early September 1969, it took a full week before Muammar Qaddafi, then just twenty-seven years old and a captain in the Libyan army, was publicly announced as the chairman of the Revolutionary Command Council (RCC) that would lead the new Libyan Arab Republic. The RCC included ten other military officers, all of the relatively junior rank (captain or major). They called themselves the Free Officers, inspired by the pan-Arabism of then-President of Egypt, Gamal Nasser.

Qaddafi insisted that he was leading a revolution. It was initially a coup, in the sense that Qaddafi took power through a sudden and decisive operation backed by the threat of force. However, this was no mere palace revolution, in which power simply shifts from one leader to the next. The coup was swiftly followed by an outpouring of mass demonstrations and expressions of popular support for change. Moreover, in the years to come, Qaddafi's regime would transform the political, economic, and social affairs in his country. In the early 1970s, Qaddafi's regime might have been called simply autocratic, but by the mid 1970s, it was highly revolutionary.

The young republic, 1969–1975

The RCC was preoccupied with consolidating its power in the early years of the revolutionary republic. The Free Officers came from

[8] D. Yergin, 2008 [1991]: 577.

modest backgrounds, most of whom had received little education outside of the military. As such, the RCC had to rely on others for many
of the bureaucratic and technical positions, especially in the oil industry, that were crucial for the functioning of the Libyan government
and the economy. Since the king's Western advisors left the country
after September 1969, the RCC had little choice but to continue the
employment of many of the bureaucrats.

Nonetheless, a new constitution was drafted, formalizing the role
of the RCC as the highest political authority of the government. The
constitution was "temporary" and was supposed to be swiftly replaced
by a permanent one, but this never happened, and Libya continued
without a formal constitution for the rest of Qaddafi's reign.[9] By the
end of 1970, the RCC was directly in charge of most of the government. All military officers above the rank of major were removed and
replaced with RCC loyalists, even as the total size of the army more
than doubled.[10] The military became a new instrument for advancement under the revolutionary regime, and thousands of young men
took advantage of it.

Two of the first acts of the new regime were to shut down the
American and British military bases on Libyan soil and to expel the
large Italian expatriate community. These acts were popular and stoked
the nascent nationalism of the Libyan masses. Qaddafi himself railed
against the presence of foreigners, and used it to justify his revolution.
Expelling the foreigners was also profitable – in the short run – for
the new government, as it nationalized the large land holdings of the
Italian community. Much of this land was then redistributed to political favorites.

The early years of the regime also saw significant changes in Libya's
oil industry. While the RCC was unable to dislodge the technocrats in
the Ministry of Oil, it was able to transform the country's relationship with the foreign oil companies. In January 1970, Qaddafi warned
the heads of the twenty-one oil companies operating in Libya that he
would shut down production unless the posted price of Libyan oil was

[9] In 1977, at the height of the revolution, a declaration was issued that
  rearranged many of the political structures of Libya, and thus functions as
  a revised constitution. However, it explicitly rejects the notion of formal
  government, and therefore the need for a constitution.
[10] K. Pollack, 2002: 360.

increased. Initially, the RCC turned on Occidental Petroleum, a relatively small independent oil company that got more than 90 percent of its global production from Libya, and was thus dependent on continued production. The RCC threatened Occidental remorselessly until it agreed to a 20 percent increase in royalties and an increase in the price of oil. Eventually, all of the other oil companies would do the same.

The strong-arm negotiating tactics used by the Libyans on the oil industry had geopolitical consequences. Initially it was Deputy Prime Minister Abdel Jalloud and the owner of Occidental Petroleum, Armand Hammer, who were the two principal negotiators. Jalloud had considerable negotiating leverage: Libya was supplying 30 percent of Europe's oil, the Suez Canal was still closed after the 1967 Arab–Israeli War, and an explosion next to a major pipeline in Syria had just cut off a sizeable portion of Saudi Arabia's oil from Western markets. That meant that Jalloud was in a position to squeeze the oil markets through cutbacks, and Hammer was desperate to continue production. Hammer asked Qaddafi's hero Nasser to intervene diplomatically, which the Egyptian president did, but to no avail. Back in the United States, Hammer went to the CEO of Exxon to try to get temporary oil supplies; he even went to Lyndon Johnson's ranch in Texas to try to put together a trade of US warplanes for Iranian oil, through which Hammer would receive some of the oil; again with no success. Yet the Libyans were turning up the heat. First they employed Abdullah Tariki, the radical and anti-Western former Saudi oil minister, as a counselor in the negotiations. Next they threatened to nationalize Occidental's operations. Then, as Hammer sat down to negotiate with the Libyans, Jalloud placed his .45 revolver down on the table directly in front of Hammer. Hammer feigned confidence, but throughout the negotiations with Jalloud, he would fly back from Tripoli to Paris each night to avoid being "detained" in the country.[11]

When the deal finally closed, it gave Qaddafi's revolutionary regime a huge boost in international prestige and domestic legitimacy. Domestically, the population saw the new regime as delivering economic prosperity while at the same time defending the national patrimony against foreign interests. Internationally, the Libyans had broken a principle of "fifty-fifty" profit-sharing between the oil companies and the producing states that had stood as the worldwide

[11] D. Yergin, 2008 [1991]: 578–579.

industry standard for more than twenty-five years. As a direct consequence of this deal, Iran demanded a renegotiation of its profit-sharing
arrangement with the oil companies, and other countries swiftly followed. This, in turn, encouraged Libya to further increase its taxes
and royalties, setting off a leapfrogging set of price increases in the
global marketplace. Ultimately this culminated, in conjunction with
the Arab–Israeli War, in the dramatic price increases of 1973. Libya
was a leading participant in the oil embargo, and maintained it longer
than any other country. Moreover, the 1973 crisis enabled a wave of
nationalizations of American and British companies inside Libya by
the Libyan National Oil Company.

While Qaddafi used changes in the oil industry as fuel for his revolutionary movement, he was more cautious with Islam. He stressed
that Islam should constitute a direct relationship between an individual and God, and should not be used for political purposes.
However, this too had a political purpose: it sidelined the *ulema*
(Islamic clergy) from politics, and made them aware that organized
opposition would not be tolerated. Nonetheless, the revolutionaries
did seek to establish their religious bona fides by banning alcohol,
closing many nightclubs and Catholic churches, and re-introducing
Islamic principles to criminal punishments. Still, the RCC was far less
willing to fuse Islam with revolutionary goals than their counterparts
in Iran a decade later.

In the early 1970s, Qaddafi experimented with a number of attempts
to redesign the political institutions of the country, nominally to move
the state toward popular rule. First, in January 1971 he announced the
creation of the Popular Congresses, which were supposed to appoint
representatives to the national parliament, who would then directly
elect the president. When these failed, Qaddafi announced the creation of the Arab Socialist Union (ASU), modeled on Nasser's party in
Egypt. In 1972, Qaddafi made any political activity outside of the ASU
punishable by death. The ASU was supposedly a vanguard party, but
it too failed to mobilize the general Libyan population, and quickly
became populated by the middle-class and young bureaucrats looking for advancement. Having failed in its first two efforts, the RCC
proposed in 1973 to create 2,400 Popular Committees within Libya's
enterprises and public organizations, as a means of establishing direct
popular rule. Yet the proposal did not go far enough for Qaddafi's
taste, as it excluded the most important economic sectors from popular

management. Qaddafi refused to sign it into law, exposing a rift in the RCC.

For the first four years of the revolution, the RCC had ruled the country as a group, and Qaddafi played the part of *primus inter pares*. The young regime survived its first counter-coup attempt in December 1969, and by 1973 was firmly in control of the country. However, tensions within the government were beginning to show. In November 1974, a split between two factions of the RCC became public for the first time, pitting Qaddafi and his followers against those who objected to his growing personal power and the rising costs of his foreign adventures. Thus in August 1975, RCC members Bashir Hawadi and Umar al-Muhayshi led a coup attempt. The attempt failed, and when the dust cleared just five members of the RCC were left standing, clearing the way for even more draconian methods of repression and political control. From this point on, Qaddafi had complete command over the country.

The Green Book and the height of the revolution

With political power now consolidated in his hands, Qaddafi renewed his efforts to build an Arab "Jamahiriyya." In 1975, he published the first volume of *The Green Book*, his revolutionary text modeled on Mao's *Little Red Book*. In it, Qaddafi introduced a new Arabic word, Jamahiriyya, meaning a state ruled directly by its people without representative government. He argued that electoral representation is a false democracy because as much as 49 percent of the population can be ruled by those for whom they did not vote. Instead, *The Green Book* laid out a utopian vision in which individuals directly managed the state by themselves. Qaddafi described a system based on hundreds of Basic People's Congresses (BPCs) that would involve the entire population. These BPCs would appoint Basic People's Committees in charge of local administration, and a General People's Congress (GPC) would legislate nationally, using a General People's Committee as a kind of executive cabinet. This enormous set of committees was celebrated in one of *The Green Book*'s populist slogans, *lijan fi kulli makan*, meaning "Committees Everywhere."[12] On March 2, 1977, the state was officially renamed the Socialist People's Libyan Arab Jamahiriyya.

[12] D. Vandewalle, 2006.

Despite the rhetoric of popular rule, Qaddafi used this system to entrench his personal power in four important ways. First, political activities were legally restricted to participation in the BPCs, making all other activity or forms of opposition illegal. Second, foreign policy decisions were excluded from the competence of the BPCs. Qaddafi thus had total control over the state's foreign policy decisions. Third, the actual power of the BPCs and the GPC was limited by the fact that the national Secretariat – where the real power lay – was de facto appointed by Qaddafi rather than the people. The RCC was formally abolished, but Qaddafi remained the commander-in-chief of the armed forces (along with Abu Bakr Yunis Jabr). Finally, Qaddafi also created a set of Revolutionary Committees that existed in parallel to the state's formal structure, providing Qaddafi with another tool by which to manipulate policy outcomes.

The publication of the second volume of *The Green Book*, entitled *The Solution of the Economic Problem: Socialism*, radically altered the economic and social relationships of the country after 1977.[13] Qaddafi declared that citizens would no longer be salaried employees, who can be exploited by capitalist enterprises; yet he also rejected the Marxist solution of state-owned enterprises. Instead, the people would become "partners in production," and by 1980 most of the important large industries were put in the hands of the BPCs – with the exception of the crucial oil and banking industries. Business owners were sidelined, traders were abolished, and entrepreneurs were described by Qaddafi as parasites. Qaddafi also sought to abolish certain kinds of property ownership, including housing. The slogan *al-bayt li sakinihi* ("the house belongs to those who live in it") captured the essence of Libya's new policy: renting real estate was mostly forbidden, and all non-occupied buildings were nationalized. New programs of agricultural land reform altered the landscape of rural Libya.[14]

Limits to the revolution

In 1981, the country's long oil boom finally peaked. Before it began, Libya was a desperately poor country, with GDP per capita estimated at $25 in 1951. Thirty years later, Libya had an income of at least

---

[13] A. Obeidi, 2001.   [14] D. Vandewalle, 2006.

$5,000 per capita.[15] Yet the 1980s would see a precipitous fall in Libya's fortunes. The global price fell rapidly until 1986, when it sold for under $10 per barrel. Other forces were at work, too: Libya's oil production was declining, in part because of a lack of capital investment since the revolution. The non-oil economy was stagnating due to the revolutionary policies restricting private enterprise and property ownership. Qaddafi's aggressive foreign policy and military adventurism, described below, also resulted in increasing economic sanctions by the United States and others. As a result of its foreign and domestic policy, and the global price reductions, Libya's oil income fell by at least half by the mid 1980s.

Gradually, Qaddafi realized that the revolution's current course could not continue. After the United States bombed one of his residences in 1986, killing his daughter, Qaddafi was incensed, but his people were not: "One saw more demonstrators in Khartoum and Tunis than in Tripoli, where the number of foreign journalists outnumbered Tripolitanians."[16] The *zahfs* (waves) of popular revolutionary fervor, previously well-attended, no longer enjoyed popular support. Accordingly, Qaddafi changed the direction of the revolution over the next few years, often in complete reversal. The *zahfs* were replaced by two waves of *infitah* (liberalization), which relaxed some of the domestic economic and political restrictions. The first one, beginning in 1987, led to some political prisoners being released, thousands of security files on Libyan citizens destroyed, permission for exiles to return, and relaxed travel restrictions to Tunisia. In 1988, Qaddafi personally participated in the destruction of the central prison of Tripoli and used a speech from the prison's tower to chastise (ironically) those who had used the revolution for their own purposes. *The Great Green Charter of Human Rights in the Era of the Masses* was also issued in 1988. Yet this first set of reforms lacked real substance, and focused on politically symbolic actions. The second set of reforms, beginning in 1990, initiated more significant economic reforms by reducing the bloated state bureaucracy, closing some unprofitable state enterprises,

---

[15] The 1981 figure is given in constant 2000 US dollars, as reported in the World Development Indicators. Other estimates are even higher: D. Vandewalle (2006) states that Libya's income per capita was $10,000 in 1981.

[16] A. Frachon, 1986.

allowing joint-stock companies, allowing businesses to open foreign currency accounts, and promoting tourism.

While there was a substantial change in the direction of the revolution from the late 1980s onwards, real progress was limited and often the reforms represented only a thin veneer of liberalization. To the West, moreover, the Libyan regime appeared as violently aggressive as ever, and perhaps even more so: Libyan terrorists were responsible for the bombings of PanAm flight 103 over Lockerbie, Scotland, in 1988 and the French UTA 772 airliner of Niger in 1989. It would take almost another decade – a decade of massive geopolitical change and deepening isolation for Libya – to see a major public reversal in Qaddafi's foreign policy.

The Arab Jamahiriyya abroad: 1969–1991

Libya's foreign policy under King Idris had been peaceful and oriented toward cooperation with the West, particularly the United States and Britain. The Kingdom also established full diplomatic relations with the Soviet Union in 1955. Libya did not engage in any militarized interstate disputes during the nearly two decades under King Idris.

Qaddafi and the Free Officers that came to power in September 1969 brought revolutionary ideas to Libya's foreign policy as well as its domestic policy. Inspired by Egyptian President Nasser, Qaddafi sought for more than a decade to unify and lead the Arab world. He also used Libya's rising oil revenues in the 1970s for military purchases and to develop a nuclear weapons program. By the 1980s, Libya had grown increasingly dissatisfied with the status quo on a number of fronts, and engaged in militarized conflicts with neighboring Chad and Egypt, with the United States, and elsewhere. Despite some reluctance at home to foreign policy activism, Qaddafi made Libya one of the most strongly revisionist states on earth.[17] I divide this activism into four components: interstate military conflicts; support for foreign insurgencies and terrorism; aggressive diplomacy and pan-Arab movements; and military expenditures and nuclear weapons program.

---

[17] Moderates in Libya's foreign ministry, who might have applied a brake on some of Qaddafi's expansionist projects, were largely eliminated (C. Wright, 1981).

Interstate military conflicts

Libya instigated or engaged in multiple militarized interstate disputes during 1969–1989. Its first major military campaign came in the 1973 October War between Egypt and Israel. Qaddafi was displeased to be left out of the planning of the war, but nonetheless lent Egypt thirty fighter jets and pilots, which saw heavy action in the war. Still, the 1973 war was not Libya's creation, nor was it one of the primary belligerents. Four other militarized disputes are much more informative with regard to Libya's foreign policy behavior during this period: those with Chad, Egypt, Tanzania, and the United States.

First, Libya engaged in a series of overlapping conflicts with its neighbor to the south, Chad, which were complicated by Chad's prolonged civil war. Initially, Libya supported and actively assisted the National Liberation Front of Chad (FROLINAT) against President Tombalbaye's regime. In 1973, Libya invaded the Aouzou strip, a border area between the two countries that was believed to be rich with mineral and uranium deposits. Libya's active role in the fighting stopped during the mid 1970s, but resumed in 1976 when Libyan troops began incursions into central Chadian territory. In 1977 a Chadian rebel leader named Goukouni Oueddei invaded with Libyan support (including active participation of Libyan ground troops from 1978 onwards), eventually capturing the capital and becoming president in 1979. In 1980, Goukouni lost power and Libya militarily intervened again, this time winning a major victory. In 1981, Chad and Libya announced their intention to unite as a single country, a move that was widely denounced by other African nations as a step in Qaddafi's expansionist agenda to create an "Islamic Empire" spanning most of northern Africa from Senegal to Sudan.

The Libya–Chad unification effort, engineered by Qaddafi with little enthusiasm from his Chadian ally Goukouni, met with widespread resistance and did not succeed. Libyan forces withdrew from Chad in late 1981 and redeployed to the Aouzou strip. Goukouni Oueddei and his chief rival, Hissène Habré, battled for control of the country for the next three years; France and Libya were significantly involved throughout this conflict. In 1984, France and Libya signed a bilateral accord in which they agreed to leave the country, but Libya only partially withdrew, leaving 3,000 troops to occupy the northern part of Chad. Habré, now in control of most of the country, used the next two years to consolidate his control, and in 1986 was again in a position to wage war against Libyan forces. French troops were redeployed in 1986 to assist Habré, specifically bombing Libya's air base Ouadi Doum that Qaddafi had constructed in northern Chad. Libyan forces were finally driven out of Chad in the "Toyota War" of 1987 (so-named because Toyota trucks were used to carry soldiers). Libya was thus engaged in a series of overlapping conflicts in Chad, occasionally supporting multiple sides, for fifteen years from 1973 to 1987.

The second significant conflict, between Libya and Egypt, was shorter and more intense. Despite several national unification attempts in the early 1970s, Libya's relationship with Egypt deteriorated rapidly in this decade, and reached its nadir in July 1977.[18] For three days, Egypt and Libya fought an intense military battle on their mutual border. Egypt mobilized over 40,000 troops in three heavy divisions and twelve commando battalions, vastly outnumbering the Libyan forces. At the time, Libya's entire military consisted of an estimated 32,000 troops, of which only eight battalions (roughly 5,000 troops) were stationed on the border with Egypt.[19] Nonetheless, Libyan troops were motivated by the fact that Egypt had sought peace with Israel. In June 1977, Qaddafi called for a march on Cairo from Libya to demonstrate for the cause of Arab nationalism, and he also called on Egyptians to overthrow Sadat. When thousands of Libyan demonstrators arrived at the border with Egypt on June 20, Egyptian troops stopped them, only to be fired upon by Libyan artillery. Egypt responded with airstrikes deep into the country on each of the next three days; Libya's air force also attacked Egypt. Other Arab leaders urged reconciliation, and a ceasefire was announced on July 24.

The third major conflict was Libya's involvement in the Ugandan war with Tanzania in 1978–1979. Tensions between Uganda and Tanzania had been building since Tanzania had given sanctuary to Milton Obote, the man overthrown by Uganda's President Idi Amin. In 1978, Idi Amin faced a mutiny within his military, some of whom fled across the Tanzanian border. Amin pursued the mutineers and when Tanzania-based Ugandan exiles joined the fighting against Amin's Ugandan troops, he declared war against Tanzania. Further, he sent troops to invade and annex part of the Kagera region of

[18] M. Deeb, 1991.   [19] K. Pollack, 2002: 365.

Tanzania, which he claimed belonged to Uganda. Tanzania mobilized quickly and counter-attacked, forcing the Ugandans to retreat. Libya sent 2,500 troops to aid Amin, equipped with T-54 and T-55 tanks, armored personnel carriers, artillery, and warplanes. With Uganda's forces falling into disarray, Libya's troops were soon on the front lines of battle. However, they were significantly outnumbered. Tanzanian forces captured Kampala on April 10, 1979, forcing Idi Amin to flee the country, first to Libya and then to Saudi Arabia.

Fourth and finally, Libya had a series of military conflicts with the United States in the 1980s.[20] The US–Libya relationship progressively deteriorated throughout the 1970s and 1980s. One source of friction centered on the Gulf of Sirte (Sidra), a 300-mile-wide body of water on Libya's northern coast. Qaddafi claimed territorial ownership over the entire Gulf, even though this was not supported by the International Law of the Sea; in 1973 he declared the territory to be demarcated by a "Line of Death." The United States disputed this interpretation, and was prepared to use its naval and air power to enforce its view. Between 1981 and 1989, the United States and Libya clashed militarily at least four times in and around the Gulf.[21] In 1981, two Libyan Sukhoi Su-22 Fitter fighter aircraft were shot down by two US Navy F-14 Tomcats; a similar incident occurred when two more Libyan planes were shot down in 1989. In 1986, following the bombing of a German disco, allegedly by Libyan agents, the United States bombed a number of targets on Libyan soil, including Qaddafi's personal compound in Tripoli. Widely interpreted as an assassination attempt, the US attack failed in part because of a telephone call from Malta's Prime Minister Bonnici, forewarning Qaddafi so that his family could be rushed out of their residence in the Bab al Aziziya compound moments before the bombs dropped. Qaddafi escaped injury but his fifteen-month-old adopted daughter Hanna was killed and two of his sons were injured. At least forty Libyans died in the attack overall; two US Air Force captains were also killed when their plane was shot down. Libya is reported to have engaged in a number of retaliatory attacks, using Scud missiles and hostage executions in Lebanon and elsewhere.

[20] R. St. John, 2002.   [21] K. Pollack, 2002.

Support for foreign insurgencies and terrorism

In the first two decades of Qaddafi's rule, Libya supported approximately thirty revolutionary groups and foreign insurgencies around the world.[22] Despite its small size, Libya's oil wealth gave it significant resources to provide assistance to such groups, and its African location gave it proximity to a large number of states with major internal disputes. The details of these activities are highly uncertain due to their covert nature. Nonetheless, the groups supported by Qaddafi can be loosely placed into three categories. First, there were a number of anti-Israeli groups that trained in Libya or received material support, such as Abu Nidal and the Palestinian Liberation Organization (PLO). Second, Libya supported one or both sides in several African internal conflicts or civil wars, including those in Guinea-Bissau, Mozambique, Somalia, Zimbabwe, Namibia, South Africa, and Angola. He also organized a number of assassination or coup attempts, such as in Chad (1971) and Sudan (1972). Third, there were a number of rebel groups outside of Africa that received Libyan aid, such as the Irish Republican Army (IRA), the Black Panthers in the United States, and various groups in Nicaragua, El Salvador, Grenada, and Guatemala.[23] Qaddafi also stood accused of trying to assassinate a number of world leaders such as US President Reagan and Saudi Arabia's Crown Prince Abdullah.[24] To the extent that there was an underlying theme in Libya's interventions, it was the struggle against colonialism and imperialism.

Libya also sponsored three major acts of international terrorism in the late 1980s. In 1986, a bomb in a German discotheque exploded, killing three people and injuring over 200. On December 21, 1988, Pan Am Flight 103 was destroyed by a bomb while in the air over Lockerbie, Scotland, killing all 243 passengers and sixteen crew members. In 1989, the French airliner UTA Flight 772 was bombed in midair over Niger, killing all 156 passengers and fifteen crew members. While

---

[22] The precise number of groups that received aid by Libya is unknown. In 1989, the US government estimated at least thirty groups (D. Vandewalle, 2006: 132). This estimate is consistent with reports by independent scholars of Libya, e.g., M. El Warfally, 1988.

[23] M. El Warfally, 1988.

[24] M. El Warfally, 1988; P. Tyler, 2004. Note that the alleged attack on Crown Prince Abdullah did not occur until 2003. In both cases, there is considerable uncertainty and little public evidence.

the Libyan government officially denied sponsoring all three incidents, it was widely believed to have done so. In 2002 Libya offered $7.2 billion in compensatory payments to the Lockerbie victims' families as part of a process of resuming normal international relations with the UN, the United States, and European countries.

Aggressive diplomacy and pan-Arab movements

When Egyptian President Nasser died in 1970, Qaddafi appointed himself as the guardian of Nasser's legacy and the leader of the pan-Arab movement. This self-appointed role was hardly welcomed by the leaders of the other Arab nations, and eventually the relationship would grow into mutual antagonism. Nonetheless, in the early 1970s, the Arab world was still stung by their defeat by Israel in 1967 and the failures of the non-aligned movement. For a time, Qaddafi represented a fresh face and a boldness that was much desired in the Arab world. His speeches attacked both friends and foes alike with a sense of righteousness that might have frustrated his political purposes, but which resonated with the masses in Libya and beyond.

Libya's pan-Arab foreign policy led to seven different national unification attempts with other Arab states. Initially, Libya's foreign policy was disorganized as the new government consolidated its power domestically, but it soon became more active. Qaddafi pursued a different Arab national unification plan in each of the first five years of his regime: in 1969 with Egypt and Sudan (the Tripoli Charter); in 1971 with Egypt and Syria (the Benghazi Treaty); in 1972 with Egypt alone; in 1973 with Algeria (the Hassi Messaoud Accords); and with Tunisia in 1974 (the Djerba Treaty). Of these, the most developed unity attempt was the Federation of Arab Republics, which was ratified by popular referendum in Libya, Egypt, and Syria in 1972.[25] Still, the three countries disagreed over the terms of the merger and it never came to fruition. When Libya and Egypt's relationship cooled in the mid 1970s, the drive for Arab national unification faltered. Libya tried twice more in the 1980s, with Chad in 1981 (the Tripoli Communiqué)

---

[25] Tunisia and Libya signed an agreement in 1974 to unify under a single constitution, single army, and single president (with the Tunisian President Bourgiba as leader, and Qaddafi as Minister of Defense) as the Arab Islamic Republic, but it quickly fell apart.

and Morocco in 1984 (the Oujda Treaty), before turning away from pan-Arabism permanently.[26]

Qaddafi's commitment to Arab nationalism was not limited to national unification attempts, and often focused on the battle against Israel. Qaddafi was deeply disappointed to be left out of the consultations between Arab leaders in advance of the 1973 war with Israel. Nonetheless, he urged the Arab League to take hardline positions against Israel and worked to disrupt US attempts to forge a peace accord in the late 1970s. Libya also sought to convert a number of state governments against Israel; by 1973, twenty-seven African states had broken diplomatic ties with the state of Israel, in part due to lobbying and pressure from the Libyan government.[27] By the middle of the 1970s, the Libyan government was openly and increasingly supportive of radical Palestinian groups. Several of them, including the Abu Nidal group, the Popular Front for the Liberation of Palestine, and the Palestinian Islamic Jihad moved their operational base to Libya.

The diplomatic relationship between the United States and Libya deteriorated throughout the 1970s, before becoming actively hostile in the 1980s.[28] Libya was initially cautious after 1969, officially adopting a neutral geopolitical position. For its part, the United States hoped that Libya could be kept outside the Soviet orbit, and that Libya's close business ties to the United States, especially in the oil business, could be maintained.[29] Still, Libya nationalized three US oil companies in 1974, and Abdel Jalloud visited the Soviet Union to conclude the first major Soviet–Libyan arms agreement. The following year, the United States announced restrictions on sales of strategic equipment and certain types of aircraft to Libya; in 1977, the Department of Defense added Libya to its list of potential enemies. In December 1979, Libyans attacked the US embassy in Tripoli and set it on fire; a few weeks later, the US State Department added Libya to its list of state sponsors of terror, on which it would remain for more than two decades. By 1981, all American diplomats withdrew from Libya, and the United States banned travel to Libya and closed the Libyan embassy in Washington. The incoming Reagan administration was particularly hostile to Qaddafi's regime, banning all exports except food and

---

[26] D. Vandewalle, 2006.
[27] *Libya: A Country Study*, 1989.
[28] G. Simons, 2003.   [29] D. Vandewalle, 2006.

medicine to Libya in 1982. This was followed in 1985 by a US ban on oil imports from Libya, and finally all financial transactions in 1986. In the wake of a terrorist bombing in West Berlin in 1986, President Reagan would publicly call Qaddafi a "mad dog of the Middle East." Days later, the United States would bomb Tripoli via airstrikes.

Qaddafi used international events, both peaceful and hostile, as rhetorical devices for his revolution at home and to justify further aggressive action abroad. His personal charisma was magnified by his ability to portray the battles with the United States and Israel as a heroic defense of national honor and defiance in the face of unjust imperialism. Yet his rhetoric may have become a self-fulfilling prophecy, as the popular legitimacy he gained from the symbolic conflict made militarized conflict desirable.

Military expenditures and nuclear weapons development program

Libya's military capabilities were severely limited when Qaddafi took power. Following the 1969 coup, the new government acted to restructure and enlarge the military. Sanusi army officers (i.e., those from the same tribe as the deposed King Idris) were removed, and the defense forces of Cyrenaica and Tripolitania were incorporated into the regular army. The size of the army doubled in 1969–1970. The biggest expansions were yet to come: as oil money flowed in during the 1970s, military expenditures increased rapidly. In the decade 1973–1983, Libya's arms purchases were an estimated $28 billion (current dollars), a staggering 14 percent of the country's GDP.[30] The air force had over 500 combat aircraft and the army bought nearly 3,000 tanks. In 1981, Libya's total economic development spending reached $10 billion, an enormous sum for a country with a population at the time of just three million people, but this still left $11 billion to the discretion of the government. Much of that money was spent on military purchases and international adventures. At the time, Libya was at war with neighboring Chad; the military was consuming almost

---

[30] K. Pollack, 2002: 362. The military expenditure figure was checked by the author with the Libyan Ambassador Ali Aujali in a personal interview, and it was not disputed, though it remains an estimate with some uncertainty. The GDP estimate is based on the World Development Indicators.

a quarter of the state's official budget by 1984 (and perhaps more in extra-budgetary expenditures).[31] Libya's increased spending also gave it access to increasingly sophisticated weaponry, as the Soviet Union became one of Libya's principal suppliers.

In 1970, Libya began a nuclear weapons development program. For most of the 1970s, Libya attempted to purchase an "off the shelf" weapon, thereby allowing it to skip over the demanding process of developing the weapons technology indigenously. Developing the technical expertise to build a bomb was necessarily a long-term venture, as Libya's scientific personal and engineering capacity at the time of the revolution was very low. Libyan officials made several trips to China, and at least one to India, in order to try to purchase nuclear weapons, but the efforts were not successful.[32] Libya did succeed in purchasing 1,200 tons of yellowcake uranium from French-controlled mines in Niger. At the same time, Qaddafi also announced that he intended to entice Arab scientists away from the United States to work on a nuclear program in Libya.[33] In 1979, the US government cut off aid to Pakistan, claiming that Libya and Saudi Arabia were financing the Pakistani program in exchange for the nuclear technology. In the early 1980s, Libya was reported to have purchased nuclear-capable missiles from West Germany, and also appears to have attempted to purchase a uranium tetrafluoride processing plant from a Belgian supplier, used for making bomb-grade nuclear material.[34] Qaddafi's public statements during the 1980s were contradictory, but on at least one occasion he declared that he would deploy nuclear-tipped, long-range Soviet missiles if he felt that a US attack was imminent.

Libya's nuclear weapons program was covert throughout this period, though most major states appear to have had at least some knowledge of it. The nominal secrecy was important because Libya had ratified the Nuclear Nonproliferation Treaty in 1975, thereby formally agreeing not to develop or acquire nuclear weapons. Libya operated the 10-megawatt nuclear research reactor at Tajura, acquired from the Soviet Union, under IAEA regulations.[35]

---

[31] D. Vandewalle, 2006.

[32] Libya's offer to India was reportedly to pay India's entire foreign debt of $15 billion in exchange for a nuclear weapon (K. Timmerman, 1992).

[33] *New York Times*, 1975.   [34] K. Timmerman, 1992.

[35] A. Cordesman, 2004.

After the US airstrikes on Libya in 1986, the nuclear weapons program was discussed at the General People's Congress (GPC), the highest body in the formal government (though, as discussed above, it was not actually in control of executive decisions). The GPC gave the executive branch a blank check to protect the regime with what a senior official described as "any necessary means and weapons." Qaddafi argued that "[i]f we had possessed a deterrent – missiles that could reach New York – we would have hit it at the same moment [as the US attack on Libya in 1986]. Consequently, we should build this force so that they and others will no longer think about an attack ... The world has a nuclear bomb, we should have a nuclear bomb."[36] However, just two years later, the official policy of the Libyan government reversed, when it called for the destruction of nuclear weapons worldwide.

At some point after the US airstrikes, the Libyans became focused on developing a full nuclear weapons program, complete with indigenous expertise and technicians, rather than simple "off the shelf" purchases. This effort became most intense during the mid 1990s, but it was matched with a simultaneous effort to use the nuclear program as a bargaining chip in the reconciliation of Libya's differences with the West, as discussed below.

The receding tide of the revolution: 1991–2010

By the time the Cold War ended, a significant change was already underway in Libya. The tide was turning in Qaddafi's revolution domestically and, more slowly, in its foreign policy as well. While the *zahfs* of revolutionary change had mobilized the masses in the 1970s, they no longer attracted much support by the late 1980s.

Libya's declining economic fortunes did not help the cause. The decline was driven by four factors. First, the global price of oil collapsed in the 1980s. Second, for Libya the decline in price was aggravated by the fact that US and some Western European countries had restricted imports of Libyan oil. This left Libya in the position of needing customers, often found only by offering steep price discounts to Eastern European states. Third, the volume of Libyan oil production was falling (see Figure 6.1), in part due to the lack of capital investment

[36] L. Spector, 1990: 183.

since most foreign oil companies had left the country. According to a Libyan official, this was made worse by the US restrictions on spare parts and pressure from the US government on all foreign oil companies to avoid dealings with Libya.[37] Fourth, the international sanctions imposed first by the United States and then the UN gradually began to take effect. According to the Libyan government's estimate, the UN sanctions cost Libya $5 billion per year after 1992.[38] Libya's inability to import high-technology goods hurt its industries, causing delays in maintenance and upgrades in the oil refinery and airline industries until the sanctions were lifted in 1999. Business uncertainty increased, medical supplies were restricted, and tourism to and from Libya declined. Consequently, the state's economic malaise reinforced the lack of political enthusiasm for Qaddafi's revolutionary ideals.

One other crucial factor contributed to the change in Libya's revolution: the collapse of the Soviet Union in 1989–1991. The Soviets provided Libya with much of its military weaponry and equipment, as well as political support and a counterweight to the mutual antagonism in the US–Libya relationship. With the Soviet Union gone, Qaddafi had new concerns about national security and the relationship with the West. Also, many of Libya's principal oil customers in Eastern Europe fell into a state of economic disarray, adding to Libya's economic woes.

The retreat and redirection of the revolution was visible in both domestic and foreign policy. Domestically, Libya engaged in two waves of liberalization (*infitah*), described earlier. In terms of foreign policy, Qaddafi finally abandoned his efforts toward Arab nationalism, having been consistently spurned or ignored by other Arab leaders for at least a decade. Instead, Qaddafi turned his efforts increasingly toward African politics. His new approach, however, involved far less military action and support for violence than it had in the past. In the period 1991–2010, Libya engaged in no major militarized interstate disputes.

Qaddafi also sought reconciliation with the West. The Libyans were interested as early as 1992 in reaching a rapprochement with the United States, and sought confidential negotiations to this end.[39]

---

[37] Ambassador A. Aujali, personal interview with the author, March 31, 2009.
[38] Ambassador A. Aujali, personal interview. The estimate of the cost is based on figures from the Bank of Libya.
[39] G. Hart, 2004.

It faced two major obstacles: first, it stood accused of several major terrorist actions, most notably the Lockerbie bombing; second, the United States and others suspected (correctly) that Libya was developing nuclear weapons. Libya simultaneously increased its efforts to develop or acquire a nuclear bomb *and* sought to negotiate an end to its weapons program in exchange for normalized diplomatic relations.[40] Libya's quiet overtures to the West were largely unsuccessful until the end of the 1990s, when the UN sanctions were suspended. Qaddafi's conciliatory response to the events of September 11, 2001, and the subsequent US desire for allies in the Arab world, opened further opportunities for negotiations. On December 19, 2003, Qaddafi announced Libya's decision to dismantle all components of its nuclear weapons program, and to halt the development of missiles with a range of more than 300 kilometers. Libya's cooperation with international inspectors led to significant information about the nuclear proliferation network of Pakistani engineer A. Q. Khan. These moves were welcomed by the United States and Europe. In 2005, a bidding process for Libyan oil exploration and development resulted in eleven of fifteen blocs being awarded to US companies. In 2006, the United States announced its renewal of normalized diplomatic relations with Libya, and in 2008, the Secretary of State paid an official visit to Tripoli.

Operation of causal mechanisms

Libya's history provides us with significant material for evaluating the causal mechanisms hypothesized in Chapter 2. The causal mechanisms, and their interactions, are explored through three distinct questions.

Did the revolutionary government make Libya more aggressive?

Qaddafi's revolutionary government, especially in the first two decades of its rule, was aggressive in its foreign policies. In large part, this was due to Qaddafi's personal preferences and his ambitions to be a major actor on the world stage. The emergence of a leader with Qaddafi's characteristics was not inevitable, however, and was made

[40] M. Braut-Hegghammer, 2008.

much more likely due to the political circumstances surrounding his rise to power. In 1969, there were multiple plots for a *coup d'état* circulating in Tripoli; Qaddafi's succeeded, in large part, because he and his Free Officers Movement were the boldest and the first to strike. The fact that he was only twenty-seven years old and a rather junior military rank (captain) at the time of the coup illustrates his ambition and high tolerance for risky actions. Even then, in the tumultuous first few months and years of the regime, Qaddafi could have been replaced by another leader, perhaps more moderate. Further, moderate members of Qaddafi's own Revolutionary Command Council who viewed Qaddafi as too radical attempted a coup in 1975. Yet he survived as a leader, through a combination of shrewdness, political ability, risk-tolerance, and luck. These characteristics allowed Qaddafi to advance a popular but radical pan-Arabist vision, which delegitimized moderates and positioned himself as the leader of a revolution. Thus Qaddafi's boldness, underpinned by a willingness to accept considerable risk in pursuit of his political objectives, was a key characteristic in his rise to power.

The revolutionary government also imposed few constraints on Qaddafi, leaving him a free hand in foreign affairs, especially after 1975. The many committees of the regime had no real power over foreign policy decisions or implementation. Qaddafi faced even fewer constraints on his leadership than did King Idris, and consequently was able to aggressively pursue his foreign policy objectives. There were some but not many domestic constraints on King Idris. For instance, a declaration of war needed the approval of Idris' cabinet, and the government's budget and expenditures were monitored and approved by a bicameral legislature, including the elected House of Representatives. Moreover, under the federal structure of Libya prior to the constitutional reforms of 1963, the provinces could obstruct new taxes, thereby potentially limiting Idris' ability to wage a military campaign. Still, some caution is warranted in evaluating the role of institutional constraints as a contributing factor to Libya's foreign policy. There were some but not many domestic constraints on the king, and it is not clear how binding they were as Idris did not attempt to lead the country into war. Adding to the analytical challenge, Qaddafi faced few institutional constraints in the 1990s and 2000s, but Libya largely avoided major international conflicts during this period. Thus the correlation between the level of domestic constraints and aggressive foreign policy is weak. The lack of domestic institutional constraints does not explain on its own Libya's aggressiveness of the 1970s and 1980s. Still, it likely served as an enabling condition.

Did oil generate incentives for aggression and conflict?

Oil income is hypothesized to reduce the leader's risk of domestic punishment for foreign policy adventurism, and to increase the state's military expenditures. There is evidence that both of these effects were present in Libya. As documented above, military expenditure consumed a large portion (at least 25 percent in some years) of the state's revenues, reaching levels that would be highly unlikely in the counterfactual case where Libya was not a petrostate and oil did not provide a rich source of income.

Moreover, Qaddafi was able to use the state's oil income to obtain for himself a certain amount of political autonomy that would have been difficult to achieve in its absence. Virtually the entire population was economically dependent on the distributive functions of the state, particularly during the period 1969–1989. In these years, private business was hindered and state-owned enterprises provided most of the population with essentials such as food and housing. This mode of economic distribution meant that clientelism dominated Libya's political life, creating a network of hierarchical relationships with Qaddafi at the top. The rentier nature of the state meant that Qaddafi was simultaneously able to satisfy the demands of his domestic constituency even as he pursued costly foreign policy activities. When other political leaders, even members of his own Revolutionary Command Council, urged that more of the oil money be spent on economic development and less on military affairs, he was able to override their objections, at least so long as the oil revenues remained high. Only once oil revenues declined and the general economy began to suffer in the late 1980s and 1990s did economic development and reform become a greater priority than military adventures.

Note that Qaddafi's political autonomy, which was in large part generated by oil income, was distinct from a mere lack of domestic institutional constraints. Even an autocrat without oil income can face few institutional constraints. By contrast, Qaddafi's political autonomy stemmed from having excess resources at his disposal even after having satisfied domestic political demands. He was then free to use the excess oil money in multiple ways, such as buying military weapons, domestic political loyalty, or security forces for domestic repression.

Did oil generate incentives to avoid aggression and conflict?

Oil is also posited to decrease the state's propensity for international conflict by increasing the incentives for peaceful international economic links. In Libya's case, there is little direct evidence of this effect if one observes only its behavior in international politics: Libya was generally more aggressive during times of high oil income, and less aggressive during times of low oil income. In combination with Libya's revolutionary government, the conflict-enhancing effect of oil appears to be the dominant factor.

However, it is possible that oil still provided conflict-reducing *incentives*, even if these incentives were overshadowed by other factors. Consider three stylized facts. First, the Libyan oil industry suffered as a result of Libya's aggressive foreign policy, particularly with the closure of the US embassy in Tripoli in 1980 and the departure of US companies such as Exxon from Libya in 1981. In addition to the decline in oil volume (see Figure 6.1), Libya's oil revenue also suffered as a result of price discounts that it was compelled to offer due to its foreign policy and the sanctions it faced. Second, it was foreseeable that Libya's foreign policy would create significant financial costs and risks for its oil industry, even if the exact costs were not calculable. And third, it seems clear that Libyan officials were aware of these potential costs. Qaddafi himself argued during the 1970s that "people [Libyans] who have lived for five thousand years without oil can live without it a few more years to achieve their legitimate rights."[41] This statement came in the context of the battle over pricing in the 1970s, but it reflected an awareness of the costs of engaging in any conflict that might jeopardize the state's oil exports. When asked in 2009 about whether the impact on the oil industry was considered in Libya's foreign policy decisions in the 1970s and 1980s, Libyan Ambassador Ali Aujali recalled, "Of course, officials knew there would be a cost, but that was the time of Arab nationalism."[42] Collectively, these considerations suggest that Libya did face a significant economic incentive to avoid international

---

[41] D. Yergin, 2008 [1991]: 578.
[42] Ambassador A. Aujali, personal interview.

conflict because of its oil industry, but chose to bear the costs in pursuit of its foreign policy objectives.

Still, the evidence should not be overstated. Consistent with my argument, the conflict-enhancing effects of oil appear to have outweighed any conflict-reducing effects in Libya's case. As we shall see in the chapter on Saudi Arabia, the conflict-reducing effects of oil are more directly observable in the behavior of a non-revolutionary government.

Conclusion

Consistent with the theoretical expectations described in Chapter 2, Libya instigated many militarized interstate disputes, and its foreign policy was most aggressive, during its most revolutionary period. The impact of oil revenue on the state's domestic politics follows the hypothesized causal mechanisms. Oil powerfully shaped Libya's domestic politics by creating a clientelistic political culture whereby the leader of the state was able to offer economic benefits in exchange for political quiescence. This political culture reduced Qaddafi's risk of domestic punishment for foreign policy adventurism. Furthermore, Libya's aggression was facilitated by a flood of oil income, which provided Libya with resources both to expand its own military capability and to support a series of foreign insurgencies and acts of international terrorism. Consequently, the modern history of Libya offers considerable support to the argument that revolutionary governments that arise in petrostates constitute a special threat to international peace.

7 | *Iran*

The greatest threat to Islam in Iran since the revolution
has been the experience of living under the Islamic Republic.

– Mehdi Bazargan

Of all of the political transformations to occur in petrostates, the Iranian Revolution of 1979 was perhaps the most dramatic. The fall of the Shah and the return of Ayatollah Khomeini set in motion a series of social, political, and economic transformations that profoundly recast public life in Iran from then onwards. The revolutionary regime also was and continues to be perceived as an aggressive actor by its neighbors. Post-revolutionary Iran has been involved in a series of international conflicts that include the Iran–Iraq War, the American embassy hostage crisis, and the tensions surrounding Iran's alleged nuclear program.

As with the previous two chapters, one of the principal aims of this chapter is to evaluate the theory posited in Chapter 2. The actual history of Iran, however, does not fit neatly in a box. For instance, although Iran has been aggressive in many instances, it has also been remarkably restrained at other times, even in the face of significant threats and provocations from other countries, not least of which came from the United States. This chapter therefore tries to capture the complexity and contradictions of Iran's domestic and foreign politics. Only by recognizing that complexity can we hope to learn from it.

As usual, the first step is to consider the value of the key variables for each time period under analysis, exploiting the variation over time within the country case. If my theory is correct, the actual behavior of Iran should match the theory's predictions based on the explanatory variables. Table 7.1 provides a brief summary of the values of the key variables: the aggressiveness of the state's foreign policy, the presence of revolutionary government, and the presence of oil income.

Table 7.1 *Summary of key variables in Iran, 1945–2010*

Iran	1945–1951	1951–1953	1953–1978	1979–1989	1989–1996	1997–2005	2005–2010
IV: Revolutionary regime	No	Slightly	No	Highly	Mixed	Mixed	Mixed
IV: Petrostate	No	No	Yes	Yes	Yes	Yes	Yes
Foreign policy:							
with Iraq	Cooperation	Cooperation	Friction	War	Conflict	Conflict	Complex
with United States	Alliance	Complex	Alliance	Conflict	Sanctions	Sanctions	Sanctions
with Israel	Cordiality	Cordiality	Cooperation	Hostility	Hostility	Hostility	Hostility
with USSR	Distrust	Distrust	Distrust	Distrust	Distrust	Distrust	Distrust
with UAE	n.a.	n.a.	Friction	Friction	Friction	Neutral	Neutral
with Afghanistan	Cordiality	Cordiality	Cordiality	Friction	Friction	Conflict	Friction
DV: Aggressiveness							
Expected value	Low	Low-Moderate	Low	High	Moderate	Moderate	Moderate
Actual value	Low	Low	Low-Moderate	High	Moderate	Moderate	Moderate

Note: For more information about the labels used in this table, see Figure 3.1.

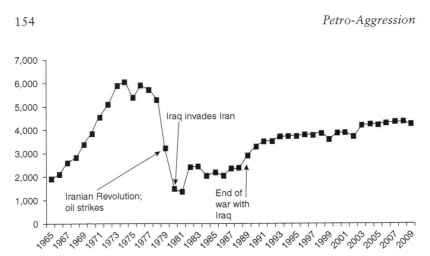

Figure 7.1 Iran's oil production 1965–2009, thousands of barrels per day
Note: Production data are from BP Statistical Review of World Energy, 2010.

First, consider the country's oil income. Despite its long history in Iran, the oil sector was a relatively minor part of the economy until the 1950s because the level of production was low and Iran's government received a relatively small share of the industry's profits. Oil production expanded rapidly after the Shah was returned to power in 1953, and in the early 1970s Iran's share of the profits from the oil industry exceeded 50 percent for the first time. By the mid 1970s, oil income constituted three-quarters of the government's revenues. Revolution and war decreased Iran's oil production, but even so almost 60 percent of the government revenue came from the oil sector during the 1980s.[1] In part, this was because price movements offset Iran's lean production in 1979–1980. In 2010, the oil sector continued to be responsible for roughly 60 percent of government revenue.[2] Thus while the total amount of revenue fluctuated considerably, Iran's high degree of economic dependence on the oil sector from the 1950s onward did not. Figure 7.1 shows Iran's oil production over time.

Second, consider the type of regime in Iran. The variation over time is described in this chapter, with special attention to the revolutionary government that came to power in 1979. Ayatollah Khomeini led a mass uprising against the Shah, forcing the latter to flee Iran. Khomeini then explicitly set out to transform the country socially and politically. He

[1] H. Amirahmadi, 1990: 165.   [2] PressTV, 2010.

replaced the monarchy with an Islamic republic, in which the people had votes but a rather limited influence in the overall direction of the government. The constitution was completely overhauled; the political power of the clergy was enhanced enormously; the name, flag, and symbols of the country were changed; women's rights were curtailed; and social practices were modified, sometimes by force. The regime's hardliners fought for control of the country, suffering assassinations, bombings, and a full-fledged civil war that peaked in the summer of 1981. Economically, the country was characterized by a mixture of socialist planning, populist distributive policies, and regime-controlled patronage to the *bazaaris*, the influential merchant middle class. Iran's population grew exponentially in the 1980s and then leveled off in the 1990s, reflecting the regime's changing attitudes about fertility and birth control.

Next, consider foreign policy. As expected by the theory, Iran's foreign policy was highly aggressive under Ayatollah Khomeini, and continued to be moderately aggressive after 1989. The combination of oil income and revolutionary politics created conditions for a sharp increase in the state's aggressiveness. However, Iran's neighbors and other states were also aggressive. For instance, the Iran–Iraq War was instigated primarily by Iraq. Still, Iran's actions prior to the onset of war, and especially during the war when Iran rebuffed all peace offers and went on the offensive, demonstrate the revolutionary government's aggressiveness. Moreover, the regime has explicitly sought to "export the revolution" since 1979, resulting in a long series of semi-official and covert military campaigns. While many petrostates have supported foreign insurgencies financially or rhetorically, Iran's behavior is unique. Iran is distinguished by the deep and integral role it played in the creation and operation of Hezbollah in Lebanon; by its connections with Hamas in Palestine, the Mahdi Army and the Supreme Council of Islamic Revolution in Iraq, and other foreign insurgents; and by the Iranian military's direct role in fighting on foreign soil as part of civil or international conflicts. Lastly, Iran's increasing efforts to develop nuclear weapons over the last two decades, in the face of widespread international condemnation, magnify the perception of Iran as an aggressive state.

Therefore the politics of Iran are broadly consistent with the argument of this book, but the link between the explanatory factors and Iran's foreign policy is not as simple as a mechanical correlation. Table 7.1

indicates that in the key revolutionary period under Khomeini's leadership, 1979–1989, Iran was indeed highly aggressive, in contrast to its earlier behavior. Yet the mixed nature of the regime since Khomeini's death – partly run by revolutionary fundamentalists, and partly run by democratic institutions – makes it difficult to classify cleanly or formulate clear theoretical expectations for its foreign policy. Thus it is not surprising that Iran's actual foreign policy had both conciliatory rhetoric under President Khatami (1997–2005) and aggressive posturing under President Ahmedinejad (2005–present). Nonetheless, even during Khatami's presidency, Iran's actions have brought the regime into recurring conflict with states in its neighborhood and beyond.

The rest of this chapter explores the hypothesized causal mechanisms in the context of the historical evidence. It is organized in five parts. The first section focuses on Iranian politics prior to the revolution of 1979. The second section focuses on Iranian domestic politics since 1979, with particular attention to how revolutionary politics and oil income affected the regime. The third section maps Iranian foreign policy since 1979, which has been aggressive in various overt and covert ways. The fourth section revisits Iran's political history in the context of the three analytical questions used in previous chapters to highlight the role of the key causal mechanisms. A short conclusion considers the trends in contemporary Iranian politics.

Iranian politics to 1979

In 1941, the UK and the Soviet Union jointly invaded Iran and displaced its ruler, Reza Shah Pahlavi. Although the invaders wanted to continue Iran's supply of oil to Britain and use of Iran as a land corridor to Russia's allies, they did not want to directly rule the country. Accordingly, they turned over administration of the country to Mohammad Reza Shah, the twenty-two-year-old son of the previous Shah. Upon his accession, the Shah promised to cooperate fully with the Allied Forces in World War II. He also took a number of steps to improve his standing with the Iranian public, including a promise to reign, not rule, as a constitutional monarch.

This promise led to ten years of highly contested politics. Although the king was head of state and controlled the armed forces, he did not control the bureaucracy or much of the country's system of patronage. Power was hotly contested by the royal palace, the cabinet, the *majlis* (parliament), and the urban upper and middle classes. In the period 1941–1954, twelve prime ministers headed thirty-one different cabinets while 148 individuals filled 400 cabinet posts.[3]

This period culminated in the leadership of Muhammad Mossadeq, who became prime minister in 1951. Mossadeq led a nationalist movement that sought to liberate Iran from the influence of foreign powers, most especially the British government. At the center of this movement was the oil industry. Iran's oil industry began in 1901, when an exploration concession was granted to William Knox D'Arcy. D'Arcy was acting on behalf of a group that would soon become the Anglo-Persian Oil Company (later the Anglo-Iranian Oil Company, AIOC, and subsequently BP), after the first commercial oil well was drilled in Iran in 1908. The British government considered Iran as a vital source of oil supply to its empire, especially after Sir Winston Churchill converted the British naval fleet from coal to oil in 1912.[4] By the 1940s, Iranians were deeply dissatisfied with British control of Iran's oil industry. Mossadeq sought to capitalize on that dissatisfaction and nationalize the industry. Thus in April 1951, Mossadeq created the National Iranian Oil Company (NIOC) and opened negotiations with AIOC to transfer control. When AIOC resisted, Mossadeq ordered NIOC to take over the oil wells, pipelines, refineries, and offices throughout the country.

As prime minister, Mossadeq continued over the next two years to challenge the status quo. Especially important was his confrontation with the Shah in 1952, in which he asserted that as prime minister, it was his right and duty to appoint the war minister and the military chief of staff, as well as other members of the cabinet. This directly challenged the Shah's traditional control over the military. Mossadeq also cut the palace budget, appointed anti-royalists as ministers, placed royal charities under government supervision, isolated the Shah from foreign ambassadors, and transferred the royal estates back to the state. By July 1953, Mossadeq's followers were publicly exploring the feasibility of replacing the monarchy altogether, and transforming Iran into a republic.

On August 19, the CIA and MI6 launched a coup, deposing Mossadeq and returning the Shah to power. An Iranian General, Fazlollah Zahedi, replaced Mossadeq as prime minister, but real authority was given

[3] E. Abrahamian, 2008: 100.   [4] D. Yergin, 2008 [1991].

back to the monarch. Thirty-two Sherman tanks rolled into central Tehran, surrounded key positions, and proclaimed Zahedi to be the Shah's designated prime minister. Although the Shah claimed that the coup was bloodless, the *New York Times* estimated that the battle left more than 300 dead.[5] In the long-run, the coup seriously compromised the legitimacy of the monarchy in the eyes of the Iranian people. At a time when radical nationalism and anti-imperialism dominated the Middle East and Africa, the coup permanently tied the Shah to the British, the United States, and the Anglo-Iranian Oil Company.

Although the oil industry was important to Iran starting with the D'Arcy concession in the early part of the twentieth century, Iran was not a petrostate in the early 1950s. In the 1930s and 1940s, oil revenues constituted less than 15 percent of government revenue, and thus an even lower percentage of its overall economy.[6] In part, this was because Iran continued to receive a rather meager share of the profits from the industry even after a global standard was set when Venezuela signed the "50–50" agreement in 1947 to split profits with the oil companies. It was not until the 1954 consortium agreement, after the Shah had returned to power, that Iran received a 50 percent share of the profits.

The Shah and the "great civilization"

By 1960, Iran had become a petrostate. In a typical year during the 1960s, oil accounted for approximately 70 percent of foreign trade and more than 60 percent of the government's revenues. The oil industry thus supplied the Shah with the resources to consolidate power among the military, the bureaucracy, and the system of court patronage. The military was the most important of these three pillars: during the period between 1954 and 1977, the military's budget grew twelvefold and its share of the annual budget increased from 24 to 35 percent. Its personnel expanded from 127,000 to 410,000 individuals if the gendarmerie (60,000) is included. The Shah also created, in 1957, an intelligence service known by its Persian initials, SAVAK. SAVAK eventually grew to have more than 5,000 full-time employees, and as an organization was responsible for some of the more ruthless

[5] K. Love, 1953.
[6] F. Fesharaki, 1976: 19.

methods of repression used to keep the government in power. Thus the combination of patronage and repression we have already observed in other chapters was also evident in Iran. These tools of patronage and repression would shortly take on a new character and context in the wake of the revolution of 1979.

In 1963, the Shah undertook a set of reforms that he labeled the "White Revolution." This so-called revolution was *not* revolutionary in the sense used in this book. Instead, the White Revolution was a collection of reforms from above, explicitly designed to pre-empt a Red Revolution from below, which was the great fear of the Shah and his Western supporters. The White Revolution centered principally on land redistribution, designed to modify and modernize the Iranian economy.[7] It also extended the franchise to women and made improvements to the country's educational system. While significant, these changes were not accompanied by a change in the political regime, and they paled in magnitude to the transformations observed in a true revolution, such as the one in 1979. Still, one important consequence of the White Revolution was that it was by design costly to the class of rural notables that owned much of the agricultural land. This decision came back to haunt the Shah at the end of his reign when the rural land-owning class, traditionally allies of the monarchy, did little to support him politically.

In terms of foreign policy, Iran was pro-Western, pro-royalist, and highly active.[8] The Shah was highly ambitious with regard to Iran's international prestige as a way of legitimizing his regime at home. The United States viewed Iran and Saudi Arabia as the "twin pillars" of stability (and anti-Communism) in the Middle East, and the Shah reveled in the role of being one of the United States' favorite partners in the region. This meant that Iran was active in the region, supporting fellow monarchs against local insurgencies. More serious for Iran was the ongoing friction with Iraq over control of the Shatt al-Arab, as discussed in Chapter 5.

Despite the Shah's ambitions, Iran was basically non-aggressive under the Shah, as it had no real expansionist policy or appetite for territorial conquest.[9] In 1955, Iran joined the Baghdad Pact with Iraq, Turkey, Pakistan, and Britain, which was designed to be a regional

[7] J. Stempel, 1981.
[8] R. Burrell and A. Cottrell, 1974; S. Chubin and S. Zabih, 1974.
[9] F. Halliday, 1979.

equivalent to NATO. Although the Pact soon fell apart, it signaled the Shah's (and his Western supporters') desire to preserve the regional status quo. Iran's border disputes did not escalate into a major conflict, and the Shah contented himself with building up his military's advanced weaponry.

One telling illustration of the difference between revolutionary and non-revolutionary leadership was the Shah's reaction to the Baathist rise to power in 1968, in comparison to Saddam Hussein's reaction to the Iranian Revolution of 1979. The Shah feared and disliked the Baathist regime for multiple reasons, including its pan-Arab ideology, its anti-monarchical republicanism, its revolutionary socialism, and its anti-Western stance. In 1968, the Shah also perceived Iraq to be weak and internally divided, as it had just suffered its tenth *coup d'état* in a decade. Consequently, Iran reinitiated the struggle over the Shatt al-Arab, and a number of border clashes ensued. Still, the Shah did not have the appetite to mount a major invasion of Iraq. Unlike Saddam a decade later, the Shah did not react to the emergence of a neighboring revolutionary regime by going to war, perceiving the risks of a major war as too great. The Shah was therefore content to let relations improve, leading to the 1975 treaty between Iran and Iraq (the Algiers Pact). Indeed, the relationship between the two countries was remarkably cordial in the late 1970s until the Shah's fall.

The road to 1979

In October 1971, the Shah decided to celebrate the 2,500th anniversary of the Iranian monarchy with a grand gala near the ruins of Persepolis. Estimated to cost tens or even hundreds of millions of dollars, this event would come to epitomize the arrogance, wastefulness, and corruption of the Pahlavi court. The 1970s brought rapid economic changes to Iran, but the gains were unevenly distributed and caused significant social and political challenges. Moreover, the Shah had already acquired a set of powerful domestic opponents.

The Shah's greatest enemy, the Ayatollah Khomeini, was not yet in the country. Khomeini actively opposed the Shah's regime in the 1960s, for which he was imprisoned and then sent into exile. Initially sent to Turkey, Khomeini moved in 1965 to Iraq, where he would spend more than a decade. Khomeini became an active force among the Shi'a population in Iraq, preaching of the necessity of Islamic government.

The Baathists viewed this as subversive, and in 1978 Saddam asked him to leave. Khomeini then traveled to a suburb of Paris, where he and his followers plotted his return to Iran.

What caused the Iranian Revolution? Various detailed explanations have been offered by scholars, and this book does not seek to provide a new answer to that question.[10] Still, given the importance of Iran's oil industry, it is natural to ask specifically about the oil industry and its role, if any, in the revolution.[11] Clearly, oil revenues flooding into Iran, especially after 1973, contributed to the country's rapid economic transformation and the corruption in the Shah's court. As argued in Chapter 10, however, this alone does not constitute evidence that oil caused the Iranian Revolution, for two reasons. First, many other petrostates, such as Saudi Arabia and Indonesia, experienced similar economic upheaval without having a revolution. Indeed, in some states, such as Venezuela, rapid economic development funded by an oil boom was associated with a period of uncommon stability and nation-building. This suggests that some other factor was present in Iran and not in other petrostates. Second, revolutions also occurred in the 1970s in countries that did not have any oil at all, such as Cambodia, Nicaragua, and Ethiopia – so the mere facts that Iran had a large oil sector, and a revolution occurred, do not imply that one caused the other. I do not mean that oil played no role whatsoever in Iran's revolution. But the evidence does suggest that, at the very least, other important causal forces were at work.

Iranian domestic politics since 1979

Following widespread protests, the Shah departed from Iran on January 16, 1979. Two weeks later, Khomeini returned to Iran after more than fifteen years in exile. By mid February, the Shah's final prime minister, Shapour Bakhtiar, was forced from office, and the new regime began. It brought with it a huge number of changes. It abolished the monarchy, and in March 1979, a popular referendum established Iran as an Islamic republic, by a vote of 98 percent in support. A new constitution followed in December, establishing the role of a Supreme Leader (Khomeini), a separate presidency, a Guardian

---

[10] C. Kurzman, 2004; M. Milani, 1994; T. Skocpol, 1982.
[11] A. Cooper, 2008.

Council, an Assembly of Experts, and a *majlis* (parliament). A new set of revolutionary courts was established, which eventually merged with the rest of the national justice system after the abolition of secular law in 1982. In due course, the regime became more radical, for instance by substantially restricting the rights of women and imposing Islamic codes of dress and behavior. Foreign trade was nationalized, as were many industries. Table 7.2 indicates the timing of key events in the new republic.

In addition to the formal government, three other important institutions emerged. First, the Islamic Revolutionary Council (IRC) was secretly formed to guide the provisional government and shape the design and implementation of the new constitution. The core of the IRC was appointed directly by Khomeini, and it included both members of the radical clergy, such as Beheshti, Rafsanjani, and Khamenei, as well as more moderate members such as Bazargan and Bani-Sadr. Gradually, however, the radical members of the Council began to dominate. Second, scores of revolutionary *komitehs* emerged throughout Iran. Some of these *komitehs* were directed by the IRC, but many other *komitehs* were created spontaneously and were more loyal to regional or ethnic leaders. The pervasive *komitehs* served a number of political functions, as well as being a vehicle for local governance and distribution of public goods. Third, the Islamic Revolutionary Guard (IRG) was created from the merger of several armed militias that were loyal directly to Khomeini. The IRG served as a parallel military structure and internal security force in the early years of the republic, while the loyalties of many officers in the regular military were suspect. Gradually the IRG grew into a massive organization with military, internal security, and commercial functions.

The rise of the radical clergy under Khomeini

Over the period 1979–1983, the revolutionaries gradually shed the domestic political allies that initially gave them their support, and the regime became increasingly radical in character. In the early days of the regime, there was a wide array of political actors active in Iran that vied for influence. Most of them explicitly supported an Islamic republic, but some did not; and among those that did, there were wide disagreements about precisely what form an "Islamic republic" should

Table 7.2 *Timeline of key events in the Iranian Revolution*

Date	Event
January 1979	The Shah departs Iran
February 1979	Khomeini returns from exile; PRG established with Bazargan as PM; revolutionary courts are established and begin executions
November 1979	US embassy seized by radical Iranian students, Bazargan resigns
December 1979	New constitution established; Bani-Sadr elected president in January
July 1980	The Shah dies in Egypt
September 1980	Iraq invades Iran
January 1981	US hostages are returned as Reagan becomes president
June 1981	Bani-Sadr is impeached as Iranian president
June 1981	IRP headquarters is bombed; Mujahedin violently oppose the regime
August 1981	President Rajai is assassinated by Mujahedin; civil war escalates
October 1981	Khamenei elected president; beginning of the end of civil war
December 1981– July 1982	Iraq sues for peace; Iran rejects all peace proposals
July 1982	Iran invades Iraqi territory for the first time
May 1983	Tudeh and all other political parties except the IRP are outlawed

take. Although Khomeini was clearly the most important political actor at the time, it was still far from certain that he would control the government. Khomeini's triumph was a testimony to his political skill, his ruthlessness against opponents, and his relentless drive to impose his political vision. Initially Khomeini sought to work with a broad coalition of allies while his core supporters took control of the state. Accordingly, he appointed Mehdi Bazargan as prime minister and leader of the Provisional Revolutionary Government. Bazargan was a prominent and long-time opponent of the Shah, but a moderate. Bazargan was well-known for his honesty and advocacy for democracy, which appealed to the liberal intellectuals and educated middle classes of Iran.[12]

At the risk of simplification, six principal groups can be identified among the dozens of political organizations in Iran during this period. First, the Islamic Republican Party was created and led by Khomeini's core group of radical supporters and militant clergy. Second, the lay Islamic radicals were led by the Liberation Movement, members of which included Bazargan, Ayatollah Taleqani, and Abulhassan Bani-Sadr, who would become the first president of Iran. Third, the moderate clerics (*ulema*) were led by Ayatollah Shariatmadari, who was associated with the Muslim People's Republican Party (MPRP). Fourth, the Mujahedin-e Khalq was a leftist Islamic radical group that violently opposed the Shah's regime, and initially supported Khomeini. Fifth, the Tudeh Party was the principal communist party of Iran, originally founded in the 1930s. Along with the Fedai Khalq (Majority), the Tudeh Party represented a secular Marxist-Leninist ideology. Sixth, the National Front founded by Muhammad Mossadeq represented the coalition of liberals most devoted to democracy. Karim Sanjabi, one of the National Front's leaders, served as the first foreign minister in the Provisional Revolutionary Government. In addition to these six major groups, there were a number of important regional and ethnic organizations, some militant opposition groups like the Paykar and the Furqan, and numerous independent parties and revolutionary *komitehs*.

As the new regime was being built, Khomeini frequently allowed a wide-ranging public debate between moderates and radicals on contentious issues, before ultimately siding with the radicals. In doing so, he preserved the appearance of serving as an unbiased mediator and spiritual guide to the revolution. For instance, he insisted that the first elected president of Iran should not be a cleric, thereby disqualifying many of his core supporters, and clearing the way for a political alliance with moderates. However, Khomeini consistently sided with the fundamentalists on the secretive Islamic Revolutionary Council whenever they clashed with the nominal leaders of the government, first under Bazargan and then under Bani-Sadr. Later, as Khomeini consolidated his power and Iranian politics grew more radical, Khomeini

[12] D. Menashri, 1990.

removed his objection to a clerical president, paving the way for Ali Khamenei to take office.

The first stage of the revolution came to an end in November 1979 with the hostage-taking at the American embassy. Iranian students stormed the embassy with help from members of the Islamic Revolutionary Guard. Although Khomeini did not know about the plan in advance, he soon decided to support the students and manipulate events to take advantage of the hostage crisis. For the radical members of the regime, there were four significant benefits. First, the move was enormously popular with the Iranian public and showed the regime's resolve to stand against the United States and "imperialism." Second, the classified papers seized at the embassy, which were swiftly published by the Iranian regime, delegitimized the United States. They also allowed the revolutionary regime to identify which Iranian officials had been talking to US agents, thereby exposing "enemies of the revolution." Third, the crisis radicalized the Iranian public and rallied support for the upcoming constitutional referendum on December 1. Fourth, it allowed the Iranians to disrupt any covert plans that the United States might have to launch a coup to reinstate the Shah, as they had in 1953. Yet for the moderates in the Iranian government, the storming of the US embassy was anathema to good governance. Thus the Provisional Revolutionary Government came to an end, when Bazargan and his cabinet resigned in protest.

Table 7.3 shows the subsequent stages in the movement in the support for the government over time, as the radical revolutionaries gradually shed their moderate allies. The process of radicalization in Iran is important for my argument because it had consequences for the aggression in Iran's subsequent foreign policy. Not all of the original supporters of the revolution had aggressive foreign policy preferences, but these actors were gradually marginalized. Consistent with the argument I developed earlier, revolutionary politics in Iran acted as a selection mechanism for a particular type of radical leadership.

The first stage of this progression was in Khomeini's deteriorating relationship with the Grand Ayatollah Shariatmadari. Although Shariatmadari had opposed the Shah and was initially sympathetic to Khomeini's revolution, he publicly opposed Khomeini's views on *velayat-e faqih*, the guardianship of Islamic jurists. As the leading Grand Ayatollah in Qom in 1979, Shariatmadari's views could not be lightly dismissed by Khomeini, and Shariatmadari had a significant

Table 7.3 *The radicalization of the Iranian revolutionary government*

Period	Government leader	Allies	Opponents
February 1979–November 1979	Bazargan	Islamic Republican Party MPRP National Front Liberation Movement Mujahedin-e Khalq Tudeh Fedai-Khalq (Majority)	Kurdish/ethnic groups Paykar Fedai Khalq (Minority) Furqan
February 1980–June 1981	Bani-Sadr	Islamic Republican Party Liberation Movement Mujahedin-e Khalq Tudeh Fedai-Khalq (Majority)	*As above, plus:* MPRP National Front
June 1981–August 1981	Rajai	Islamic Republican Party Mujahedin-e Khalq Tudeh Fedai-Khalq (Majority)	*As above, plus:* Liberation Movement
October 1981–July 1982	Khamenei	Islamic Republican Party Tudeh Fedai-Khalq (Majority)	*As above, plus:* Mujahedin-e Khalq
July 1982–August 1989	Khamenei	Islamic Republican Party	*As above, plus:* Tudeh Fedai Khalq (Majority)

public following. However, after several attempts at reconciliation, Khomeini placed Shariatmadari under house arrest. This led to wide-spread protests by Shariatmadari's supporters. Seeking to avoid a violent civil war, Shariatmadari called for his supporters to stand down, thereby implicitly accepting defeat. He was subsequently sidelined from Iranian politics and died under house arrest in 1986.

The next major schism was with the new president, Bani-Sadr. Bani-Sadr had been with Khomeini in Paris before the revolution and initially he enjoyed Khomeini's full support. However, Bani-Sadr was not a member of the Islamic Republican Party (IRP) and was a rival of Ayatollah Beheshti, the IRP's leader and the head of Iran's judicial system. This rivalry soon led to friction. As Bani-Sadr did not have a party of his own, he moved closer to moderate leaders of the Mujahedin and the National Front, putting him on a path that would ultimately lead to his downfall. The IRP had control of the *majlis* and the judiciary, and soon sought to limit Bani-Sadr's executive powers. In May 1981, the *majlis* authorized the IRP prime minister, Mohammad-Ali Rajai, to appoint top officials to forty national institutions, thereby usurping the president's constitutional authority. This led to a showdown in June 1981, in which Khomeini supported the *majlis'* decision and impeached Bani-Sadr. After a brief call for popular "resistance to tyranny," Bani-Sadr went into exile in France.[13]

By July 1981, the IRP had lost many of its moderate allies. Heretofore the struggle was mainly political, but in the second half of 1981 the regime's enemies grew increasingly violent. The Mujahedin-e Khalq, the Marxist-Leninist group which had initially worked with the IRP, now sought to destroy it. On June 28, 1981, they set off a bomb in the conference hall of the IRP headquarters, which killed the secretary-general of the IRP, Ayatollah Beheshti, and seventy other senior leaders. In August of the same year, the opposition struck again, this time assassinating President Rajai and Prime Minister Bahonar.

The violent insurrection only increased the radicalization of the regime's supporters. Ali Khamenei, who had already been seriously wounded in a separate explosion in June, became the new president in a landslide election. His election was significant because he was the first cleric to serve as president. Khomeini had reversed his earlier decision to keep the presidency secular, and was now prepared to

---

[13] N. Keddie, 2006.

have his fundamentalist camp dominate all branches of government. Moreover, his government increasingly repressed its opponents. The political struggle in Iran became a full-fledged civil war, in which open battles lasted hours or even days. The Mujahedin estimated that they killed 1,200 religious and political leaders of the regime, but government's official executions tallied 4,400 by July 1982, and many more unofficial deaths are suspected.[14] In addition, by the end of 1981 more than 35,000 political dissidents were imprisoned.

By the fall of 1981, the armed rebellion was clearly losing. The Mujahedin tried and failed to disrupt the presidential elections of October 2. By sticking to the election schedule, Khomeini showed his resolve in the face of violence and his commitment to securing legitimacy for the regime through the popular vote. The high voter turnout demoralized the opposition, and the regime's security forces continued to score victories. Within three weeks, Rafsanjani was able to claim that the government had destroyed 90 percent of the "main opposition forces."[15] Then in February 1982, the government raided a Mujahedin safehouse in Tehran, leading to the deaths of ten central committee members of the organization. With the organization's remaining senior leaders in exile, the Mujahedin were forced to sharply curtail their resistance activities.

With the opposition silenced, the regime no longer needed the last major element of the revolutionary coalition, the Tudeh Party. While the Tudeh supported the revolution's anti-monarchy, anti-Western, and leftist economic ideology, the Tudeh frequently opposed the regime's dictatorial tendencies and the Islamization of Iran. As time wore on, the Tudeh's concerns about the regime became more pronounced. In large part, this had to do with the conduct of the Iran–Iraq War. By late 1981, Saddam Hussein was already indicating that he would welcome a peace settlement. The Iranian regime, by contrast, chose to go on the military offensive. In July 1982, as Iran invaded Iraqi territory for the first time, the Tudeh publicly opposed the government's decision to take the offensive in the war. This led to further conflicts, ending in the formal dissolution of the Tudeh Party in May 1983. Simultaneously, the government outlawed all political parties except the IRP.

The consolidation of the regime in late 1981 set the stage for an aggressive foreign policy and a new approach to the war against Iraq.

---

[14] R. O'Kane, 2000.   [15] D. Hiro, 1985: 198.

Even as the IRP shed its political alliances with moderates and grew increasingly radical, it was able to maintain the support of the Iranian people. It did this, in part, by using the same tools used by fellow revolutionaries, Saddam Hussein and Muammar Qaddafi: oil-funded patronage and repression.

Oil revenues and the consolidation of power

Iran's oil wealth provided the revolutionary regime with resources in two ways. First, oil production was a direct source of income for the government. Despite promises by revolutionary leaders in 1978–1979 to permanently lower the country's oil production and even eliminate oil exports, the government eventually sought to maximize production.[16] At the end of 1981, the government desperately needed the revenues, as its foreign reserves were down to $500 million, just two weeks' worth of imports. As a member of OPEC, Iran did not want to officially undercut the OPEC price, but Iran quietly let it be known in Europe and Japan that it was offering steep discounts for its oil.[17] By early 1982 fresh orders for Iranian oil began to arrive, and production rapidly increased to meet them. The influx of revenue provided Iran with crucial resources just as it sought to take the offensive against Iraq.

Second, Iran's oil wealth indirectly provided the revolutionaries with a huge additional resource: the accumulated assets of the Pahlavi monarchy and its supporters. The new regime created dozens of *bonyads* (foundations), which collectively controlled a sizeable fraction of the entire Iranian economy (currently estimated at roughly 20 percent of GDP).[18] The largest of these *bonyads* was the Mostazafan Foundation, which was created in 1979 as the successor to the Pahlavi Foundation. The Mostazafan Foundation acquired all of the royal family's assets, as well as many industries and properties seized by the revolutionaries. It was (and continues to be) the second largest commercial enterprise in Iran, after the national oil company. The Foundation served as a mechanism to support the poor and redistribute wealth.[19] Inevitably, this also meant that it acted as a vehicle of patronage for the regime to reward its supporters.

[16] S. Bakhash, 1982.   [17] D. Hiro, 1985.
[18] A. Molavi, 2005: 176.   [19] A. Saeidi, 2001.

The revolutionary government used its oil revenue to bolster its popular support while fighting enemies both at home and abroad. It did this in four ways. First, and perhaps most importantly, the state heavily subsidized or rationed basic commodities, especially food. In the early 1980s, subsidies cost the public exchequer $1.9 billion per year, or 5 percent of the national budget.[20] The subsidies and rationing of imported goods were always directed first at meeting the needs of the lower classes; the middle and upper classes could obtain what they desired on a black market tolerated by the government, often at double or triple the official prices. The government's goal with the subsidies was consciously political: it wanted to ensure that the majority of the population saw the government as meeting their needs. Similarly, the second major use of oil revenue was an Islamic system of social security, also designed as a populist measure to satisfy the demands of the population. Together, the subsidies and social security system cost the public purse $4 billion, a striking figured compared to the military budget of $4.2 billion in the midst of a major war.[21]

The third major use of the oil revenue was to vastly increase the number of individuals directly employed by the government, thereby making them clients of the state. The central bureaucracy grew from twenty ministries with 304,000 civil servants in 1979 to twenty-six ministries with 850,000 civil servants in 1982.[22] The new ministries included intelligence, revolutionary guards, heavy industries, higher education, reconstruction crusade, and Islamic guidance. In addition, the state's role in the economy expanded dramatically. The Mostazafan Foundation alone employed 85,000 employees and took control of 140 factories, 470 agrobusinesses, 100 construction firms, sixty-four mines, and 250 commercial companies.[23] The state was responsible for no less than 50 percent of all of Iran's industrial output.[24] The state also provided benefits to hundreds of thousands of volunteers in the paramilitary and militia groups like the *Basij-e Mostazafan*, who participated in the war and in internal security operations. The ranks of the military and the Iranian Revolutionary Guard also swelled considerably with the war against Iraq, bringing the armed forces to a total

[20] D. Hiro, 1985: 216.   [21] D. Hiro, 1985: 208, 216.
[22] E. Abrahamian, 2008: 169.
[23] E. Abrahamian, 2008: 178; D. Hiro, 1985: 253.
[24] H. Amirahmadi, 1990: 189.

of 500,000 personnel.[25] In total, the public sector was responsible for four-fifths of all new jobs in post-revolutionary Iran.[26] This vast increase in the size of the state was of course paid for by oil money, which despite fluctuations brought an average of over $15 billion a year throughout the 1980s.

Finally, the government used oil money to compensate war victims. The war with Iraq killed 170,000 Iranians and injured twice as many by the spring of 1984.[27] The regime was anxious not to lose the support of the people for the war. Accordingly, it cast the war in religious terms, labeling the war dead as martyrs who would receive unimaginable rewards in the afterlife. Khomeini himself said that "war can be as holy as prayer when it is fought for the sake of defending Islam."[28] But the regime also recognized that material considerations could help prevent demoralization and bolster support for the war, so it liberally rewarded the families of the dead. By 1986, the regime had already channeled over $5 billion through two foundations dedicated to war victims.[29] It paid a fallen soldier's family compensation of $24,000 and full salary as pension, and an additional $60 per month for each of his children until they came of age at eighteen.[30] It also assisted the family in renting, buying, or building a house.

Iran's oil sector was all the more important because the rest of its economy was suffering. Only a small number of factories were operational, and an even smaller number were profitable. Agriculture was also performing poorly, which the government tried to address by providing free chemical fertilizers and cheap loans to small farmers. The reality was that Iran's economy was critically dependent on the oil sector and imported goods. This dependence was made clear in 1981, when Iran's main oil terminal at Kharq Island was hit by the Iraqis, and Iran's oil shipments dropped to a low of 300,000 barrels per day.[31] The shortfall in oil exports led to a severe economic crisis and trade imbalance. Two of the revolution's central promises had been to conserve Iranian oil by curtailing production and to sharply reduce Iranian trade with the West. In late 1981, however, the government abandoned those promises because it needed oil revenue to sustain

[25] E. Abrahamian, 2008: 176.   [26] H. Amirahmadi, 1990: 189.
[27] D. Hiro, 1985: 236.   [28] Quoted in D. Hiro, 1985: 215.
[29] H. Amirahmadi, 1990: 68.   [30] D. Hiro, 1985: 239.
[31] D. Hiro, 1985: 206.

its populist economic agenda and continue the war. Thus within three years of the revolution, Iranian leaders sought to take full advantage of oil production and revenues.

By the middle of 1983, the revolutionaries had consolidated their regime and put in place the oil production and populist economic policies that would sustain their popular support. The war with Iraq dragged until 1988, imposing a huge cost on both countries in human and economic terms. Yet the leaders of both countries were able to use oil revenues to fund their war machines and sustain patronage networks at home, thus perpetuating the war until August 1988.

Iranian politics since Khomeini

Khomeini died on June 3, 1989. The following day, Ali Khamenei was selected Supreme Leader by the Assembly of Experts. This selection was controversial. For several years, the Grand Ayatollah (*marja*) Hossein Montazeri had been groomed to serve as the Supreme Leader following Khomeini, but in the years prior to Khomeini's death, they fell out. This disagreement created a challenge for Khomeini, as Montazeri was clearly the most qualified on religious grounds to serve as Supreme Leader, and the constitution called for such qualifications to be preeminent. Heedless, Khomeini called for Assembly to revise the constitution to allow Khamenei to be designated his successor even though he was not a *marja*. With the amendment in place, Khamenei became Supreme Leader, and Rafsanjani replaced him as president.

After Khomeini's death, the power sharing between the president and the Supreme Leader took on increased importance. While Khomeini lived, there was never any real question about where the locus of political power existed. In the years since 1989, however, the elected president has been able to guide Iran's government, with a limited degree of independence from the Supreme Leader. In part this is because the position of prime minister was abolished, giving the president more power; and in part, it is because Khamenei is not as revered as Khomeini was.

The dual nature of Iran's government, led by both president and Supreme Leader, affects the extent to which Iran can be classified as a revolutionary government after the death of Khomeini. There is no precise "endpoint" to a revolution, of course, and generally a state that has experienced a revolution gradually becomes less revolutionary as old institutions are replaced with new ones and the original cast of revolutionary leaders disappear from the scene. In Iran's case, the Supreme Leader Ali Khamenei was an active leader in the revolution: he joined Khomeini's movement in 1962, was one of five clerics in Khomeini's inner circle to found the Society of Militant Clergy in the 1970s, was arrested repeatedly for his role as organizer in the revolution, and was later a member of the Islamic Revolutionary Council and president of Iran.[32] Similarly, Akbar Rafsanjani, president from August 1989 to August 1997, was a senior revolutionary leader and a member of Khomeini's inner circle. Yet Mohammad Khatami, who became president in 1997, was not a significant leader of the 1979 revolution. Neither was Mahmoud Ahmedinejad, elected president in 2005. Consequently, Iran can be thought of as a mixed case, in which some original revolutionary leaders still participate in the government of Iran, but the government as a whole is not as revolutionary as it was under Khomeini.

The 1990s brought various attempts to reform domestic policy, many of which failed. As president, Rafsanjani sought to consolidate the revolutionary regime and reform Iran's war-weary economic policy. Rafsanjani sought to adopt structural adjustment policies in pursuit of a modern, market-based economy in which Iranian industries were integrated with the rest of the world. However, his reforms were largely stymied by opposition in the *majlis*, and the state continued to play a major direct role in the economy. In 1997, Khatami was elected president as an outsider and a reformer. Many observers expected him to ease Iran's repressive domestic policies and foster cooperation with the West. Indeed, he encouraged liberals in the *majlis* to pass more than 100 reform bills, including those that banned all forms of torture; expanded women's rights; eliminated legal differences between Muslims and non-Muslims; and transferred power to supervise elections away from the Guardian Council.[33] However, most of these bills were vetoed by the conservatives in the Guardian Council. Khatami later described his presidency as a failure in most respects, as he was unable to significantly liberalize Iran.

At the end of Khatami's two terms as president in 2005, the mayor of Tehran Mahmoud Ahmedinejad was elected. He is the leader of the

[32] B. Moin, 2000; J. Murphy, 2008.
[33] E. Abrahamian, 2008.

Alliance of Builders of Islamic Iran, a highly conservative organization, and as mayor of Tehran he reversed many of the liberal reforms
of previous mayors. His early career is uncertain; many observers
suspect that he was a member of the Islamic Revolutionary Guard
in the 1980s, but his official biography disputes this. He champi-
ons a populist economic agenda and is aided politically by his own
lower-class background. His domestic policies are highly conservative, in sharp contrast to those favored by Khatami. The differences
between the two presidents were also significant in foreign policy.

Foreign policy of Iran since 1979

Iran's foreign policy became significantly more aggressive after the
1979 revolution. While the Shah boasted of his ambitions to make
Iran a superpower and spent lavishly on his military, his regime participated in few interstate conflicts. By the late 1970s, his government
had cordial relations with Iraq, Israel, and the United States. Iran's
chief rival was Saudi Arabia, but this was largely a competition for
prestige and influence, rather than a violent conflict.

By contrast, the Ayatollahs sought to violently export their ideology and Islamic form of government to neighboring countries. They
adopted the slogan "Death to America," swore their lasting enmity to
Israel, condemned the Saudi regime, opposed the USSR, fought with
the UAE over disputed territory, and supported multiple insurgent
groups in Afghanistan. Their mantra was "neither East nor West." In
fact the regime's hostility was directed east, west, and almost everywhere else. Although it did not start its long and costly war with
Iraq, the revolutionary government's actions both prior to and during the course of the war are consistent with its overall pattern of
aggression.

Iran was not, however, the only state responsible for its conflicts.
American and Western support for Iraq during the Iran–Iraq War was
an open secret. For decades, Iran has faced hostility from almost all of
its neighbors, as well as from the United States and much of the West.
It is thus reasonable to believe that at least some of its behavior was
a reaction to the threats and provocations that Iranian policymakers perceived. Moreover, Iran's foreign policy was on some occasions
remarkably restrained when responding to provocations from external powers, particularly the United States.

The US hostage crisis

On November 4, 1979, Iranian students stormed the US embassy and took sixty-six Americans hostage. The women and black Americans were soon let go, leaving fifty-two men as hostages for a total of 444 days. After taking a few days to assess the situation, Khomeini decided to exploit the event. He did so in the knowledge that this could (and did) provoke a military response by the United States, but Khomeini decided that the benefits were worth the risks. First he ordered his friend Mohammad Khoeiniha into the embassy to act as a guide to the students and bolster the legitimacy of the hostage-takers. The students were then able to claim that their position was "taken by the Leader [Khomeini] and expressed by the students."[34]

Consequently, the storming of the embassy became a full-fledged act of aggression by the government of Iran against the United States. The United States responded with Operation Eagle Claw, a failed rescue attempt by Special Forces in April 1980. After the Shah's death in July 1980, and the invasion of Iraq two months later, the Iranians' enthusiasm for the hostage situation began to wane, and negotiations between the United States and Iran made progress. This eventually led to the Algiers Accord, which specified the conditions under which the hostages were to be released. In exchange, the United States agreed to unfreeze approximately $8 billion in Iranian assets. In a final act of pique against President Carter, Iran did not release the hostages into US custody until twenty minutes after Reagan had been sworn in as president.

The Iran–Iraq War

Iraq invaded Iran in September 1980.[35] As such, the Iran–Iraq War can be understood as an example of Iraqi aggression. Yet Iran's behavior immediately prior to and during the war provides ample evidence of Iranian aggression as well. Prior to Iraq's invasion in 1980, Khomeini espoused a policy of "exporting the revolution" to Iraq and called for Iraqi Muslims, especially Shi'a Muslims, to rise up in opposition to Saddam Hussein. Iranian troops were also provocative on the border, leading to multiple shots fired across the Shatt al-Arab. After Saddam's

---

[34] B. Moin, 2000: 227.   [35] S. Chubin and C. Tripp, 1988.

declaration of war on September 17, Iraqi troops swiftly captured the province of Khuzestan and parts of other territories. By March of 1981, however, Iraq's advance had stalled. Iranian forces were not as weak as the Iraqis had imagined, and Iraqi losses began to mount.

Although it was still emerging from revolutionary domestic turmoil, Iran had a number of significant advantages in the war. First, it had a much larger population than Iraq, meaning that it frequently had two or three times as many soldiers fighting on the front-lines as the Iraqis did. Second, Khomeini successfully cast the war as a religious battle between Iran's Islamic government and Iraq's secular dictator.[36] His propaganda was made more effective by the fact that the United States, France, and other secular countries (including eventually the USSR) were supplying Iraq with advanced weapons. Third, Iraq overestimated the extent to which the residents of Khuzestan would welcome the invading Iraqi army. As it turned out, national pride triumphed over regional and ethnic differences in Iran. The combination of these factors provided Iran with access to vast numbers of boys and young men willing to serve as "human waves" to attack Iraqi forces. Iran slowly pushed Iraq back to its original borders. In June 1982, Iran liberated Khorramshahr, the largest port of Khuzestan and the last significant part of Iranian soil held by Iraqi troops.

The war was then at a turning point. Should Iran continue the war by invading Iraq or should it accept peace? Saddam Hussein had already publicly offered peace on multiple occasions, notably in December 1981, again in April 1982, and again in June 1982.[37] When Iraq reported on June 29 that its troops had left Iranian territory entirely, Iran called it "a lie." The UN Secretary General, the Organization of the Islamic Conference, and the Non-Aligned Movement all made significant attempts at mediation. The United Nations Security Council unanimously passed Resolution 514 on July 12, 1982, calling for an end to the war. Perhaps most significantly, the Arab League put forward a peace proposal, including war reparations worth 40 billion British pounds ($70 billion) for Iran, financed in large part by Saudi Arabia and the Gulf monarchies. Iran rebuffed the offer.

A large segment of Iranians wanted peace. The doves on the Supreme Defence Council, as well as leaders of the Tudeh Party and

---

[36] D. Menashri, 1990.   [37] D. Hiro, 1985: 208–211.

the Liberation Movement, argued forcefully that if Iran invaded Iraq, it would lose the sympathy that Iran had aroused in Muslim communities around the world, thereby undermining Iran's legitimacy.[38] The hawks argued that attacking Iraqi territory would stop any further attacks from Iraqi forces, particularly their artillery, and it would allow Iran to capture Iraqi oilfields around Basra near the Iranian border. The hawks won. By July 1982, Iran's oil sales were more than covering its military expenses, the Mujahedin had been crushed, strong internal patronage networks had been established, and the hardliners calculated that the war was as much a domestic political asset as it was a risk, even if things went badly.

Thus for the next six years, Iran and Iraq continued one of the bloodiest and costliest wars of the twentieth century. In the end, Iran achieved no territorial gains or financial reparations, even though it could have received a huge sum of money in 1982 under the Arab League plan. Iran successfully invaded some Iraqi territory, but it soon learned what Iraq had learned in 1980: attacking was more difficult than defending. Khomeini's appeals to Iraqis to rise up against Saddam Hussein were largely ignored, as the Iraqi Shi'a chose to fight the Iranians rather than welcome them. Both sides sought to destroy the other's oil export capacity. Starting in 1984, this led to the "Tanker War," in which both sides tried to sink naval ships in the Persian Gulf carrying the other side's oil.

Iran was not, however, the only state acting aggressively. For years, American and Western support for Iraq in the conflict was an open secret. US involvement became more direct when it decided to re-flag many ships carrying Iraq's oil under the US flag. In October 1987, the US military attacked Iranian oil platforms in retaliation for an Iranian attack on the US-flagged Kuwaiti tanker *Sea Isle City*. The risk of a direct confrontation between Iran and the United States escalated still further in July 1988 when the USS *Vincennes*, operating in Iranian territorial waters, shot down a civilian airliner, Iran Air Flight 655. The US government insisted that this was a mistake, although Iran and other outside observers argued that it was deliberate.[39] Iran's reaction was remarkably restrained, in part due to its waning enthusiasm for the war.

---

[38] D. Hiro, 1985.   [39] F. Rajaee, 1993: 143.

The war finally came to an end in August 1988. Khomeini was very reluctant to accept a peace accord, yet ultimately the economic and human toll of the war grew unsustainable.[40] Despite having taken the offensive, Iran made little progress in Iraq. It was hindered by its inability to get spare parts for its American-made military equipment, especially its air force. Iran relied on weapons from Syria and North Korea, but Iraq was receiving sales from a wide variety of suppliers, including NATO and the Warsaw Pact. Iran's economy was collapsing and popular enthusiasm for the war had evaporated.[41] In the face of this reality, Iran's leaders finally accepted peace, ironically on terms much less attractive than those available six years earlier.

Additional international military incidents

With the end of the war with Iraq and the death of Khomeini in 1989, the Iranian government's foreign policy softened somewhat. Presidents Rafsanjani and especially Khatami tried to renew ties with the West and Central Asian countries. In a twist on Samuel Huntington's vision of a "Clash of Civilizations," Khatami sought to foster a "Dialogue of Civilizations." Khatami rejected the familiar slogan of "Death to America" and instead insisted his vision of the revolution was focused on life. Internationally, he met with Pope John Paul II, Jacques Chirac, and Vladimir Putin; he refused to meet with the radical Iraqi cleric Moqtada al-Sadr.

However, Iran was far from peaceful during the 1990s. Iran made a number of aggressive moves on all four points of the compass. In the west, Iran continued to attack and antagonize Iraq. Iran charged that Iraq was housing Iranian opposition groups, and consequently carried out a series of strikes in Iraqi territory in 1993–1994, primarily using fighter jets and rockets. In 1996, Iran renewed these attacks and sent troops into northern Iraq to participate in a battle between rival Kurdish groups. Again in 1997 and in 1999, Iran took military action inside Iraq. While these attacks were aimed against non-state actors rather than Iraqi troops, the Iraqi government considered them militarized violations of its sovereignty.

On its eastern front, Iran was active militarily against Afghanistan. After Taliban forces compromised the Iranian consulate, Iran deployed

---

[40] K. Pollack, 2004.   [41] N. Keddie, 2006.

200,000 troops to the border as a show of force in 1998. Iran subsequently crossed the border and claimed to have inflicted "heavy" casualties against the Taliban. In 1999, Iran also shelled Afghanistan with artillery fire after the Iranian-backed *Hizbe Wahdat* group suffered a defeat by the Taliban.

To the north, Iran came into conflict with the littoral states of the Caspian Sea over how the sea borders should be drawn. This conflict was exacerbated by the belief that the Caspian Sea held valuable deposits of petroleum and natural gas. Efforts by the Azerbaijanis to begin petroleum exploration led the Iranians to fire warning shots at foreign boats.

Finally, to the south, Iran continued to dispute the territorial control of the islands of Abu Musa, Lesser Tunb, and Greater Tunb. The UAE claimed sovereignty over these islands, but in 1992 Iran elected to expel all foreign workers on the islands, including those operating the UAE-sponsored school, medical clinic, and power-generation station. The UAE continues to dispute Iran's claim on the islands, but is not in a position to settle the matter militarily.

Since the end of the 1990s, Iran has had fewer direct interstate conflicts. Still, Iran continues to be perceived as aggressive and volatile, particularly by American and Israeli officials. Arab governments are more circumspect, but in private they are openly hostile to Iran. Omani officials explicitly describe Iranian foreign policy as aggressive and an ongoing military concern.[42] Saudi officials went so far as to ask the United States to take military action to "cut off the head of the snake."[43]

Iranian support for foreign insurgencies

Iran's military aggressiveness has not been limited to direct interstate conflicts. Since the revolution, the Iranian government has actively supported foreign insurgencies and rebel groups. To a certain extent, this is a common pattern among oil-rich petrostates, many of which use some of their oil income to sponsor insurgencies in enemy countries. Iran's behavior, however, has been extraordinary. Whereas petrostates typically provide financing and occasionally military aid to

[42] US Government diplomatic cable, August 7, 2008. www.wikileaks.org.
[43] *Guardian*, 2010a.

foreign groups, Iran's support goes considerably beyond that. Iran has a special division of the Islamic Revolutionary Guard, known as the Qods force, that is tasked with exporting the Islamic revolution. Iran has used its own troops to mobilize, train, and fight alongside rebel groups on foreign soil. Furthermore, Iran's connections to Hezbollah and Hamas are deeper and more direct than virtually any other state relationship with a non-state rebel actor.

The Qods force is an elite, covert division of the Islamic Revolutionary Guard. Its personnel size is unknown but estimates place it at 5,000 soldiers, although an expansion in 2006–2007 may have brought that number closer to 15,000.[44] The budget for the Qods force is classified and reported directly to the Supreme Leader. The force is divided into seven directorates: Iraq; Lebanon, Palestine, and Jordan; Afghanistan, Pakistan, and India; Turkey and the Arabian Peninsula; Central Asian countries; Western nations; and North Africa. The Qods forces have offices in many Iranian embassies that are closed to most embassy staff. The Qods forces are suspected of having carried out lethal operations in multiple countries. A particularly spectacular example occurred in Germany, when four Iranian Kurdish opposition leaders were killed in a restaurant in Berlin. The German courts convicted an Iranian official in 1997, along with four others in absentia, including President Rafsanjani and Supreme Leader Khamenei.[45] More recently, the Qods force is alleged to have tried to kill the Saudi ambassador to the United States in Washington, DC.[46]

Iran's ties to Hezbollah and Hamas are deep. While Iranian relations with Israel had been cordial and even cooperative under the Shah, the Islamic Revolutionary government views Israel as its enemy. Hezbollah's leaders were inspired by Khomeini and created their organization after the Israeli invasion of Lebanon in 1982.[47] Hezbollah's forces were in part directly mobilized and trained by the Qods force.[48] Iran is estimated to provide $200 million per year to Hezbollah, making it the group's principal funder.[49] Iran and Syria are suspected of exerting considerable direct influence over the organization, although they officially deny it and precise details are impossible to obtain. However, two joint operations indicate close coordination between Hezbollah

[44] A. Cordesman, 2007.
[45] A. Norton, 2009.   [46] M. Milani, 2011.
[47] A. Norton, 2009.   [48] A. Cordesman, 2007.
[49] J. Giraldo and H. Trinkunas, 2007.

and the Qods force. The first attack, in 1992, was the bombing of the Israeli embassy in Argentina, killing twenty-nine people. A second bombing of a Jewish community center in Buenos Aires in 1994 killed eighty-five people. In November 2006, warrants were issued for the arrest of former Iranian president Akbar Rafsanjani and eight other Iranian officials.[50] Leaked US diplomatic cables also suggest that the Qods force used the cover of the International Red Crescent to smuggle weapons and materials to Hezbollah during its 2006 war with Israel.[51] Iran also gives Hamas an estimated $30 million per year, plus military training and ideological support.[52] In response to the Western boycott of Hamas in 2006, Iran pledged $250 million to pay the wages of civil servants in Gaza, compensate Palestinians who had lost their homes, and support Hamas' security operations. Some observers allege that Iran works to coordinate the insurgent activities of Hezbollah and Hamas.[53]

Finally, Iran is active in fomenting insurgencies in other parts of the world. In Iraq, Iran supported Kurdish and Shiite insurgent groups continuously since the 1979 revolution.[54] Even after the end of the war and Khomeini's death, Iranian troops operated in Kurdish areas of Iraqi territory to undermine Saddam's reign. Iran's support for insurgency in Iraq continued and even escalated after the fall of Saddam in 2003. General David Petraeus testified before Congress that the United States military had found Qods operatives in Iraq and seized documents detailing the planning, approval process, and conduct of attacks that killed US soldiers in Iraq.[55] Although the White House publicly left some questions open about whether these attacks had been directly authorized by the Iranian government for diplomatic reasons, there was clearly no doubt in the mind of General Petraeus.[56] The Egyptian government has repeatedly accused Iran and Sudan of collaborating to arm, finance, and train Muslim militants to carry out violent acts of subversion in Egypt.[57] In Afghanistan, Iranian forces are believed to have supported various rebel factions for more than

---

[50] A. Norton, 2009: 79.
[51] US Government diplomatic cable, October 23, 2008. www.wikileaks.org.
[52] M. Wurmser, 2007.   [53] M. Wurmser, 2007.
[54] J. Felter and B. Fishman, 2008.
[55] A. Cordesman, 2007.
[56] J. Felter and B. Fishman, 2008.
[57] MIDs Narratives. See F. Ghosn *et al.*, 2004.

two decades. The support is typically for multiple sides in the same conflict, suggesting that different parts of the Iranian government are active without coordination. Overall, it is unclear precisely what Iran's objectives are other than to sow internecine warfare among neighboring countries.

Nuclear weapons program

Iran's foreign policy takes on a new character once its covert nuclear weapons program is considered. Iran has had a nuclear energy program for more than half a century, beginning with a nuclear reactor purchased from the United States in 1959. Under the Shah, Iran was a member of the Nonproliferation Treaty and agreed to use nuclear energy for purely civilian purposes. The Shah also appears to have had a covert operation to develop nuclear weapons technology during the 1970s.[58] However, Iran's nuclear weapons program got started in earnest in the late 1980s. In 2005, Iran publicly admitted that it purchased a nuclear enrichment "starter kit" and designs for casting and machining parts for a nuclear weapon from the Pakistani scientist A. Q. Khan in 1987.[59] Throughout the 1990s, Iran continued its efforts to develop nuclear weapons, including under President Khatami.

Officially, Iran argues that nuclear power is for purely civilian purposes. The government points to rising domestic energy consumption, and argues the country's petroleum production is needed to generate foreign currency. These assertions, however, are not credible. The reactors built by Iran are efficient for military purposes, not civilian ones. Moreover, the enormous investment in nuclear reactors diverts precious capital away from the refineries needed to resolve Iran's most serious energy problem: its rising domestic demand for gasoline.

In September 2005, the International Atomic Energy Agency found Iran to be in noncompliance with its Nuclear Nonproliferation Treaty safeguards agreement and reported Iran's case to the UN Security Council in February 2006. In 2003, Iran agreed in negotiations with Germany, France, and the UK to suspend certain sensitive activities, but this agreement broke down in August 2005. Iran has continued

---

[58] L. Spector, 1990.
[59] S. Squassoni, 2007. The Shah also may have had a covert operation to develop nuclear weapons technology during the 1970s.

its enrichment activities, repeatedly failing to meet international deadlines. Its operations are condemned by UN Security Council Resolutions 1696 and 1737, with the latter authorizing multilateral economic sanctions against Iran.

Operation of causal mechanisms

As in previous chapters, the hypothesized causal mechanisms can be probed further by considering three questions.

Did the revolutionary government make Iraq more aggressive?

The Iranian Revolution resulted in a state with highly aggressive foreign policy behavior. Evidence of the causal factors hypothesized in Chapter 2 can be identified. First, Iran's leader was politically ambitious, ruthless, and unafraid to take a calculated risk.[60] Khomeini protested against the Shah's reign in the 1960s, when it was highly dangerous to do so. He did so knowing that he would likely be arrested and possibly executed. Indeed, Grand Ayatollah Shariatmadari elevated Khomeini to the level of Grand Ayatollah (*marja*) precisely because there was a clause in the constitution forbidding the execution of *marja*. Saved from the Shah's wrath, Khomeini was sent into exile. In Iraq, he continued to preach about the necessity of Islamic government and the duty of Muslims to rise against tyranny, which certainly did not endear him to the Baathist regime. In exile, Khomeini lived under the constant threat of assassination. After he returned to Iran, the danger only increased. The government discovered multiple plots to kidnap and/or kill Khomeini in the early years of the regime. Consistently, Khomeini showed himself to be a shrewd leader willing to take risks in order to achieve political gains.

Second, the revolutionary turmoil in Iran facilitated the emergence of a leader with Khomeini's ambition and risk-tolerance. Although in hindsight it is tempting to say that Khomeini was the inevitable leader of Iran, that was far from certain in the early days of the regime. He enjoyed tremendous spiritual and popular legitimacy, but if his personality and skill set had been different, one could easily imagine Khomeini

[60] B. Moin, 2000.

playing the role that Ayatollah Shariatmadari in fact played: a popular
religious leader, who was politically active but ultimately ineffective
as a politician. Just as Nasser usurped the presidency from Naguib in
Egypt, a radical Iranian leader might have usurped Khomeini as leader
of the revolution. Yet Khomeini's combination of shrewdness, ambition, ruthlessness, and luck ensured that he never gave up the reins of
the revolution. To the contrary, he initially promoted relatively moderate leaders like Bazargan and Bani-Sadr to help solidify his hold on
power before siding with the hardliners in the factional disputes that
subsequently developed.

As expected, the revolutionary political dynamics produced a
government guided by radicals, such as Khomeini, Rafsanjani, and
Khamenei, who displaced not only liberal thinkers like Bazargan and
Sanjabi, but also other radical leaders who were still too "moder-
ate," such as Ayatollahs Shariatmadari, Taleqani, and Montazeri.[61] An
American analyst living in Iran described the political environment:

the moderates were doomed to failure in Iran for systematic reasons. They
were struggling to survive in a climate in which the political winds blew
strongly against them ... Since the revolution seemed under attack from all
sides, the new leaders who struggled to the top were precisely those with
the mentality of tough campaigners. They expected no quarter and gave no
quarter; they were ready to kill and be killed. In short, they were the extrem-
ists, the true believers.[62]

Thus the tumultuous, violent nature of Iranian politics in the late
1970s and early 1980s created a breeding ground for radical leaders.

Third, the revolution eliminated constraints on the power of the
Supreme Leader. The Shah had significant executive powers prior to
1979, but Iran was still a constitutional monarchy with some limited
checks on the Shah's authority.[63] As Abrahamian points out, the Iranian

---

[61] B. Moin, 2000.
[62] J. Bill, 1989: 268–270. I thank Michael McKoy for the reference.
[63] For instance, Article 51 of the Persian Constitution of 1906 [1907] vested the
power to declare war in the Shah, but Article 45 stated that the Shah's decrees
could only be carried out when they were countersigned by the responsible
Minister, Articles 61 and 67 made Ministers responsible to the *majlis*, and
Articles 94–101 placed the government's power to tax and spend (crucial for
conducting a military campaign) in the hands of the *majlis*. These constraints
were severely weakened after 1953, however. After 1953, the Shah had the

Revolution provided the Supreme Leader with powers unimagined by the shahs.[64] The constitution bestowed on Khomeini titles such as Supreme Faqeh, Supreme Leader, Guide of the Revolution, Founder of the Islamic Republic, Inspirer of the Mostazafan, and the Imam of the Muslim Umma. This last title was especially important: Shi'as had never before bestowed on a living person the title of Imam, with its connotations of divine infallibility. The constitution also gave the Supreme Leader wide-ranging authority, unparalleled in Iran's previous constitutions.[65] He was to "determine the interests of Islam," "supervise policy implementation," and "mediate between the executive, legislative, and judiciary." He could dismiss the president; vet candidates for office; grant amnesty; appoint the chief justice, the state prosecutor, and lower court justices; and he named six clerics to the powerful Guardian Council, which could veto any legislation passed by the *majlis*. As commander-in-chief, he had the authority to declare war and peace, mobilize the armed forces, and appoint military commanders. As if all of this were not enough, Khomeini explained that the Islamic government, being "a divine entity given by God to the Prophet" could suspend any laws on the ground of *maslahat* (protecting the public interest), another precept never before adopted by Shi'as. Khomeini's powers were so vast that he could even suspend the very laws of Islam, as he argued: "The government of Islam is a primary rule having precedence over secondary rulings such as praying, fasting, and performing the hajj. To preserve Islam, the government can suspend any or all secondary rulings."[66] Consequently, the revolutionary leader faced few constraints in pursuing risky foreign policies.

The Iranian Revolution did not wipe out all elements of political accountability, however. Unlike in Iraq under Saddam or in Libya under Qaddafi, the voices of independent political thought continued and even flourished in the early years of the revolutionary regime. Moderates expressed their opposition to the regime on a range of matters, including the war with Iraq. Gradually, as the regime consolidated its power, those voices were repressed, until in

power to dismiss his ministers or the entire *majlis* at any time, and elections were deeply flawed. Even so, dismissing the *majlis* was politically costly for the Shah, so these institutional constraints survived in a weakened form.

[64] E. Abrahamian, 2008.   [65] D. Menashri, 1990: 116.
[66] Quoted in E. Abrahamian, 2008: 165–166.

May 1983 all political parties except the Islamic Republican Party
were outlawed. Ultimately, the opposition could do little to influence
Khomeini's key followers. Thus when the Tudeh Party expressed its
opposition to the government's decision in June 1982 to invade Iraq,
it backfired: the regime viewed the Tudeh as traitorous and gradually repressed the organization.

Did oil generate incentives for aggression and conflict?

As expected, oil income increased Iran's propensity for international
conflict, both by reducing the leader's risk of domestic punishment
for foreign policy adventurism, and by increasing the state's military
capabilities. Initially, Iran's oil production suffered dramatically from
the revolution, dropping to less than a third of its pre-revolutionary
production of more than five million barrels per day, a rate that it still
has not equaled. Yet by 1982 Iran's oil industry was producing 2.4
million barrels per day, sufficient to supply Khomeini's government
with a large oil income to secure domestic political support and fund
military operations.

Khomeini used the country's oil income for political purposes,
ranging from populist subsidies, expanding the clientelist state bureaucracy, and financing the security services that repressed Iranian
opposition. Khomeini's actions indicate that he was well aware of the
vital role that oil played in Iran. For instance, while he successfully
called upon the oil workers to stage massive strikes in the final days of
the Shah's regime, once in power he almost immediately asked those
workers to go back to work. Khomeini said, "The [oil] industry is the
lifeline of the nation."[67] And as indicated above, Khomeini's government was quick to renege on its pre-revolutionary promises when, in
1981, it realized how desperately it needed to reactivate its oil sales to
the West.[68] As in other revolutionary petrostates, oil money was used
directly to garner popular support for military activities. Subsidies and
rationing of basic goods ensured that the war's impact on the economy
did not deprive the masses of essential commodities, and families of

---

[67] Additionally, Khomeini's first prime minister told oil industry workers after
the resumption of oil exports in March 1979 that the Iranian Revolution itself
would fail if oil exports were not resumed. R. Ramazani, 1987: 206–207.
[68] S. Bakhash, 1982.

war victims were well-compensated by the state. This use of the state's resources ensured that the hardliners had a free hand to pursue the war without effective domestic opposition, even after Iraq sought to make peace.

Oil income was also crucial to funding Iran's military expenditures, its covert operations and extensive support for foreign insurgencies, and its nuclear weapons program. This was not, however, unique to the revolutionary regime: the Shah spent lavishly on Iran's military, especially after the influx of oil revenues starting in 1973. Indeed, for much of the Iran–Iraq War, the revolutionary regime was essentially using up the military capital that the Shah had built. Largely due to its isolation from international markets, Iran has gradually developed a significant domestic production capacity for military equipment. Almost all of this industry is state-run and state-financed, which again relies profoundly on Iran's oil revenues.

Did oil generate incentives to avoid aggression and conflict?

Oil can also decrease a state's propensity for international conflict by increasing the economic incentives for peaceful international trade and stability in the global oil export market. Despite Iran's aggressive policies, the conflict-reducing incentives of its oil industry are observable. They are most clear in Iran's war with Iraq. Iraq devoted considerable effort to destroying Iran's oil export capacity, and Iran's leaders claimed that the first five years of the war cost the country $150 billion in lost oil revenues.[69] Iraq's first move in the war was to invade and occupy Iran's oil-rich province of Khuzestan. Iraq also repeatedly attacked Kharq Island, Iran's largest oil terminal. As Iran's leaders considered the question of whether to pursue the war, the potential and actual loss of a significant portion of the country's oil income represented a significant financial incentive to stop the war and accept a peace settlement. Further, the Tanker War illustrated each side's awareness of the vital importance of oil revenues, and the impact that their loss could have on the state. Even for Khomeini and the other hawks in the revolutionary government, the potential loss of oil revenues was a serious risk. No wonder that, even among Khomeini's inner circle, there were those who advocated for an end to the war in 1981–1982.

[69] H. Amirahmadi, 1990: 65.

Conclusion

Iran's revolutionary government and significant oil income have combined to shape the state's domestic and foreign policy over the last three decades. As expected, Iran is an aggressive state, frequently antagonizing its neighbors, the United States, and other actors in the international system with both its overt and covert actions. Concomitantly, Iran has been the target of significant aggressiveness by the United States and others. Three issues are likely to shape Iran's international affairs in the future: the violent insurgencies being fought in both of its immediate neighbors, Afghanistan and Iraq; Iran's relationship with Hamas, Hezbollah, and Israel; and Iran's (alleged) nuclear weapons development program. The frictions associated with any one of these factors could provide the basis of one or more armed conflicts, potentially on a very large scale. However, there is nothing inevitable about such an outcome.

Iran's oil industry is experiencing a difficult transition. Despite producing approximately four million barrels per day in 2008–2009, and despite having the world's third largest oil reserves, Iran's oil industry is troubled in many ways. The country has limited refining capacity, meaning that it is often a net importer of gasoline. Through 2010, Iran also heavily subsidized the price of gasoline, creating a huge fiscal burden (estimated at $3 billion per month).[70] Perhaps most seriously, Iran's upstream oil industry is aging and requires foreign investment, which has been hampered by ongoing US and multilateral sanctions. Iran's domestic consumption is also rising quickly. Unless it increases its production capacity significantly in the next decade, Iran could become a net importer of crude oil in the next decade.[71] If this occurs, the loss of export revenues for the government would be a profound shift in Iran's fiscal situation, and could even provide incentive for additional popular accountability over the government as its revenues become increasingly tax-based.

Iran's contemporary affairs are sufficiently complex that they defy precise predictions. However, to the extent that the original leaders of the 1979 revolution who occupy senior positions are gradually being replaced by men who have risen up through the ranks of the political

[70] US Government, Energy Information Agency, 2010.
[71] S. Reed, 2006.

system, Iran is likely to have a leadership with less risk-tolerance and less ideologically extreme preferences over time. Moreover, to the extent that its oil revenues are curtailed by demographic and economic factors, Iran will become less of a petrostate. These factors are good news for international peace and security.

8 | *Venezuela and the Bolivarian Revolution*

Serious leadership is needed, not irresponsible populism.

– Hugo Chávez[1]

The politics of Iraq, Libya, and Iran provide significant evidence in support of the argument that petro-revolutionary regimes tend to have highly aggressive foreign policies. Because those states are all in the Middle East/North Africa, one might wonder whether there is something special about the region itself. As I argued in Chapter 4, the evidence is strongest in the Middle East because that region is home to most of the world's petrostates, and therefore most of the petro-revolutionary governments. Yet there is no theoretical reason to expect that the argument fails outside of the region. I expect the argument to apply outside of the Middle East wherever there is both a revolutionary government and an economy dominated by the oil industry. This chapter focuses on one such case: Venezuela under the leadership of President Hugo Chávez.

From his bombastic rhetoric and activist foreign policy to his controversial political and economic reforms at home, Chávez is one of the most striking figures of recent times. Since his election in 1998, Chávez has led what he refers to as a "Bolivarian Revolution," re-shaping the institutions and policies of Venezuela. While the Bolivarian Revolution is not as swift or as transformative as some of the other revolutions examined in this book, it nonetheless constitutes a marked change in Venezuelan politics. I therefore classify Chávez's regime as moderately revolutionary. Consequently, Venezuela's foreign policy is expected to be moderately aggressive. In practice, the Chávez presidency marks a significant breakpoint, as the government has engaged in some of the most aggressive foreign policy behavior in Venezuela's history. Still, thus far it has not initiated a war or large-scale military conflict.

---

[1] Quoted in R. Gott, 2005: 188.

Table 8.1 *Summary of key variables in Venezuela, 1958–2010*

Period	1958–1974	1974–1979	1980–1989	1990–1998	1999–2010
President	multiple	CAP	multiple	multiple	Chávez
IV: Revolutionary regime	Non-	Non-	Non-	Non-	Moderately
IV: Petrostate	Yes	Yes, high revenue	Yes	Yes	Yes, high revenue
Foreign policy:					
with Colombia	No conflict	No conflict	Mild friction	No conflict	Conflict
with Guyana	Friction	No conflict	No conflict	No conflict	Friction
with Brazil	No conflict	No conflict	No conflict	No conflict	No conflict
with United States	No conflict	Mild friction	No conflict	No conflict	Hostility
DV: Aggressiveness					
Expected value	Low	Low	Low	Low	Moderate
Actual value	Low	Low	Low	Low	Moderate

Note: For more information about the labels used in this table, see Figure 3.1.

Table 8.1 evaluates the key variables in each time period 1958–2010. As the table shows, Venezuela experienced occasional periods of mild friction with its neighbors but no major conflicts until 1999. Under Chávez's regime, however, Venezuela has engaged in significant disputes with Colombia, the United States, and Guyana. This has coincided with a period of centralization of power by the president, and a dramatic increase in military expenditure.

First, consider the country's oil income. Venezuela was a petrostate for the entire period under consideration. Oil production was already almost three million barrels per day by the late 1950s. Even before the dramatic increases in oil prices in the 1970s, oil income constituted more than half of Venezuela's government revenue and 20 percent of its GDP. Over time, production levels and prices have fluctuated, but in every period oil income has been the main source of revenue for Venezuela's government. Figure 8.1 shows Venezuela's oil production over time.

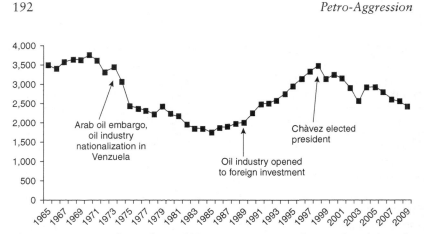

Figure 8.1 Venezuela's oil production 1965–2009, thousands of barrels per day
Note: Data on production volume are from BP Statistical Review of World Energy, 2010.

Second, as suggested by Table 8.1, there is a correlation between the emergence of a revolutionary government and a more aggressive foreign policy. Chávez rejected and replaced Venezuela's constitution, changed the legislature from a bicameral to a unicameral body, stacked the Supreme Court with his supporters, abolished presidential term limits, nationalized key industries, compromised the central bank's independence, changed the name and symbols of the country, and introduced "twenty-first century socialism" into Venezuela's politics and economy. At the same time, Venezuela's foreign policy became significantly more aggressive under Chávez's leadership, especially in relation to Colombia and the United States.

The rest of this chapter is organized in five parts. The first section focuses on Venezuelan politics prior to the emergence of Chávez. The second and third parts focus on the domestic and foreign politics, respectively, of Venezuela under Chávez. The fourth part revisits the changes in Venezuela using the three analytical questions used in previous chapters to highlight the role of the key causal mechanisms. A short final section concludes.

Venezuelan politics prior to Chávez

Venezuela's life as a petrostate began when oil production was commercialized near Lake Maracaibo in the 1920s. The dictator Juan

Vicente Gomez skillfully handled the foreign oil companies, often playing them off against one another in negotiations. Still, Venezuela received only a small proportion of the oil revenue until Romulo Betancourt, the democratizing president of Venezuela during the *trienio* period 1945–1948, raised taxes on petroleum revenue significantly. During this period, universal and direct elections were held for the first time in Venezuelan history. The fragile democracy was soon overthrown in a military coup, and was not re-established for another decade.

With the downfall of the dictatorship of Marcos Perez Jimenez in 1958, Venezuela's modern political system was established. A political agreement between the major parties, called the Punto Fijo Pact, powerfully shaped Venezuelan democracy for the next forty years. Punto Fijo refers to Rafael Caldera's house in Caracas, where the leaders of the principal parties of Venezuelan politics met to organize the re-establishment of democracy. President Romulo Betancourt, leader of Acción Democrática (AD), and Rafael Caldera, head of Partido Social Cristiano (COPEI), agreed to institutionalize a power-sharing agreement that became the backbone of a two-party system.

In 1960, Venezuela helped found the Organization of Petroleum Exporting Countries (OPEC) to organize petrostate governments and increase oil prices. The architect of the organization was the Venezuelan politician and diplomat Juan Pablo Perez Alfonso, who had worked for the Texas Railroad Commission and understood how such an organization could be used to regulate prices. Interestingly, he initially proposed an organization that included both producers and consumers, but the United States rejected this idea. OPEC was created in Baghdad with the support of Iraq, Iran, Kuwait, and Saudi Arabia. The organization would not rise to global significance until the early 1970s.

Carlos Andres Perez (known almost universally in Venezuela by his initials, CAP), was elected President of Venezuela in 1973. It was his good fortune to lead Venezuela in the period 1974–1979, just as oil revenues were skyrocketing. An energetic and activist president, CAP immediately seized on this revenue windfall and launched major new spending programs according to his vision of *La Gran Venezuela* (the Great Venezuela). CAP's initial popularity and authority allowed him to rule by decree for a year, passing more than 100 decrees in a nine-month period.[2] Still, as CAP's term continued, he was increasingly constrained by domestic politics, both in Congress, in his own party, and especially in his interactions with Fedecamaras (the business council).[3]

CAP formally nationalized Venezuela's oil industry. Much of the oil industry was already in the government's hands by the time CAP came to office. All that remained was formal nationalization, which proceeded with relatively little rancor. Employees of Exxon and Shell on one day became employees of the state-owned Petróleos de Venezuela (PdVSA) on the next day, still coming to work in the same office buildings as they had before.[4] Moreover, in the first year after nationalization, Exxon signed with Venezuela what was considered at that time the largest single oil supply contract ever made. Thus the nationalization of the oil industry in the 1970s was accomplished with relatively little conflict with international parties.

In the international arena, CAP pursued an ambitious agenda of progressive and democratic causes in Latin America. He opposed the repressive regimes in Chile and Nicaragua, helped Panama gain sovereignty over the Panama Canal, supported Cuba's re-integration into Latin American politics, and co-founded SELA, the Latin American Economic System. CAP also committed Venezuelan funds to the World Bank, the IMF, the Inter-American Development Bank, the OPEC Fund for International Development, and several regional institutions.[5] In 1974, Venezuela's official development assistance to foreign countries amounted to an astonishing 3 percent of GDP.[6] Despite this financial generosity, Venezuela experienced some friction with its Latin American neighbors during this time. Some states were suspicious of Venezuela's rising influence.[7] Bilaterally, Venezuela had diplomatic disputes with Colombia, Guyana, and Brazil, but these disputes were minor and did not become militarized.[8] The dramatic increase in

[2] H. Tarver *et al.*, 2005.   [3] T. Karl, 1997: 130–136.

[4] D. Yergin, 2008 [1991]: 649.

[5] J. Martz, "Venezuelan Foreign Policy Toward Latin America," in R. Bond, 1977: 158–169.

[6] R. Bond, 1977: 228.   [7] J. Martz in R. Bond, 1977: 189.

[8] The COW dataset records one MID involving Venezuela during this period, a "display of force" against Guyana. However, the incident was short-lived and tensions eased during this period after an agreement in 1970. Brazil constructed military bases near its border with Venezuela, but there was never a significant military dispute.

Venezuela's oil income during the 1970s also allowed the government to significantly boost its military spending.

A generation later, many observers would compare Chávez's activism both at home and abroad to that of Carlos Andres Perez. At home, both men launched massive new spending projects backed by a fortuitous rise in the price of oil, and both nationalized the oil industry (or re-nationalized it, in Chávez's case). In foreign affairs, both encouraged warmer relations with Cuba, both were generous in their use of foreign aid, and both were keen to be seen personally as symbols of Latin American unity.

Yet the differences between the two men cannot be ignored. While CAP was an activist president, he was not a revolutionary. He was a party insider, a protégé of former President Romulo Betancourt, and worked within the constitutional system supported by the Pact of Punto Fijo. Chávez did not. This led to crucial differences in the outcomes, especially in foreign policy. Critically, Venezuela saw itself in the 1970s as a democracy which, though it might have differences with the United States, was essentially a part of the West and sought friendly partnership with the United States. Indeed, CAP sought to have the United States treat Venezuela as a "special supplier" of oil, in sharp contrast to Chávez's threats of an embargo. While Venezuela desired and benefited from higher oil prices, CAP's government also worked to be a mediator and a moderating influence within OPEC rather than a price-hawk.[9] Chávez was just the opposite. And while CAP nationalized the oil industry, fair compensation was paid to the companies and a continuing relationship was established in which US corporations received large contracts. This stands in contrast to Chávez's treatment of US companies. Thus in the 1970s, contemporary analysts argued that "[a]mong those countries aspiring to an international status within the region, Venezuela is one of the most friendly to the United States. Further, Venezuelan foreign policy has in recent years been flexible, conciliatory, and constructive."[10]

By 1979, CAP was unpopular, and his party lost the presidential elections. COPEI's candidate, Luis Herrera Campins, was elected. Though he came to power by decrying the excess of government spending, Campins would soon follow in CAP's footsteps. Buoyed by a new oil

[9] F. Tugwell in R. Bond, 1977: 205.
[10] F. Tugwell in R. Bond, 1977: 220.

price boom in 1980–1981, the government launched new projects and accrued more debt. This set the stage for an economic crisis in the period following 1986, when global oil prices dipped briefly below $10 per barrel. The task of trying to manage this crisis fell to Jaime Lusinichi, who was elected president in 1984. The economic and political difficulties that ensued have been well documented by Terry Lynn Karl and Thad Dunning.[11]

During the democratic era 1958–1989, Venezuela's foreign relations were peaceful. The country did not engage in any wars or large-scale militarized incidents. In 1987, there was one incident in which a Colombian naval vessel entered Venezuelan waters, and the Venezuelan government reacted by sending F-16 fighter jets toward the ship. However, no combat ensued, and the countries retained peaceful relations: in 1989, the two countries formed the Comisión de vecindad Colombo-Venezolana (Neighborhood Commission) to bolster friendly ties and later an agreement to share military intelligence was formed.

Venezuela's cooperative and non-aggressive approach to foreign policy continued through the 1990s. Venezuela and Colombia cooperated extensively to combat the Colombian guerilla group ELN, which was operating near the Venezuelan border. In 1998, President Caldera of Venezuela authorized the Colombian army to enter and fight guerrillas on Venezuelan territory.[12] This action stands in stark contrast to the 2008 dispute between the two countries, discussed below. Thus, with the exception of occasional diplomatic friction, Venezuela's foreign relations remained cordial with all countries through the 1990s.

The rising tide of the Bolivarian Revolution: 1989–1999

In the late 1980s, political tensions were rising in Venezuela. With oil prices averaging just $18 per barrel in 1989, government revenues had dropped precipitously compared to the early 1980s and the economy suffered.[13] CAP was elected to a second term as president, in the hopes that he could return Venezuela to the glory days of the 1970s. Instead, he sought assistance from the IMF and implemented a series

[11] T. Dunning, 2008; T. Karl, 1997.
[12] *El Tiempo*, 2008.
[13] BP Statistical Review of World Energy 2010. All oil prices quoted are from this source. Note also that the WTI benchmark price is quoted, which is slightly different from the price of Venezuelan crude.

of austerity measures in the economy. This led to an unprecedented degree of popular unrest and, ultimately, the weakening of the civilian democratic regime in Venezuela.

One of the crucial events was known as *el caracazo*. On February 27, 1989, the government raised public transportation fares, sparking massive social unrest.

Caracas was sacked and looted during massive riots, with a death toll in the hundreds. The event turned out to be the opening salvo in a long string of protests against the government. At least 120 protests and forty-six strikes took place between 1989 and 1992.[14] Of course, even stable democracies have occasional protests and riots, but the scale of unrest in Venezuela was indicative of a widespread popular rejection of the governing system.

On February 4, 1992, a then-unknown army commander named Hugo Chávez Frías launched a coup attempt against the government. Chávez failed to accomplish his part of the military objectives of the coup and was ultimately captured by the government forces. He was then put on television to order his supporters to stop. This he did, concluding that his supporters must stop the fight *por ahora* ("for now"). Thus the words *por ahora* became one of his slogans and a political symbol for the years Chávez spent in jail. Even though the coup attempt failed, his brief appearance on television made Chávez a national hero and a symbol of frustration with the reigning system of democratic government.

Later that same year, a second military coup was attempted and failed. On November 27, Brigadier General Visconti and officers from the Venezuelan Air Force led the second coup attempt. This group of conspirators denied any connection with Hugo Chávez's Movimiento Bolívariano Revolucionario 200 (MBR-200). Visconti's group was more politically moderate, and even attempted to negotiate with President Perez before the coup attempt.[15] When the attempt failed, Visconti and ninety-two other officers and soldiers left Venezuela aboard a captured military plane, escaping to Peru.

It was by no means inevitable in the years 1992–1997 that Hugo Chávez would emerge as leader of the opposition to Venezuela's

---

[14] C. Marcano and A. Tyszka, 2007: 64. Some sources claim that the number of protests was even higher.
[15] S. Baburkin *et al.*, 1999.

two-party system of government.[16] There were plenty of other potential leaders, including General Visconti, Francisco Arias Cárdenas, and Teodoro Petkoff. Visconti led the second coup attempt in 1992. Francisco Arias was a member of the MBR-200, was a co-leader of the coup attempt in February 1992, and unlike Chávez, he accomplished his portion of the military objectives of the coup attempt. Yet Arias was more moderate than Chávez and split with him and the MBR-200 in 1993 because of the group's unwillingness to engage in the democratic process. Arias was elected governor of the important Zulia State, whose capital is Maracaibo, providing him with a potential platform for national leadership. Teodoro Petkoff was a former guerilla, the founder of the leftist group Movimiento al Socialismo (MAS), and a cabinet minister from 1994 to 1999. He, too, might have tapped the rising popular resentment and sought the executive leadership. However, these other leaders were either insufficiently radical or did not possess the necessary political skills (and luck) to seize leadership of the nascent opposition movement. Both Arias Cárdenas and Petkoff would eventually become presidential candidates running against Chávez, in 2000 and 2006 respectively, but neither could muster the popular support of Chávez.

The rising tide of opposition in Venezuela generated opportunities for a leader who was risk-tolerant, ambitious, and politically savvy. The coup attempt in 1992 had established Chávez's credentials as an outsider to the political system and a symbol of opposition. Though he would remain in jail until pardoned in 1996, Chávez's steady stream of visitors allowed him to communicate with the outside world and attract a body of followers. Still, when he left prison he commanded just 7 percent support for president according to national polls.[17] It was then that Chávez began to demonstrate the savvy that accompanied his revolutionary ambitions. Chávez listened to his friends and new political mentors, Luis Miquilena and William Izarra, who urged him to tone down his revolutionary rhetoric so that he could appeal to a wider audience and succeed in electoral politics. Gradually, he gathered around him individuals from both the left- and right-wing opposition to form a popular coalition that could support his bid for

[16] P. Penaloza, 2006.
[17] C. Marcano and A. Tyszka, 2007: 106.

the presidency. As the established parties AD and COPEI continued to make political mistakes in 1997 and 1998, Chávez's popularity grew.

President Perez was removed from office in 1993 on corruption charges and later that year an election was held. By then, popular antipathy towards the existing two-party system was already high. Rafael Caldera, founder of COPEI, realized that he would have to leave his own party to get elected. This was one of the early signs of the collapse of the AD-COPEI duopoly system of democratic governance.[18] Caldera founded a new party and was elected president, in large measure because he was seen as an outsider who could act as an honest broker. However, his attempts to stabilize support for the existing political institutions failed.[19]

In 1998, on the eve of Hugo Chávez's election, the support for the two-party system in Venezuela was extremely weak. The corruption and incompetence that had characterized Venezuelan democracy in the previous two decades were taking their toll. A survey conducted by Latinbarometro found that just 35.7 percent of Venezuelans in 1998 were satisfied with democracy. Electoral absenteeism and non-participation in the political process were high. Venezuelans were ready to "write a blank check" to anyone who could fix the country's economic and political problems.[20] Hugo Chávez, campaigning on populist economic themes and railing against corruption, was there to exploit that discontent.

The Bolivarian revolutionary regime at home: 1999–2010

In this political climate Hugo Chávez was elected president, and from the moment he came to office he worked to revolutionize the government of Venezuela. In his presidential inauguration ceremony, he refused to swear allegiance to the Constitution, and instead promised to replace it. Within a year, he did just that. In the years following, Chávez would continue to mobilize popular support for his Bolivarian Revolution as a way of weakening or overturning existing

---

[18] T. Dunning, 2008: 206–208.
[19] Some scholars attribute Caldera's failure to his lack of oil money needed to support popular spending projects. See T. Dunning, 2008: 207.
[20] Personal interviews in Caracas, January 2008.

political institutions, centralizing power, and introducing a new style of governance in Venezuela.

The new Bolivarian constitution

The new regime's first step after taking power was to reshape the constitution. A popular referendum mandated an election for a National Constituent Assembly to write a new constitution. This bypassed Venezuela's existing bicameral Congress, and allowed Chávez to shape the procedures of the new Assembly and its proposed constitution because his supporters won 125 of 131 seats.[21] Chávez also sought to provide a veneer of popular participation. Proposals for the new constitution circulated by means of workshops, committees, manifestos, radio, and newspapers. Altogether, 624 proposals were submitted to the Assembly, and the government claims that over half were incorporated into the new constitution.[22] It was then ratified in a popular referendum in December 1999. Copies of the constitution were distributed widely, as part of a program to give the Venezuelan people a direct, unmediated relationship with their leader and government.

Behind the populist rhetoric, the new constitution was carefully crafted to increase the power of the presidency and weaken constraints on the executive. Abandoning the provision that had prevented the incumbent president from being re-elected since democracy was installed in 1958, the new constitution increased the limit from one term of five years to two terms of six years each. (Even this limit was abolished by referendum in 2009, and Chávez states that he intends to remain in office until 2030.) The constitution eliminated the bicameral Congress and replaced it with a unicameral National Assembly which can pass legislation into law with a single vote. The autonomy of the Central Bank was compromised. The new constitution also eliminated congressional oversight of the military, allowing the president to more easily stack the military's top ranks with friendly generals. (By 2001, Venezuela had more generals and admirals than Mexico and Argentina combined.[23]) These measures significantly increased the power of the presidency in relation to the rest of the government. Though the 1999 constitution left the Supreme Court largely untouched, President

[21] S. Ellner, 2008: 111.   [22] S. Collins, 2005.
[23] C. Marcano and A. Tyszka, 2007: 260.

Chávez enacted a law in 2004 expanding the Court from twenty to thirty-two members. Because there were already five existing vacancies, Chávez was then able to simultaneously appoint seventeen new judges to the bench – a majority – all of whom were Chávez loyalists. This was condemned by Human Rights Watch and other international groups as crippling the independence of the judiciary.[24]

One of the changes enacted by the 1999 Constitution was to modify the official name of the country to the Republica Bolívarana de Venezuela ("Bolivarian Republic of Venezuela"). This change was made at the personal insistence of President Chávez, and its symbolism is important. Simón Bolívar, the leader of the nineteenth-century independence movement in Latin America, is held in the popular imagination in Venezuela as a mixture of saint, warrior, and cult hero. Chávez has successfully tied his political movement to Simón Bolívar.[25] Thus by renaming the country a "Bolivarian Republic," Chávez was in effect declaring that his political movement was inextricably connected to the national spirit of the country itself.

Bolivarian Circles and para-statal organizations

President Chávez created the Bolivarian Circles (*Circulos Bolívarianos*) in 2000, one of a number of new para-statal organizations established to organize and mobilize the supporters of the Bolivarian Revolution. These Circles were community-level organizations that were nominally decentralized, grassroots organs of participative democracy. Estimates of the membership of the Bolivarian Circles vary widely, ranging from 120,000 to 2.2 million.[26] President Chávez personally conducted a mass induction ceremony involving over 20,000 new members on December 17, 2001. The primary purpose of the Circles was to provide political support for Hugo Chávez.[27] The Circles also conducted public works, such as setting up medical services, providing childcare, and cleaning parks.

Despite their nominal status as decentralized and grassroots organizations, the Bolivarian Circles were dependent on, and supportive of,

---

[24] Human Rights Watch, 2006.
[25] See also S. Collins, 2005.
[26] G. Morsbach, 2002; also see K. Hawkins and D. Hansen, 2006.
[27] K. Hawkins and D. Hansen, 2006.

the leadership of Hugo Chávez. The opposition alleges that hundreds of army-issue weapons were distributed among the Bolivarian Circles in a bid to turn them into a fighting force that could sustain the government in the event of civil conflict.[28] When political opponents spoke out against these organizations, they were violently persecuted.[29] Even *chavistas* (supporters of Chávez) observed that activists who "challenge the charismatic leader in an effort to assert their autonomy are likely to find themselves marginalized and frustrated."[30]

The structure and purpose of the Bolivarian Circles bear a striking resemblance to similar organs of "participative democracy" in repressive countries such as Cuba and Libya. It is widely suspected that Chávez modeled the Bolivarian Circles on the Cuban Committees for the Defense of the Revolution (CDRs). Like the Circles, the Cuban CDRs are designed to provide public services at a neighborhood level and to report "counter-revolutionary" activity. In Libya, the equivalent organizations are called Revolutionary Committees, which like the Bolivarian Circles, establish clientelistic relationships with the state leadership. It seems likely that Chávez got the idea for the Bolivarian Circles from Castro and Qaddafi. In all three countries, the organizations served the same three purposes: build and maintain political support for the revolutionary regime; distribute public services; and provide information about potential threats to the regime.

The Bolivarian Circles were replaced over time by other organizations, such as the Communal Councils (local governance), the Misión Miranda (the militia), and the Movimiento V Republica (the political party MVR, later PSUV). The Circles received relatively low levels of financial funding from the central government. When better-funded organizations capable of distributing more material benefits from the state were formed by the Chávez government, the Bolivarian Circles

[28] Retired Vice-Admiral Jose Rafael Huizi-Clavier publicized documents that showed that Bolivarian Circles had arms caches containing hundreds of 9mm pistols and AK-47 assault rifles (G. Morsbach, 2002).

[29] For instance, Ernesto Alvarenga, a member of the opposition Solidarity Faction in the National Assembly, stated, "There is no room for criticism within the Bolivarian Circles and members have all been told to obey the president without questioning him. They are undemocratic organizations." Two bombs were sent to Alvarenga's office in Caracas in 2002, though neither managed to inflict casualties; Alvarenga was later wounded at a political protest (G. Morsbach, 2002).

[30] K. Hawkins and D. Hansen, 2006: 126.

were largely abandoned (although never formally disbanded). The more militant objectives of the Bolivarian Circles were taken up by the Misión Miranda, discussed below.

The 2002 coup against Chávez

In 2002, the Bolivarian Revolution faced a dramatic challenge: President Chávez, the former coup plotter, was himself very nearly overthrown in an attempted coup. On April 9, the leader of the largest labor organization in Venezuela called for a strike and on April 11 led an organized march on the presidential palace, Miraflores. This led to a violent confrontation with the *chavistas*. During the confrontation, snipers opened fire on the crowd and an unknown number of civilians were killed. That night, General Lucas Rincon, commander-in-chief of the Venezuelan armed forces, announced on a nationwide broadcast that President Chávez had resigned. Pedro Carmona, president of the business organization Fedecamaras, was appointed the interim president. Carmona's first decree reversed the major social and economic policies of the Bolivarian Revolution, dissolved the National Assembly and the Supreme Court, and renamed the country the "República de Venezuela."

The new government under Carmona was the shortest-lived in Venezuelan history. Carmona's decrees, especially dissolving the Supreme Court, were deeply unpopular, leading to riots in the streets. Soldiers loyal to Chávez mounted a counter-coup, storming and retaking the presidential palace. By the night of April 13, just two days after he had left, President Chávez was back in power. He denies ever resigning.[31]

The question of involvement by the United States in the coup was controversial. President Chávez alleged that he had proof of US military involvement in the coup, including radar images of US naval vessels and aircraft in Venezuelan waters and airspace, though he never produced the images. An investigation by the US State Department found no evidence that support from the US government directly contributed

---

[31] The matter remains controversial. No resignation letter bearing the signature of Hugo Chávez was ever produced. According to one first-hand account, Chávez verbally "relinquished" his power, but did not use the word "resign." See C. Marcano and A. Tyszka, 2007: 175–181.

to the coup.[32] Still, it seems clear that the Bush administration at least had foreknowledge of a coup plot prior to the attempt.[33] The White House Press Secretary did not condemn the coup and stated the events were "a result of the message of the Venezuelan people."[34] Whether or not the United States was directly involved in the coup attempt, the incident earned the Bush administration the lasting enmity of President Chávez.

In subsequent years, Chávez used this incident to stoke nationalistic sentiment and international support for his regime. Chávez frequently argued that Venezuela must equip itself militarily as a precaution against an American invasion. In November 2005, Venezuela staged a mock invasion of its territory by the United States.[35] Chávez repeatedly used the prospect of gringo imperialism to advance his political agenda.

Economic policy and government expenditure in the Bolivarian Revolution

The Chávez government enacted a wide variety of economic reforms and new public expenditures, in at least eight major areas: the *misiónes*; worker cooperatives; corporate co-management; government expropriation of private property; land redistribution; new tax enforcement; delegation of land authority to community organizations; and rejection of government links to organized business interests.[36] Collectively, these changes constituted a significant shift in economic policies and government expenditure. At least nominally, the changes were made in an attempt to increase the power of workers and the rural poor, as part of an economic program that became increasingly socialist over time. However, the government's rhetoric often masked the underlying impact of the new policies.[37] The changes made by the Chávez government progressively centralized power.

---

[32] United States Department of State, 2002.
[33] Democracy NOW! 2004; E. Vulliamy, 2002.
[34] US Government, 2002.   [35] B. Jones, 2008: 434.
[36] S. Ellner, 2008: Chapter 5.
[37] Despite the rhetoric, moves to empower workers have been abandoned for strategic state-controlled sectors such as the oil industry and the state-run electricity industry. Moreover, many worker cooperatives have been commercial failures, heavily dependent on state subsidies. S. Ellner, 2008: 128–130.

The oil industry offers an example of this centralization. In 2001, President Chávez began to re-nationalize the oil industry. Under the Hydrocarbons Law passed that year, royalties paid by private companies increased from 1–17 percent to 20–30 percent. Further, the law guaranteed the state-owned oil company, PdVSA, a majority share of any new projects, and that all future foreign investment would be in the form of joint ventures with PdVSA. In the first few years, the reforms did not greatly interfere with private operators. However, when oil prices began to rise in late 2003, the government's relationship with the foreign oil companies became an open conflict, as discussed in the next section.

The government's relationship with PdVSA changed dramatically under President Chávez. Prior to 1999, PdVSA was run as an independent company led by technocratic managers. In February 2002, Chávez appointed a new president and stacked the board of directors with political allies. The government's actions were protested as a politicization of PdVSA, and contributed to the coup in April 2002. Even after the coup attempt, resentment among PdVSA's management lingered. In December 2002, PdVSA's managers and employees locked out the company's workers to pressure President Chávez to hold early elections. The strike lasted for two months, initially bringing oil production to a virtual halt. Chávez eventually broke the strike, resulting in the dismissal of 19,000 PdVSA employees.

Since the strike, PdVSA has been under far more direct control of the government. Rafael Ramirez, the president of PdVSA since 2004, is a close ally of Chávez and has served simultaneously as the minister of energy and oil, a political position that had been kept distinct to ensure the independence of PdVSA. Ramirez explicitly stated, and Chávez agreed, that PdVSA employees owe political allegiance to the Bolivarian Revolution, and that they should vote for Chávez or leave their jobs.[38] PdVSA was delisted from the New York Stock Exchange, so its accounting practices no longer needed to comply with international standards for transparency. Most importantly, the company's revenue and assets became freely accessible to the government, which uses them for expenditure programs, including the *misiónes bolivaranas*. In 2005, the transfers from PdVSA to the *misiónes* were almost

[38] BBC, 2006.

seven trillion bolivars ($3.2 billion), more than twice the financial con-
tributions from the central government itself.

Chávez launched the *misiónes bolívaranas* in 2003 as a means of
direct service provision to the people of Venezuela, circumventing the
existing government bureaucracy. More than a dozen *misiónes* existed
by 2010, collectively representing approximately 20 percent of government expenditure.[39] Each *misión* has a specific purpose: *Barrio Adento*
provides medical services (supported by Cuban doctors provided by
Castro in exchange for subsidized oil); *Robinson* provides literacy and
adult education; *Sucre* and *Ribas* provide remedial primary and secondary school education; *Mercal* provides discounted food staples.
When launched in 2003, these *misiónes* were hugely popular, particularly with the rural and lower-class urban population.

In addition to providing social services, several of the *misiónes* have
explicitly political functions. For example, *Misión Florentino* generated support for the "No" vote in the presidential recall referendum of
2003, and others are named after events associated with Chávez (e.g.,
13 de Abril). A key feature of the *misiónes* is that they circumvent
the government's bureaucracy, often displacing services that were traditionally offered by existing institutions. Associations of professors and
doctors have expressed concern that the *misiónes* lower professional
standards and absorb resources at the expense of established institutions.[40] The para-statal financial accounting of the *misiónes* is not
transparent, and is controlled directly by the office of the president.

The *misiónes* also serve to radicalize and militarize the population.
The explicit goal of *Misión Miranda* is to form a citizen armed militia
trained in asymmetric warfare. The Chávez government defends this
force as needed in case of a US military invasion, but political opponents note that the training and weaponry of the force make it most
suitable for waging civil war or an armed revolution. The size of this
militia is unknown, but estimates place it at 80,000 people.[41] Members
of the civilian militia are required to take an oath of personal loyalty
to Chávez. Additionally, in January 2006, Chávez declared that the
new goal of the *Misión Vuelvan Caras* was to turn every "endogen-
ous nuclei of development" into "military nuclei of resistance against

[39] S. Collins, 2005: 390.
[40] S. Ellner, 2008: 133.   [41] G. Wilpert, 2007.

American imperialism" as part of a continuous program to create "citizen militias."[42] *Chavista* hardliners Alberto Muller Rojas and Eliecer Otaiza, both retired army officers, view the militias as a counter-balance to Venezuela's traditional armed forces, providing protection for President Chávez against the risk of a military coup.[43] Thus in addition to their distributive functions, the *misiónes* are designed to mobilize and radicalize the population in support of the personal leadership of Hugo Chávez.

Personalization of power under Chávez

The Bolivarian Revolution has helped President Chávez centralize power, weaken constraining institutions, and personalize his leadership over the country. One manifestation of this approach is a reliance on military officers in political positions. Military officers took over civilian positions in the Chávez government to a degree not seen in Venezuela since the military dictatorships prior to 1958. More than a hundred men in uniform occupied positions of leadership in state-run corporations, national agencies, governmental funds, and special commissions. In the regional elections in 2004, fourteen of the twenty-two candidates on the *chavista* party ticket, each of whom had been hand-picked by Chávez, were from the military realm. Consequently, the government has been continuously populated by military officers who are, by training and personality, conditioned to work in a hierarchy and follow orders from above.[44] This increases Hugo Chávez's personal control of the government.

A second component of this approach has been to ensure that non-military officials in the government are loyal to him personally. In the first year of the Bolivarian Revolution, commentators wrote that any Venezuelan who had spent time out of the country would have difficulty identifying the current government officials, so complete was the change.[45] Even after the first year, Chávez continued to shuffle his Cabinet ministers and closest advisors, typically on the basis of personal loyalty. General Alberto Rojas, Chávez's campaign chief in 1998 and later his military advisor, observed that Chávez's followers

---

[42] *El Universal*, 2006.   [43] S. Ellner, 2008: 167.
[44] F. Maso, 2004, quoted in C. Marcano and A. Tyszka, 2007: 258–259.
[45] C. Marcano and A. Tyszka, 2007: 139.

"have to feign, at the very least, absolute submission to him."[46] When they did not, they were removed at least temporarily. At the beginning of 2008, President Chávez had made 118 individual appointment changes in his cabinet since taking office.[47]

Chávez has repeatedly stated that he expected his followers to support his regime by violent confrontation if necessary. For instance, he said, "When I talk about armed revolution, I am not speaking metaphorically; armed means rifles, tanks, planes, and thousands of men ready to defend the revolution."[48] Francesco Arias Cárdenas, a co-conspirator in 1992, says of Chávez: "I think he lives in the clutches of a paranoia to preserve his power. The preservation of his power is his own personal hell, and that is why he is constantly at battle."[49]

Even *chavistas* publicly worry about the cult of personality surrounding around Chávez. Chávez's demands for absolute loyalty (e.g., "[t]hose who are with me are with me, those who are not with me are against me ... I will not accept gray areas") has elicited some expressions of concern. Gregory Wilpert, a Chávez supporter, writes:

If Chávez were to disappear from one day to the next, the entire movement would fall into a thousand pieces because it would have lost its unifying glue. This extreme dependence on Chávez also means that it is extremely difficult for Chávez supporters to criticize Chávez because every criticism threatens to undermine the project because it gives rhetorical ammunition to the opposition ... Criticism from within the ranks is rarely present and criticism from outside the ranks is easily dismissed.[50]

In sum, President Chávez has demanded more individual loyalty from his supporters, and more centralized power from his government, than any Venezuelan leader since the establishment of democracy in 1958.

Chávez also structured the government's organization to increase his personal control. As the country's oil revenues increased during the period 2002–2007 in line with global oil prices, the ranks

---

[46] C. Marcano and A. Tyszka, 2007: 274.
[47] *El Nacional*, 2008.
[48] H. Chávez, 28 November 2002, quoted in C. Marcano and A. Tyszka, 2007: 260.
[49] F. Arias, quoted in C. Marcano and A. Tyszka, 2007: 275.
[50] G. Wilpert, 2006.

of the government's bureaucracy swelled considerably. It is telling that certain areas of the government increased at a far more rapid pace than the rest of the government. Three areas of the government increased dramatically: the central offices of the Presidency, the Ministry of Defense, and the Ministry of Energy and Petroleum. Over this five-year period, the number of full-time staff in those ministries increased by 86%, 57%, and 61%, respectively, compared to 21% staff growth in the rest of the government (except education).[51] In sum, the Chávez administration spent its oil revenue in ways that increased the power of the presidency and the military strength of Venezuela. This enabled the government to engage in increasingly adventurous foreign policy.

Finally, Chávez used the media to personalize his power, most notably with his popular weekly television show, *Alo Presidente*.[52] The show is unscripted, runs between two and seven hours, and allows Chávez to tell personal stories, sing, and entertain. Chávez also makes political announcements on the show, ranging from the launch of the Bolivarian Circles in 2001 to threatening war and ordering the military mobilization against Colombia in 2008. For Chávez, the show accomplishes a number of political objectives. First, it builds and sustains popular support for his leadership. By spending hours each week in front of the camera, Chávez reinforces the message that he is the leader of his political movement and the government of Venezuela, its living symbol. Second, the television show is oriented to, and popular among, the lower classes of Venezuela who have traditionally remained outside of the political process. This allows Chávez to bring a new segment of society into his ruling coalition, and to politically educate this audience in a manner that suits the purposes of the Bolivarian Revolution. Even anti-*chavistas* acknowledge that Chávez

---

[51] The "central offices of the President" includes the Secretaria de la Presidencia, Vicepresidencia, Ministerio de Comunicación e Información, Ministerio de Participacion Popular y Desarrollo Social; the "rest of the government" does not include the enormous Ministry of Education, which includes all full-time teachers, and which also grew dramatically in this period (62 percent).

[52] The Chávez government launched a number of other media projects, including *De Frente con el Presidente* (Face to Face with the President), the predecessor to *Alo Presidente*, showing on Thursday nights; two new government newspapers called *El Correo del Presidente* and *Vea*; a new television station, Vive TV; and a new magazine, *Question*.

has been masterful at bringing in new participants to the political process.[53] Third, *Alo Presidente* stokes nationalistic, anti-American, and revolutionary sentiment among the population. Chávez uses the show to lambaste his political enemies, both foreign and domestic. For all these reasons, *Alo Presidente* has become a crucial political instrument of the Bolivarian Revolution, and a tool to personalize the power of Chávez. As one Venezuelan observed, "there is no Revolution without Chávez."[54]

Revolutionary foreign policy under Chávez: 1999–2010

Chávez transformed his country's domestic politics. At the same time, he has taken full advantage of his presidential authority to engage in an activist foreign policy. This foreign policy activism can be divided into three components: aggressive diplomacy and oil nationalization; increased military spending; and military exercises and disputes.

Aggressive diplomacy and oil nationalization

The list of diplomatic initiatives and proposed international organizations during President Chávez's tenure is long. More than 800 international agreements were signed by the Chávez government prior to 2006.[55] Venezuela pushed for the creation of four new regional oil initiatives – in the Caribbean (Petrocaribe), the Andean region (Petroandino), South America (Petrosur), and Latin America (PetroAmérica) – which would include assistance for oil developments, investments in refining capacity, and preferential oil pricing. Venezuela hosted a major OPEC meeting in 2000, successfully lobbied for a Venezuelan (Ali Rodriguez) to be selected OPEC Secretary General, and has since been a leading price hawk within the organization. In international trade, Venezuela joined Mercosur and created a new organization called ALBA, the Latin American Bolivarian Alternative, which had eight members in 2010. President Chávez announced in 2007 that Venezuela would

---

[53] Personal interviews with pollsters at Datanalysis and Hinterlaces, Caracas, January 2008.

[54] Personal interviews, Caracas, January 2008.

[55] Even this number was considered preliminary and probably too low, due to the difficulty in accounting for many of the agreements signed by other parts of the government (besides the MRE). See P. Penaloza, 2006: 164.

leave the World Bank, and instead create Banco del Sur, an alternative development bank for South America. In 2010, Banco del Sur had seven members, each of which has committed capital to finance the bank's loans.

Much of Chávez's diplomatic activity had an underlying theme of confrontation and destabilization of existing institutions. For instance, ALBA was created in reaction to the US-proposed Free Trade Area of the Americas (FTAA); Banco del Sur was created to undermine the World Bank; Petrocaribe competes with the existing Caricom. Chávez called the IMF a "revolting instrument of exploitation at the service of the world's most powerful."[56] This institutional competition has been intentional, in keeping with the Chávez government's multipolar view of world politics. Venezuela's endorsement of multipolarity was an explicit rejection of US global leadership and an implicit assertion of Venezuelan leadership in the informal coalition of states opposed to the United States.

This theme of international confrontation was also present in Venezuela's bilateral relationships. The relationship between Venezuela and the United States worsened considerably, and long-standing military cooperation arrangements were canceled. Similarly, Venezuela's relationship with Colombia declined precipitously. At the same time, Chávez worked to build an anti-US coalition. He has traveled internationally more than any president in Venezuelan history, paying special attention to US antagonists: Russia, Iraq, Syria, Nicaragua, Libya, Belarus, and Iran. President Chávez developed a strong relationship with Iranian President Ahmedinejad, who awarded Chávez with Iran's highest honor for his defense of Iran's nuclear policy.[57] Iran also invested in cement and automotive manufacturing projects in Venezuela, and in 2007, the two countries agreed to create a $2 billion social investment fund to finance additional projects in their countries as well as elsewhere.[58] In 2007, Iran Air launched a new flight route: Tehran–Damascus–Caracas.

The United States has responded in kind, casting Chávez as a threat to peace and democracy. In her confirmation hearings as Secretary

[56] *El Universal*, 2004.
[57] The award was given for Chávez's "support for Iran's stance on the international scene, especially its opposition to a resolution by the International Atomic Energy Agency." N. Karimi, 2007.
[58] C. Kraul and M. Mogollon, 2007.

of State, Condoleezza Rice called Chávez a "negative force in the region."[59] In 2000, US officials were appalled at Chávez's decision to visit Saddam Hussein in Baghdad, the first head of state to enter Iraq since the United Nations had imposed sanctions in 1990. Between 2000 and 2001, Venezuela went from the tenth to the first largest recipient of funds from the US National Endowment of Democracy in Latin America, much of which was allotted to opposition groups.[60] The United States also provided additional funds through its Office of Transition Initiatives. The United States has stopped arms sales to Venezuela from American suppliers and has sought to block sales from other countries. It also opposed Venezuela's candidacy for one of the rotating seats on the UN Security Council. In 2008, US Representative Connie Mack submitted a bill to Congress calling for Venezuela to be designated a state sponsor of terrorism in response to Venezuela's support of the FARC in Colombia, though the bill did not pass.

The Chávez government has also been active in supporting leftist causes in Latin America. This policy extends beyond the traditional government-to-government diplomacy and in some cases appears to have led to direct intervention in electoral politics. In August, 2007, a Venezuelan-American entrepreneur named Guido Antonini Wilson illegally carried $800,000 in cash into Argentina, allegedly from President Chávez, to help finance Christina Kirchner's presidential campaign in Argentina in the October 28 election.[61] Also on Wilson's private plane were four officials from Venezuela's PdVSA and three Argentine government officials. President Chávez also appears to have intervened covertly in other Latin American countries such as Bolivia and Nicaragua, but this is inherently difficult to confirm. To support Chávez's foreign policy initiatives, Venezuela launched a number of new media operations. One of these was Telesur, an international cable station meant to rival CNN and other major networks. By 2008, Telesur was supported by seven other countries, and had a clear leftist political agenda.[62]

Venezuela's oil wealth played a direct role in President Chávez's diplomacy in three ways. The first is obvious: it has funded an enormous array of initiatives, from media to foreign aid to military spending. Those activities became increasingly extravagant as oil prices rose, but

---

[59] CNN, 2005.   [60] S. Ellner, 2008: 199.
[61] Reuters, 2007b.   [62] B. Jones, 2008: 429.

were curtailed as prices fell in late 2008. According to one Venezuelan NGO, President Chávez offered more than $37 billion (US) in foreign aid to more than thirty countries in the period 2002–2007, though the actual amount disbursed is likely considerably lower than the amount promised.[63] Second, Chávez has used the prospect of cheap oil and preferential access to oil supplies as a carrot to attract diplomatic partners and participation in his initiatives. For instance, Venezuela offered oil to Cuba and other members of Petrocaribe at preferential rates; in exchange, Venezuela has received among other things the services of Cuban medical doctors.[64]

Third, Chávez used investment in Venezuela's oil industry as a tool of international confrontation and geopolitical re-alignment. In 2004, Chávez announced an increase in the royalties paid by foreign oil companies, primarily Exxon-Mobil, Total, Shell, Chevron, and Conoco Philips. The announcement, made on Chávez's weekly show *Alo Presidente*, was authorized by the 2001 Hydrocarbons Law and was the first in a series of steps to "re-nationalize" the oil industry. The government then began to apply pressure on the companies to surrender a controlling stake of their operations to PdVSA, which would continue as joint ventures. By 2005, all of the major companies except Exxon had agreed to such arrangements.[65] In 2007, the companies were again compelled to renegotiate deals, this time in Venezuela's Orinoco region.[66] Again, it was Exxon that refused to sign an agreement. As the Exxon–Venezuela dispute became more severe, the company then took the matter to court in the United States, the UK, and the Netherlands, requesting and receiving in 2008 a court order to freeze more than $12 billion of PdVSA's international assets.[67] The final outcome of the dispute between Exxon and Venezuela is not yet known.

Behind President Chávez's efforts to re-nationalize the oil industry was an explicit geopolitical agenda. US and Western European companies were specifically targeted for tough treatment and economic renegotiation. In reaction to Exxon's court victory in 2008, Chávez threatened to place an embargo on oil sales to the United States. This

[63] Fundacion de Justicia y Democracia, 2008.
[64] It is widely suspected that the services of an unspecified number of Cuban security personnel were also included in this deal. The exact terms of the agreement have not been released publicly.
[65] G. Morsbach, 2002.   [66] Reuters, 2007a.
[67] Reuters, 2008.

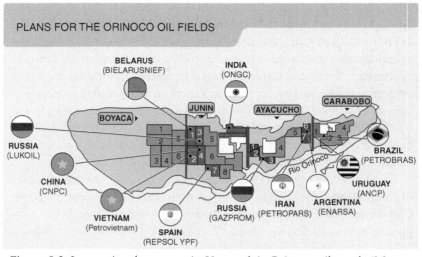

Figure 8.2 International partners in Venezuela's Orinoco oil patch (Magna Reserva)

follows an earlier threat to embargo oil sales to Western Europe. Neither of these threats has been realized, and many observers do not see them as credible. Nonetheless, the threats alone have consequences, as oil markets assign a political risk premium to the price of oil, and companies spend resources negotiating with the Chávez government and trying to estimate future risk. In contrast to this treatment of the US and its allies, the Chávez government has worked hard to lure foreign investment from states in its "multipolar" coalition such as Russia, China, Iran, and even some with little or no technical expertise, such as Belarus and Uruguay. Figure 8.2 highlights the diversity of new foreign partners in Venezuela's Orinoco belt.

Military spending

Many conflicts in Latin America are militarized even when they are not violent, and consequently military expenditures can be an important tool of posturing in interstate bargaining.[68] Venezuela's military expenditure has risen dramatically under President Chávez, due in part to the rapid rise in the country's oil income. Obtaining valid

[68] D. Mares, 2001.

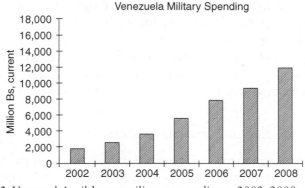

Figure 8.3 Venezuela's oil-boom military expenditure, 2002–2008

estimates of how much a state spends on its armed forces is not easy. In theory, publications by the Stockholm International Peace Research Institute (SIPRI) and the Institute for International Strategic Studies (IISS) should be tailor-made for this analysis. However, those publications are subject to significant methodological constraints, particularly because they focus so heavily on budgetary expenditure, thereby ignoring large extra-budgetary purchases. Accordingly, the estimates of Venezuela's military expenditure shown here are based on my original research. The details of the estimation methodology and data sources are described elsewhere.[69]

Figure 8.3 shows the estimates of Venezuela's military expenditure, measured in millions of bolivars. These data show how military expenditure has increased rapidly under the Chávez government, keeping pace with the rapid rate of economic growth during the oil boom. This growth in military expenditure has led to a dramatic increase in the number of military personnel. In 2002, the number of military personnel was less than 100,000; just six years later, it was somewhere between 160,000 and 250,000.[70] Venezuela's weapons purchases have also increased, especially from potential US rivals. Venezuela established military-technological ties with China through the acquisition of two squadrons of Chinese-built Karakorum-8 trainer jets and ground radars, notably replacing similar US-made equipment. President Chávez has announced more than $4 billion of military

[69] J. Colgan, 2011c.   [70] J. Colgan, 2011c.

purchases from Russia, including 100,000 Kalashnikov rifles, twenty-four Sukhoi fighter planes, and fifteen helicopters. These military expenditures represent an aggressive increase in Venezuela's military capability. US Director of National Intelligence Michael McConnell testified to Congress that Venezuela's military build-up is probably three to four times what would be needed for external defense.[71]

Military exercises and international disputes

The aggressive international diplomacy and increase in military expenditure under President Chávez did not result in Venezuela engaging in a full-blown war in the period 1999–2010. This is consistent with Venezuela's long history of peaceful international relations: it has not once engaged in a foreign war since its struggle for independence in the nineteenth century. The lack of militarized conflict is also partly due to the strength of its potential adversaries. For instance, a direct military confrontation with the United States, Chávez's principal rhetorical adversary, is clearly infeasible for Venezuela. Chávez is therefore limited to running military exercises to annoy the United States, such as the Russian–Venezuelan naval exercises in 2008.

Nonetheless, Venezuela has engaged in a number of disputes with its immediate neighbors since 1999. The smaller of these disputes is with Guyana, focusing on a territorial claim dating back to the nineteenth century. The Chávez government rekindled Venezuela's claim, and the dispute led to low-level armed conflict. For instance, in 2007, Venezuelan military personnel used explosive devices to destroy two Guyanese gold-mining dredges that allegedly were poaching on disputed territory.[72]

Venezuela's more significant disputes were with Colombia. In these disputes, the Chávez government has taken aggressive actions, in part because Colombia is an important US ally in the region. These actions brought Venezuela and Colombia to the brink of armed conflict in 2008, but the friction had been building for some time. Since at least 2000, the Chávez government has been suspected of providing material support to the Colombian rebel group FARC (Revolutionary Armed

---

[71] M. McConnell, February 27, 2008 – see Congressional Research Service, 2008.
[72] A. Sanchez, 2008.

Forces of Colombia) and allowing them safe haven in Venezuela near the border of Colombia.[73]

In 2007, Colombian President Uribe and his appointed negotiator Piedad Córdoba asked President Chávez to facilitate the humanitarian exchange of hostages from the FARC. As documents from the FARC would later show, Chávez and Córdoba were working together to turn the hostage negotiations into a public relations coup. FARC documents reported that Chávez hoped the rendezvous would give him "continental and world renown."[74] In the event, Chávez's role in the hostage negotiations was short-lived. President Uribe suspended Chávez and Córdoba's role in the FARC negotiations when they violated his condition that they contact the Colombian military only through official channels, rather than directly. In reply, Chávez stated that he was putting bilateral relations with Colombia "in the freezer" and suspended all trade ties. Uribe responded that Chávez was attempting to legitimize terrorism and that he was pursuing an expansionist program on the continent.[75] President Chávez further aggravated the Colombian government in January 2008 by expressing his support for the FARC and requesting European governments to remove the FARC and ELN from their list of terrorist groups. He added that the two groups have a "Bolivarian" goal that "we respect."[76]

On March 1, 2008, Colombia launched a military attack on a leader of the FARC, Raul Reyes, at a guerrilla camp just inside Ecuadoran territory. The attack resulted in the death of twenty people, including Reyes and other members of the FARC.[77] The Colombian armed forces were allegedly alerted to Reyes' position because of an intercepted satellite phone call from President Hugo Chávez, informing Reyes that three FARC hostages had been released.[78] Ecuadoran President Correa condemned the incident as a "massacre" and an act of aggression on the part of Colombia.[79] President Chávez echoed Correa's sentiments. Both Venezuela and Ecuador withdrew their ambassadors from Bogota

---

[73] For instance, a FARC defector told a special investigation by the Colombian government that he witnessed four Venezuelan helicopters and two fighter planes invade Colombian airspace in 2000 and provide cover for FARC guerilla forces retreating over the border. http://newsmine.org/content.php?ol=war-on-terror/venezuela/venezuela-aids-farc-rebels.txt.

[74] M. O'Grady, 2008.   [75] Telesur, 2007.

[76] CNN, 2008.   [77] *El Mundo*, 2008.

[78] *Noticias 24*, 2008.   [79] BBC Mundo, 2008.

and expelled the Colombian ambassadors from their own countries in protest of the attack.

Although it was Ecuador's territorial sovereignty that had been impinged, Venezuela's reaction was at least as strong as Ecuador's. On March 2, President Chávez used his weekly television program, *Alo Presidente*, to ratchet up the crisis, calling President Uribe a liar and a lackey of North American imperialism. Still on air, Chávez then ordered ten battalions of the Venezuelan armed forces to the border with Colombia. On March 4, President Uribe announced that Colombia intended to bring charges against Hugo Chávez with the International Criminal Court for the crimes of funding terrorism and genocide (by the FARC).[80] The same day, Venezuelan cabinet minister Elias Jaua announced that Venezuela was closing its border with Colombia. President Chávez threatened to nationalize Colombian investments in Venezuela, and warned that a Colombian incursion into Venezuela would be a cause for war. The contrast could not have been sharper between Chávez's actions and those of his predecessor, President Caldera, who invited the Colombian military into Venezuelan territory in its battle against the FARC in 1998.

Militarily, the crisis ended swiftly. The Colombian foreign minister Fernando Araujo apologized to Ecuador, and on March 9, Venezuela re-established normal diplomatic ties with Colombia. A series of questions about the links between the FARC and the Venezuelan government remained unanswered, however. During the March 1 incursion, the Colombian government recovered a set of FARC computer files. According to Colombia, the files show that Venezuela gave the FARC $300 million in support and was assisting the FARC in obtaining 50 kilograms of uranium. Colombian Vice-President Francisco Santos stated that the FARC was planning to build a "dirty bomb," although the motive may have been to sell the uranium for profit.[81] A letter from FARC leader Manuel Marulanda to President Chávez thanked the Venezuelan government for its assistance in the war against the Colombian government. The FARC also offered their "modest knowledge in defense of the Bolivarian Revolution" in case of military aggression from the United States.[82] The computer files were sent

---

[80] BBC, 2008.   [81] *Guardian*, 2008.
[82] Press conference of General Óscar Naranjo, 2008.

to Interpol for an investigation, which found no evidence that the Colombian government had tampered with the contents.

In addition, the FARC computer files revealed plans to overthrow the Colombian government and replace it with a revolutionary regime with ties to Venezuela. Piedad Córdoba, Chávez's partner in the FARC hostage negotiations, was one of twelve individuals named in the files as members of the transitional government once the FARC had toppled the current regime in Colombia. The files also showed that she received money from President Chávez to build her political support. This is consistent with President Uribe's earlier statements that he believed Chávez wanted a revolutionary FARC government in place in Colombia, and Chávez's alliance with the FARC was part of an expansionist project.

The fallout from Venezuela's relationship with the FARC continued for months after the immediate crisis. In September 2008, the US government froze the assets of three senior members of the Venezuelan government: ex-Interior Minister Ramon Rodriguez Chacin, senior intelligence director Henry de Jesus Rangel, and military intelligence chief Hugo Armando Carvajal Barrios. A US government official stated that the Venezuelans had "armed, abetted and funded the FARC, even as it terrorized and kidnapped innocents."[83] Minister Rodriguez Chacin later resigned from the Interior Ministry for what he called personal reasons.

President Chávez denies any wrongdoing in connection with the FARC. He argued that he "worked his heart and soul out to put them [Colombia] on the road to peace."[84] He denies arming or funding the rebel group, and dismissed Interpol's findings as ridiculous.[85]

Operation of causal mechanisms

Did the revolutionary government make Venezuela more aggressive?

The breakdown in Venezuela's *Punto Fijo* system of two-party democracy in the 1990s created an opening for a new leader to emerge. As discussed earlier, it was hardly inevitable that Hugo Chávez would

[83] J. Forero, 2008b.   [84] Agence France Presse, 2007.
[85] J. Forero, 2008a.

be the man who became president. Yet Chávez succeeded due to a combination of risk-tolerance, ambition, political charisma, and luck. As expected by the theory, a period of domestic political upheaval facilitated the rise of a leader who had those characteristics. Chávez's risk-tolerance was demonstrated in various acts prior to coming to power, most notably his willingness to organize a secret revolutionary organization while still an active member of the military, and the attempted coup he led in 1992. His ambition to alter the status quo is also evident in a variety of ways, perhaps most clearly in his socialist ideology. This has consequences both domestically and in foreign policy. For example, Chávez often refers to Venezuelans as *Gran Colombians*, referring to the Republic of Colombia in the era of Simón Bolívar, which included modern-day Venezuela, Colombia, Ecuador, and Panama, as well as portions of other countries. He openly discusses his desire to re-unify the people of South America. This rhetoric, along with his support of leftist groups and his interventions in the domestic politics of other countries, has led many observers to suggest that he has expansionist ambitions.

The Bolivarian Revolution also allowed Chávez to weaken the political constraints on the executive and consolidate power in his hands. Consider the formal institutions and procedures identified in Table 3.1, and how they changed over time. The constraints on the Venezuelan presidency were fairly constant in the pre-Chávez period 1958–1998, with the exception of the twelve-month period in which CAP was Congressionally-authorized to rule by decree. Under Chávez, however, the institutional constraints were weakened considerably and permanently. The legislature was changed from a bicameral to a unicameral body, the Supreme Court was stacked with Chávez supporters, presidential term limits were abolished, the central bank's independence was compromised, and the military was more directly controlled by the president. Large portions of the national oil income are channeled through off-budget accounts that Chávez is able to access directly without meaningful oversight. On the other hand, the Constitution now provides for a mechanism for a popular referendum on presidential recall (though this depends on a fair electoral system, which is in doubt). On the whole, Chávez had more direct control over the government of Venezuela than any previous president since 1958.

The combination of an ambitious, risk-taking leader and the lack of significant domestic political constraints generated Venezuela's most aggressive foreign policy behavior in many decades. As observed above, Venezuela's relationships with Colombia and the United States have deteriorated dramatically. Where there was once considerable military cooperation, there is now recurrent friction and the potential for militarized conflict.

Did oil generate incentives for aggression and conflict?

Oil played a direct role in the foreign policy behavior of Venezuela in at least three ways. First, oil income provided the financial resources to fund its major military purchases and support for foreign groups like the FARC. Second, privileged access to oil was offered to allies in exchange for goodwill and political support. Third, oil production policy was used to expropriate assets from foreign multinational firms, and to offer production opportunities to new potential allies as part of Venezuela's multipolar geopolitical strategy. Efforts to gain allies were taken in the context of a re-alignment of Venezuela's geopolitical alliances, primarily away from the United States and its allies such as Colombia. Thus oil was used both as an income source and a direct instrument of an aggressive foreign policy.

Oil also played an indirect role in foreign policy by bolstering the power of the presidency under Hugo Chávez. Chávez used PdVSA and the government's oil income to make dramatic changes to the structure of the government and economic policy. In particular, Chávez's populist and distributive policies have bolstered his popularity and allowed him to centralize power. At the same time, the increased military expenditure facilitated by the oil money created and strengthened patron–client relationships between Chávez and the military. As expected by the theory, oil income has provided Chávez with considerable political autonomy.

The effect of oil income can only be understood by examining its interactions with domestic politics and the preferences of the state leadership. It is true that as oil prices and revenues increased, Venezuela's behavior changed: its military spending increased, its diplomacy became more aggressive, and its treatment of US and European oil companies became harsher. Conversely, as oil prices and revenues fell, Venezuela's behavior changed in the opposite direction. However, it would be a mistake to believe that the oil market alone determines Venezuela's foreign policy. While the variation in oil income can help to explain some aspects of the state's foreign policy – such as its relationship with the foreign oil companies – it does not explain more fundamental preferences and geopolitical alignments, such as Venezuela's relationship with the United States and Colombia. Increased oil income might expand Venezuela's military, but only under revolutionary leadership was Venezuela's military mobilized for war. And while both CAP and Chávez used abundant oil income to fund foreign aid, only Chávez used it in a way that sought to undermine existing international organizations and treaties, such as the World Bank, Caricom, and the FTAA. The differences in preferences between the revolutionary government of Hugo Chávez and the non-revolutionary governments that preceded him are far more important in determining the behavior of Venezuela than mere changes in the country's oil income. As we have seen in this chapter and elsewhere, it is the interaction between oil income and a revolutionary government that creates the most powerful incentives for international conflict.

Did oil generate incentives to avoid aggression and conflict?

The theory developed in Chapter 2 also suggests that oil provides incentives for international cooperation, especially with important importers of oil. This is certainly the case for Venezuela. In the period 1958–1998, Venezuela was one of the United States' staunchest allies. As both a cause and consequence of this relationship, Venezuela lobbied Congress to be treated as a "special supplier" of oil to the US market in the 1970s. Another indicator of this positive relationship is that Venezuelans' views of Americans have traditionally been more positive than those in other South American countries, although that tendency has weakened in the last decade.[86] Once Chávez came to power, the Venezuela–US relationship clearly deteriorated, especially after the tacit approval by the US of the coup attempt against Chávez in 2002. Yet despite Chávez's threats of an oil embargo, Venezuela has never enacted one, and the United States continues to be Venezuela's largest market for oil exports. Moreover, while there has been considerable friction between the Venezuelan government and foreign-owned oil companies (especially American-owned), Chávez has

---

[86] Pew Research Center, 2007.

chosen to be conciliatory on occasion, particularly when oil prices are low and Venezuela is in need of higher oil incomes to balance its budget. Consequently, it seems clear that oil is providing incentives for Venezuela to avoid a total break with the United States, and to continue its long-standing cooperation.

Conclusion

Hugo Chávez and his Bolivarian Revolution have emerged as one of the most important political phenomena in modern Latin American politics. Analytically, the historical development of the Chávez regime provides an opportunity to test the theoretical framework developed in previous chapters. In turn, the theoretical framework offers a way of understanding and analyzing the behavior of the Bolivarian Revolution.

The Chávez regime is neither as revolutionary at home nor as prone to militarized interstate disputes as some of the petrostates in the Middle East. Yet as this brief history demonstrates, both elements are present. President Chávez has quite dramatically reshaped the domestic political institutions of Venezuela, with significant social and economic implications. Venezuela's foreign policy also has been far more aggressive and provocative under Chávez than under any previous president. Nowhere is this more evident than in Venezuela's relationship with Colombia, where Chávez has supported revolutionary rebel groups and mobilized Venezuelan troops against the Colombian government.

Three aspects of this analysis are worth highlighting in light of the overall theory on oil and revolutionary regimes. First, domestic dissatisfaction in Venezuela enabled the rise of a radical leader, which in turn made international conflict substantially more likely. As documented above, it was far from inevitable that Chávez would become president in the 1990s. Second, Venezuela's oil income is an integral part of its politics, especially under the leadership of President Chávez. Oil income enabled Chávez to centralize political power in his hands and radicalize the domestic political discourse. Finally, oil income played an essential part in Venezuela's foreign policy in multiple ways.

After more than a decade, it is still not yet clear how the Bolivarian Revolution will unfold. In many ways, the combination of oil politics and a revolutionary regime has influenced Venezuela in ways that the proposed theoretical framework would suggest. Still, as time marches on there is likely to be a certain amount of political fatigue with the revolutionary regime, making it somewhat less likely that Venezuela will get into serious international conflict.

9 | *Saudi Arabia*

We do not use oil for political purposes.
                    – Advisor to Crown
                       Prince Abdullah

The Kingdom of Saudi Arabia is the most important petrostate in the world. With an estimated 260 billion barrels in oil reserves, almost a quarter of the world's total conventional supply, and the largest surplus production capacity, Saudi Arabia is the biggest player on the global oil market. In contrast to other countries studied in this book, Saudi Arabia was never revolutionary: it is a monarchy led by one of the oldest ruling dynasties in the world. This contrast makes it an excellent case to consider the political effects of oil in the absence of revolutionary government.

Saudi Arabia's foreign policy is marked by two themes: the incentives for international cooperation generated by oil, and the checkbook diplomacy made possible by oil income. These themes highlight the fact that oil has multiple effects on the foreign policies of petrostates, and that the net impact is not always to increase the state's propensity for aggression and conflict. Indeed, Saudi Arabia has largely avoided initiating direct interstate conflict. This is not to say that the Kingdom's foreign policy is pacifist. It has used its ample financial resources to fund proxy wars and foreign insurgents. Yet the net effect of oil, in combination with a leadership that is generally risk-averse, has been to encourage Saudi Arabia to seek cooperation with powerful states and ensure that its oil exports continue to flow. This is most clearly seen in the US–Saudi relationship, which is a special focus of this chapter.

Consider the variables in Table 9.1, which summarize the key characteristics of Saudi Arabia 1945–2010. First, Saudi Arabia has not had a revolutionary government. To the contrary, the country is ruled by the Saudi monarchy, which has resisted any radical shifts in the

225

Table 9.1 *Summary of key variables in Saudi Arabia, 1945–2010*

Saudi Arabia	1945–1967	1967–1973	1974–1999	2000–2010
IV: Revolutionary regime	Non-	Non-	Non-	Non-
IV: Petrostate	Yes	Yes	Yes	Yes
Foreign policy:				
with United States	Cooperation	Embargo and cooperation	Cooperation	Complex
with Egypt	Proxy conflict	Warming	No conflict	No conflict
with Yemen	Complex	Warming	No conflict	No conflict
with Israel	Hostility	Conflict	Hostility	Diplomacy
with USSR/ Russia	Hostility	Hostility	Proxy conflict	No conflict
with Gulf monarchies	Mild friction	Cooperation	Cooperation	Cooperation
DV:				
Aggressiveness				
Expected value	Low	Low	Low	Low
Actual value	Low-Moderate	Moderate	Low	Low

Note: For more information about the labels used in this table, see Figure 3.1.

political, economic, or social institutions of the country. Since 1953, when the first king of the modern Saudi state died, the country has been ruled by a succession of his sons: Saud, Faisal, Khalid, Fahd, and Abdullah. Each of these kings has made major decisions, and in some cases enacted significant reforms in the Kingdom. There have even been some struggles for power within the royal family. Nonetheless, the basic Saudi regime has remained constant, and the basic political, economic, and religious relationships have been modified only gradually through time. There have been attempts to overthrow the existing regime, but none have been successful.

Saudi Arabia is clearly a petrostate, in the sense that its oil sector dominates the national economy and its international exports. Of course, there has been some variance in the production and revenues from the Saudi oil sector. Figure 9.1 shows Saudi oil production over time. Production increased relatively modestly until the late 1960s,

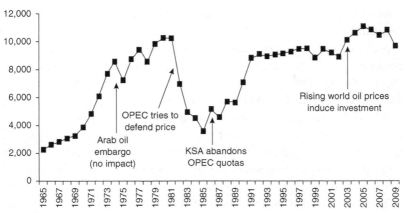

Figure 9.1 Saudi oil production, 1965–2009, thousands of barrels per day
Note: Data from BP Statistical Review of World Energy, 2010.

then rapidly increased to 8.6 million barrels per day in 1974. At the same time, the Arab oil embargo and price shocks of 1973–1974 dramatically increased Saudi oil revenues. Interestingly, the oil embargo of 1973–1974 made almost no impact on Saudi Arabia's oil production and exports. The state's oil revenues continued to increase until 1980–1981, when both production and prices peaked. From then on, oil production, prices, and revenues fell until 1986, when Saudi Arabia significantly increased its oil production, driving prices still lower but increasing the state's overall revenues. Saudi production and prices stabilized through much of the 1990s at about nine million barrels per day and $25 per barrel respectively. Saudi oil revenues skyrocketed again during the 2003–2008 oil boom. Despite this variation, Saudi Arabia has remained a petrostate throughout, due to its enormous oil reserves and production capacity. Even in lean years, Saudi Arabia's oil income forms the lion's share of its government revenues and GDP.

Finally, consider Saudi foreign policy. Throughout the postwar era, Saudi Arabia has avoided direct interstate military conflict, although it has occasionally funded foreign insurgents in active conflicts. In the 1960s, Saudi Arabia experienced a serious military conflict with Egypt as part of Yemen's civil war, but it was primarily a defensive conflict for Saudi Arabia, and it did not seek to initiate armed hostilities. In 1967–1973, Saudi Arabia supported the Arab side in two wars against Israel, but its actions were principally economic and Saudi troops did not fight against Israelis (in contrast to Libya, which was also not a front-line state). The Arab–Israeli War put strain on the Saudi–US relationship, climaxing in the Arab oil embargo in late 1973. Yet even then, Saudi policy was secretly cooperative with the United States, and became openly cooperative as soon as the embargo was over. During the 1970s and 1980s, the Saudis used checkbook diplomacy to fund insurgents against the USSR, and support Iraq against Iran. Clearly, Saudi Arabia has not had a pacifist foreign policy. Yet its actions reveal a reluctance to engage in direct interstate military conflicts. Overall, the Saudi foreign policy has been remarkable for the extent to which it has avoided initiating interstate fights, especially in a region steeped in such conflict.

The theory thus passes the first test. The rest of this chapter is organized in three main sections. The first section offers an historical narrative describing Saudi Arabia's foreign policy over time. Its history is divided into four periods: prior to 1967, 1967–1973, 1974–1999, and 2000–present. The second section analyzes the hypothesized causal mechanisms as they operated in Saudi history. Finally, the last section compares Saudi Arabia and Libya, which were similar in many respects prior to the onset of Qaddafi's revolutionary government in Libya. This comparison highlights the importance of domestic politics in explaining the net effect of oil on a state's international relations.

Saudi foreign policy

Saudi politics prior to 1967

In February, 1945, US President Franklin Roosevelt met in person with King Abdul Aziz ibn Saud aboard a US Navy cruiser in the Suez Canal. The historic meeting on the USS *Quincy* solidified a de facto alliance between the two countries. The partnership is characterized by a commitment by each party: the United States assists Saudi Arabia in its military defense against foreign enemies (and, to a lesser extent, internal enemies); and Saudi Arabia cooperates with the United States in the global oil market. Neither of these commitments has ever been formalized, but both are reflected in numerous public statements by leaders of both countries in the postwar period, most explicitly in the Carter Doctrine. The meeting also foreshadowed a continuing source of tension in the relationship: regarding Palestine, Roosevelt promised that the United States would never assist the Jews against the Arabs.

King Abdul Aziz died in 1953. The royal succession was peaceful, but a power struggle soon developed between the new King Saud and his brother Faisal, the Crown Prince. The political struggle continued for almost a decade, until in 1962 Faisal effectively seized power.[1] In the face of additional pressure from senior members of the family, Saud backed down and abdicated from the throne in March 1964. At no point did this within-family power struggle become revolutionary.[2]

During this period, Saudi Arabia maintained a peaceful policy with most of its Gulf neighbors, as well as Iran, Iraq, Jordan, and the United States.[3] As Saud and Faisal worked to consolidate power domestically, their priorities were more focused on preserving and defining the nature of their regime than on overturning the international status quo.[4] However, Saudi Arabia was also involved in a serious international dispute with Egypt over Yemen during this period.

The relationship with Nasser started relatively well. King Saud invited Egyptian officers to replace the American advisors to the Saudi military in 1954, and Egypt and Saudi Arabia signed a mutual defense treaty in 1955.[5] King Saud also supported Nasser in the 1956 Suez Canal crisis. However, as time went on, the Saudis grew concerned about the revolutionary "Free Officers" inspired by Nasser, especially those within Saudi Arabia who launched a coup attempt in 1955. By

---

[1] King Saud's indecisiveness about the military conflict in Yemen played a major role in Faisal's rise to power. G. Gause, 1990: 61.

[2] In the midst of this struggle, another Saudi Prince, Talal, became a Nasser loyalist and sought to radically reform the regime. However, Talal never garnered much support, failed to revolutionize the regime, and fled to Cairo. M. al-Rasheed, 2002; W. Bowen, 2008; T. Hegghammer, 2009.

[3] One exception to this pattern was the Al Buryami dispute between Saudi Arabia and Oman and Abu Dhabi (today part of the UAE). This was a minor dispute over a patch of territory that lies at the intersection of the three countries. In 1951, Abu Dhabi and Oman asked the British government to negotiate a settlement with the Saudis on their behalf. In an attempt to pre-empt the settlement, and encouraged by the Americans in Aramco, forty Saudis rode into the Al Buraymi oasis in 1952 and claimed the area for the Kingdom. In response, Oman and Abu Dhabi raised an army, but the standoff never resulted in violence. The territorial issue was referred to international arbitration in Geneva, and eventually settled peacefully in April 1975. This was primarily a diplomatic rather than military affair: the tiny Saudi force was never sufficient to mount an effective attack, no casualties occurred, and the outcome was settled by diplomatic arbitration. A. Brown, 1999; J. Meagher, 1985.

[4] S. Hertog, 2010.   [5] J. Kechichian, 2001.

September 1956, the Egyptian and Saudi relationship had soured.[6] In the 1960s, the relationship between the two states would face a severe test over the Yemeni civil war.[7]

In 1962, Abdullah al-Sallal deposed the Imam al-Badr of Yemen in an effort to create the first non-monarchical regime on the Arabian Peninsula. Nasser supplied the republicans with thousands of Egyptian troops, leading Saudi Arabia to break off relations with Egypt in 1962. The Saudis provided money and materials for the opposite side, the Yemeni royalists. As Egyptian planes began a series of attacks on the Saudi border with Yemen, the Saudis used their economic power in another way: they asked for help from their chief oil customer, the United States. The United States responded swiftly, using fighter planes in the Dhahran Airfield to act as a deterrent against Egypt, as well as sending warships and more aircraft to the Kingdom. Saudi Arabia mobilized its own military to defend its border with Yemen, but it relied primarily on the United States for defense and on the Yemeni royalists for offense.

Significantly, the dispute between Egypt and Saudi Arabia was always a proxy war and never became a direct military conflict. Indeed, Crown Prince Faisal "sought at all costs to avoid a direct confrontation with the Egyptians."[8] Saudi Arabia's primary objective was to prevent the spread of revolutionary instability, not helping the royalists to victory. When Faisal became king in 1964, he maneuvered diplomatically with the United States and Egypt towards a peaceful solution. In August 1965, Egypt and Saudi Arabia signed the Jeddah Agreement, by which both countries promised to stop all assistance in the Yemeni civil war. Both sides' interventions officially came to a halt in June 1967 with the outbreak of the Arab–Israeli War. King Faisal recognized the Yemen Arab Republic in 1970 and subsequently provided the Yemenis with significant financial payments.[9]

Despite the tense relationship with Egypt and Yemen, Saudi foreign policy in this period was essentially conservative in character.[10] To

---

[6] It was alleged that King Saud so feared Nasser that he paid £1.9 million for a (failed) assassination attempt against the Egyptian president (M. al-Rasheed, 2002; R. Bronson, 2006).

[7] For an interesting exploration of politics in Saudi Arabia and Yemen, see K. Chaudhry, 1997.

[8] G. Gause, 1990: 61.   [9] M. al-Rasheed, 2002.

[10] M. Kerr, 1971.

a large extent, the Saudis were preoccupied with consolidating their regime at home, which was greatly facilitated by growing oil revenues. However, when the regime perceived a threat to its legitimacy or territorial security, it did not hesitate to use its financial and economic power in pursuit of foreign policy objectives. Indeed, Saudi Arabia's rising oil industry provided it with a flexible instrument, for uses ranging from funding Yemeni fighters to eliciting support from the United States.

Saudi foreign policy, 1967–1973

The period 1967–1973 saw a change in the foreign policy of Saudi Arabia. The Kingdom was a rather reluctant member of the Arab coalition in the 1967 war against Israel, but the consequences of the Israeli victory represented a shock to Saudi Arabia's heretofore conservative policy. Moreover, the US support of Israel during and after the 1967 war created a deep rift in the US–Saudi relationship that sowed the seeds of subsequent Saudi decisions, up to and including the momentous oil embargo of 1973.

In May 1967, the Saudis followed Jordan and Syria's lead in goading the Egyptians to war against Israel, using radio announcements to publicly question Nasser's commitment to the Arab struggle. Still, the Saudis stood to lose much from the war: if Israel won, the United States and by implication its ally Saudi Arabia would be criticized for the Arab defeat; if Egypt won, a victorious Nasser would gain even more stature and popularity in the Arab world. King Faisal was thus only a reluctant participant in the war. In May 1967, he was in Europe and intentionally delayed his return to Saudi Arabia as a way of avoiding the demands on him to support Egypt against Israel.[11] The Kingdom eventually sent 3,000 troops, but only to southern Jordan, far from the active fighting. The war began on June 5, and by June 11, the Arab states had lost decisively. Egypt lost Sinai and Gaza; Syria lost the Golan Heights; Jordan lost East Jerusalem and the West Bank; and Nasser lost the leadership of the Arab world.

The Six-Day War put enormous strain on the relationship between the United States and Saudi Arabia. The Arab states were furious with the United States for supporting Israel, and on June 6, Egypt, Algeria,

[11] R. Bronson, 2006.

Sudan, Syria, Yemen, and Iraq broke off diplomatic relations with the United States. Saudi Arabia did not, a result of the US–Saudi ties built by oil. Nonetheless, Faisal needed to do something to show his domestic constituency that he was taking action. On June 7, Saudi Arabia joined Iraq, Kuwait, and Algeria in their oil embargo against the United States and the United Kingdom. The 1967 embargo was primarily a symbolic act. Although nominally it lasted until September 1, it effectively ended just four days after it began, as Saudi oil minister Yamani and his Kuwaiti counterpart announced on June 11 that oil exports would return to normal levels. Moreover, even at the height of the embargo, King Faisal secretly agreed to supply the US military with oil and jet fuel for its operations in Vietnam and elsewhere in Asia. Faisal knew that the US military would be seriously inconvenienced by a disruption in Saudi oil supplies, and he wanted to mitigate the damage done to the US–Saudi relationship. The king also guaranteed the safety of American Aramco employees in Saudi Arabia, in light of the anti-American protests taking place inside the Kingdom.[12]

The real damage to the US–Saudi relationship took place in the aftermath of the war. Israel had more than doubled its territorial size in 1967, at the expense of the Arab states. The United States did nothing to pressure Israel to return its conquered territories. This stood in contradiction to the solemn promises to Saudi Arabia made by five US presidents from Roosevelt to Johnson that the United States would protect the territorial integrity of all Middle Eastern states. The anger generated in the aftermath of the Six-Day War would help motivate Saudi actions against US and Israeli interests in the next six years. In August 1967, Arab leaders met in Khartoum and declared their three slogans: *lai'itiraf, la mufawada, la sulh* ("no recognition, no negotiation, no treaty [with Israel]"). The Khartoum meeting was also important for the decision by Saudi Arabia, Kuwait, and Libya – the three states with the highest per capita oil revenues at the time – to fund the front-line Arab states, namely Egypt, Syria, and Jordan. Saudi Arabia added the stipulation that it would only fund Egypt once the latter had completed its withdrawal from Yemen. Once again, the Kingdom was reaching for its preferred instrument of foreign policy: checkbook diplomacy. Rather than engage in military conflict directly, the Saudis were content to fund others.

[12] R. Bronson, 2006; A. Brown, 1999; R. Vitalis, 2007.

Saudi Arabia's use of financial power found further expression in 1969. In a meeting in Rabat, Morocco, the Palestinian Liberation Organization (PLO) was recognized as the sole legitimate representative of the Palestinians. The Saudi government directly gave the PLO 3.72 billion riyals (USD 992 million) in the fourteen-year period from 1978 to 1991, not counting additional contributions from semi-state and non-state actors in Saudi Arabia.[13] Saudi financing of the PLO was a crucial factor in making the organization financially sustainable, and it also helped Saudi Arabia move closer to the center of Arab politics. The Saudis supported various factions within the PLO and provided huge sums of money to Palestinian training camps in Lebanon, Syria, and Jordan.[14]

King Faisal also used Saudi Arabia's increasing financial power to fund Islamic organizations such as the World Muslim League (founded in 1962) and the Organization of the Islamic Conference (founded in 1969). Faisal hoped that these organizations would help Saudi Arabia seize a leadership role in the Muslim world on the basis of its special position in Islamic heritage as the home of Mecca and Medina. This pan-Islamic vision was an important alternative to pan-Arabism because it offered a popular ideology that was compatible with the existing nation states of the Middle East and was therefore non-threatening to the Saudi regime. Indeed, the World Muslim Congress declared that "those who disavow Islam and distort its call under the guise of nationalism are actually the most bitter enemies of Arabs, whose glories are entwined with the glories of Islam."[15] Pan-Islamism also widened the scope of the Middle East political dialogue to include states like Iran and Pakistan, which Saudi Arabia sought to use to dilute the influence of then-pre-eminent Egypt. In the wake of Nasser's defeat in the 1967 Arab–Israeli War, this pan-Islamic vision gained a certain degree of momentum.

One reflection of Saudi Arabia's rising stature in the Arab world, and its changing relationship with Egypt, was that when President Sadat began to consider a new war against Israel in the 1970s, he consulted extensively with King Faisal and asked for his help. As late as 1972, King Faisal was deeply reluctant to use an oil embargo as a weapon against the United States, for two reasons. First, despite

---

[13] T. Hegghammer, 2010.   [14] A. Vasilev, 1998.
[15] A. Sindi, 1980.

growing tensions in the US–Saudi relationship, the de facto alliance was one of the foundations of Saudi foreign policy and King Faisal did not want to act against the United States lightly. Second, the Saudis recognized the very limited impact of the 1967 Arab oil embargo and initially believed the same would be true in the 1970s.[16] However, in 1973 Faisal realized that the global oil market had changed, and he grew increasingly frustrated with the US position on Israel. Eventually, Faisal gave Sadat the commitment that he sought: half a billion dollars for Sadat's war chest and a commitment to impose an oil embargo.

On October 6, 1973, Egypt and Syria struck Israel. It quickly became apparent that unless the United States supplied Israel with desperately needed materials, Israel could lose the war. Even when the United States chose to supply the Israelis, the Saudis remained reluctant to break off relations. Still, other Arab states were agitating for an embargo, and on October 20, Saudi Arabia finally agreed. The oil embargo, as it unfolded over the next five months, dramatically re-shaped the global oil industry and Saudi Arabia's position in the world. In mid 1973, the price of oil was $2.90 per barrel; by December it was $11.66. In some cases panicked buyers were willing to pay far more than the posted international price, and there were shortages in the United States and elsewhere. Yet even by the end of 1973, the Arab producers were beginning to relax the production restrictions. Officially the embargo against the United States did not end until March 18, 1974, but Saudi Arabia and others were selling oil into the markets well before then. Saudi Arabia did this largely because Faisal realized that the United States and the West could not bear both the huge price increase and the production cuts associated with the embargo. Moreover, Faisal also allowed Saudi Aramco – the national oil company – to make secret oil shipments to the US troops in Vietnam, to ensure that US military operations would not be compromised.[17] These steps allowed Saudi Arabia to mitigate the real cost of the oil embargo for the United States, even as it used the embargo as a public statement of displeasure about US policy toward Israel.

Saudi Arabia's military involvement in the 1973 war was limited to a token number of active troops. This stood in contrast to the military efforts of "front-line states," principally Egypt and Syria, and to many

---

[16] R. Bronson, 2006.   [17] A. Brown, 1999.

other Arab states that were at least as geographically distant from Israel as Saudi Arabia. Libya and Algeria sent significant armed forces and squadrons of fighter jets; Iraq also sent a small force. In total, the Arab countries would add 100,000 troops and at least 650 tanks to Egypt and Syria's front-line forces.[18] In comparison, Saudi Arabia's military contribution was puny.

As usual, the Saudi leaders chose to use the Kingdom's economic and financial power as their chief instrument of foreign policy, rather than military action. In effect, Saudi Arabia's oil industry provided it with an alternative to interstate military conflict. Moreover, as suggested in Chapter 2, oil also generates incentives to avoid armed conflict: it generates a strong financial incentive for a petrostate to preserve peaceful and cooperative international relationships, to avoid a disruption to the oil trade. This second effect was especially pronounced in the US–Saudi relationship in the years following 1973.

Saudi foreign policy, 1974–1999

Well before the end of the oil embargo in March 1974, Saudi Arabia returned to its usual conservatism in its foreign policy, especially with regard to maintaining and rebuilding its friendship with the United States. The leaderships of both countries acknowledged that it was far too dangerous and costly to willfully oppose the other.[19] High-level officials began to work closely again, particularly on economic and military matters. In June 1974, only three months after the official end of the embargo, Prince Fahd and other senior Saudi officials arrived in Washington to sign a multi-pronged agreement of cooperation between the two countries. The agreement called for the establishment of a Joint Commission on Economic Cooperation and a Joint Security Cooperation Commission that brought together officials from both governments to devise strategies for Saudi economic development and defense modernization.

In practice, this agreement was the start of a massive program of "petrodollar recycling." The goal was to ensure that the vast sums of money that the United States was now spending on OPEC oil were returned to the United States in the form of investments and

---

[18] A. Rabinovich, 2005: 54–55.
[19] R. Bronson, 2006: 123.

payments for weapons. For Secretary of State Henry Kissinger, the real objective was to "create incentives for the [oil-]producing nations to become responsible participants in the international economy."[20] In other words, Kissinger wanted to make sure that Saudi Arabia was a stakeholder in the United States' economic success, such that the Kingdom would never again have an incentive to embargo its oil sales. US Treasury Secretary William Simon was an eager partner in this effort, as he was concerned about the United States' rapidly growing balance-of-payments deficit. Between 1972 and 1973, the US bill for foreign oil jumped from $3.9 billion to $24 billion. While not all of the United States' oil money was headed to Saudi Arabia, the payments were sufficiently large to create a strong financial incentive for cooperation between the two countries. This is exactly what happened: by 1976, Saudi Arabia had invested $60 billion in the United States, and its military purchases had jumped to more than $5 billion per year compared to just $0.3 billion in 1972.[21] One American military officer commented, "I do not know of anything that is nonnuclear that we would not give the Saudis."[22] This kind of cooperation is all the more striking considering how soon after the embargo it occurred.

In March 1975, King Faisal was assassinated by one of his nephews. The assassination was a personal act of revenge for the assassin's brother, who had been killed by Saudi police in a demonstration in 1965.[23] Faisal's brother Khalid reluctantly became king, ruling until 1982, though much of the real power lay with the Crown Prince Fahd. Khalid and Fahd continued rebuilding the relationship with the United States and focused on spending the Kingdom's rapidly rising oil income. The 1970s saw dramatic spending and investment projects in Saudi Arabia, along with a certain amount of social change and modernization.

The year 1979 was a momentous one in the Middle East. In Iran, the Shah was toppled and the Ayatollah Khomeini came to power. Leaders of the Saudi regime were justifiably concerned that this could inspire a similar effort to topple their own monarchy, and they did not have to wait long to see such an attempt. In November 1979,

[20] H. Kissinger, 2000: 677.
[21] R. Bronson, 2006: 122–127. The Saudis also had other motives for the weapons purchases, including patronage, prestige, and alliance building with the United Sates (G. Nonneman in P. Aarts and G. Nonneman, 2006).
[22] J. De Onis, 1974.   [23] M. al-Rasheed, 2002.

tens of thousands of Shiite Muslims in Kingdom's Eastern Provinces rose up and staged an unprecedented *intifada* against the Saudi regime in the towns of Qatif, Saihat, Safwa, and Awamiyya.[24] The National Guard was called in and a violent confrontation ensued for seven days, until the rebellion was put down. Almost simultaneously, a religious leader named Juhayman al-Utaybi and several hundred armed followers seized the Grand Mosque of Mecca and held hundreds of hostages inside.[25] Again, the Saudi regime responded with force, using helicopters and artillery in a major assault to re-take the mosque. The military won, but at the cost of more than 400 dead and over 1,000 injured, including hundreds of pilgrims. Although the two uprisings were put down, they had a profound effect on the Saudi regime.[26] Henceforth, it constantly sought to burnish its religious credentials to ensure the stability and continuation of the regime. It did this in part by pouring money into religious institutions at home and abroad.[27] In 1986, the regime even changed the king's official title to the Custodian of the Two Holy Mosques.

The 1979 uprisings, in combination with the Soviet invasion of Afghanistan and the outbreak of the Iran–Iraq War in 1980, also served to strengthen the bond between the United States and Saudi Arabia. President Reagan continued the Carter doctrine laid out in 1980, which stipulated that an attempt by any outside force to gain control of the Persian Gulf region would be regarded as an assault on the vital interests of the United States, and would be repelled by military force. To enforce this doctrine, Carter created the Rapid Deployment Joint Task Force, which was enlarged and became Central Command (Centcom) under President Reagan. The United States significantly increased its military spending and presence in the Persian Gulf region.[28] It also helped the six monarchies create the Gulf Cooperation Council as a bulwark against Iranian aggression.[29]

As part of the implicit US–Saudi alliance, Saudi Arabia spent vast sums to support the global anti-Communism effort. Most famously, the

[24] T. Jones, 2006.
[25] Y. Trofimov, 2007. Note that the siege of Mecca, unlike the rebellion in the Eastern Provinces, was not an explicit attempt to overthrow the Saudi monarchy, but it was evidence of the potential for violent instability that existed within the Kingdom.
[26] T. Hegghammer and S. Lacroix, 2007; M. Herb, 1999.
[27] T. Niblock, 2006.   [28] A. Brown, 1999: 343.   [29] G. Gause, 1994.

Saudis spent billions of dollars to support the *mujahedin* in Afghanistan, who were fighting a resistance war against the Soviet occupation. In just the years 1987–1989, the Saudis gave the Afghan *mujahedin* at least 6.75 billion riyals (USD 1.8 billion).[30] Yet Saudi financing for insurgents in the 1980s extended far beyond Afghanistan and included support for groups in Angola, Sudan, Ethiopia, Yemen, and elsewhere, wherever there was an active battle against Communists. The Saudis worked hand-in-hand with the United States, even facilitating funding for the Nicaraguan contras that lay at the heart of the Iran-contra affair. Thus the Saudi efforts to support foreign insurgencies are evidence of a certain degree of foreign policy aggression. However, there is no evidence that Saudi Arabia sought to use these insurgents as part of a program of territorial expansion. And while substantial numbers of private Saudi citizens went to Afghanistan to fight, the Saudi government did not provide them with any material support.[31]

Throughout the 1980s, the Saudis continued to make large weapons purchases, in part to solidify their relationships with powerful oil consumers. In 1986 the Reagan administration arranged for Saudi Arabia the largest foreign arms sale in US history, including five of the advanced AWACS planes.[32] The Saudis did not deal with the United States alone, however. From the 1980s onwards, Saudi arms purchases from European suppliers (British and French in particular) increased significantly, outstripping the US sales in many years. After trying and failing for years to purchase F-15 fighter-bombers from the United States, the Saudis turned to the British in 1985. This led to the giant al-Yamamah contract, the largest oil-for-arms deal in the world, which sent advanced British jet fighters to the Kingdom. Then in 1987–1989, the Chinese provided thirty-six CSS-2 intermediate-range ballistic missiles to the Saudis, a contract valued at $3 billion.[33] This was widely seen as a breakthrough in Saudi–Chinese relations, which caused considerable consternation among US policymakers. (In 1990, China and Saudi Arabia established formal diplomatic relations, and the economic and diplomatic relationship has grown stronger over time.[34]) Saudi arms purchases, made possible by its oil income, are widely seen

---

[30] T. Hegghammer, 2010.
[31] T. Hegghammer, 2011.   [32] A. Cordesman, 2003.
[33] G. Nonneman in P. Aarts and G. Nonneman, 2006: 344–345.
[34] G. Kemp, 2010.

as part of a strategy to create interdependence with great powers and thus improve the Kingdom's security guarantees.[35]

The long-standing "oil for security" arrangement between the United States and Saudi Arabia would reach its apex in 1990–1991 following Iraq's invasion of Kuwait. Realizing that Saudi Arabia's military defenses would be no match for the Iraqi military, both Saudi and American leaders feared that Saddam Hussein would attack the Kingdom. US officials requested and received permission to station hundreds of thousands of troops in Saudi Arabia as part of Operations Desert Shield and Desert Storm. Once again, Saudi Arabia used its financial muscle: the estimated cost of the war to Saudi Arabia was $55 billion, and the Kingdom continued to pay billions after 1991 in the form of US arms purchases.[36] Again, oil exports generated financial incentives for both countries to cooperate and for Saudi Arabia to spend profligately in support of its foreign policy objectives.[37]

Throughout the 1990s, the Saudis would continue to cooperate with the United States and others in trying to contain Iraq's military advances. In an oft-forgotten incident in 1994, Saddam Hussein again threatened Kuwait by positioning three divisions of the Iraqi Republican Guard consisting of 80,000 soldiers near Kuwait's northern border.[38] The United States and its coalition partners rushed troops to the region, and some of them remained in Saudi Arabia after the incident. While this was evidence of continued security cooperation between Saudi Arabia and its allies, it also led to significant tensions.

Saudi Arabia's other bilateral relationships during the 1980s and 1990s were characterized by the usual degree of diplomatic friction, but no major conflicts. Saudi Arabia's relationship with Egypt, Jordan, Yemen, and the members of the Gulf Cooperation Council were all reasonably harmonious, albeit to varying degrees. Saudi Arabia's relationship with Iran was marked by mutual antipathy, as each state saw the other as a rival in terms of regional politics and for leadership in the Islamic world. Yet despite this antipathy, and despite some significant provocations by Iran (see Chapter 7), Saudi Arabia did not seek to initiate a militarized conflict. Only with Iraq was there open

---

[35] P. Aarts and G. Nonneman, 2006.
[36] T. Lippman, 2004: 311.
[37] Saudi Arabia also created a sovereign wealth fund: see K. Diwan, 2009.
[38] S. Yetiv, 1997.

military hostility, and even there Saudi Arabia sought principally to preserve the status quo rather than to act aggressively.

Saudi foreign policy, 2000–2010

By the late 1990s, serious disagreements emerged between the United States and Saudi Arabia. In part, this was due to differences about the best approach to dealing with Iraq and the growing threat of Islamic terrorism. The 1996 bombing of Khobar Towers in Saudi Arabia killed nineteen American soldiers, and there was friction between the two countries about how best to respond to the incident. Yet the issue that created the most serious fissure in the bilateral relationship was Israel. In September 2000, the second Palestinian *intifada* broke out. Despite a last minute push at the end of his presidency, Bill Clinton was not able to secure a meaningful peace accord, and the new Bush administration elected to diminish US efforts for Middle East peace. As the fighting in Palestine went on, Crown Prince Abdullah became incensed by what he perceived as American indifference to the brutality of the Israeli military and the plight of the Palestinians. Abdullah's view was widely shared in the Arab world.[39]

Thus just prior to the attacks of September 11, 2001, US–Saudi relations were in crisis for just the second time in history (the first being the 1973 embargo). On August 27, 2001, Crown Prince Abdullah sent a sharply worded letter to President Bush. In it, he stated that he was deeply disturbed by the escalating violence in Palestine and the United States' apparent decision not to intervene. Ominously, Abdullah wrote, "We are at a crossroads. It is time for the United States and Saudi Arabia to look at their separate interests." The threat to the long-standing partnership between the two countries would soon grow even worse. Just two weeks later, fifteen Saudi nationals were involved in the 9/11 attacks. The Saudis initially showed little contrition over the role of Saudi nationals in the attack, and Abdullah publicly placed most of the blame on Israel and Zionists. In early 2001, 56 percent of Americans had a favorable view of Saudi Arabia; by December, its favorability rating had plummeted to just 24 percent.[40] In the fall of 2001, it was not clear whether the US–Saudi relationship would endure these tensions.

[39] T. Hegghammer, 2010.   [40] R. Bronson, 2006: 235.

Even with these heavy pressures on the relationship, however, oil continued to provide a massive incentive for the United States and Saudi Arabia to cooperate. The Bush administration responded to the Crown Prince's letter by promising to re-examine US policy toward the Israeli–Palestinian crisis. Bush hosted Abdullah at the president's ranch in Crawford, Texas, in April 2002 and again in April 2005. For his part, Abdullah proposed the Arab Peace Initiative, a plan for Israeli–Palestinian peace and normalized diplomatic relations between Israel and the Arab states. Moreover, since 2003, Saudi Arabia has been far more interested in cooperating with the United States on the issue of terrorism, particularly after it suffered a number of attacks by terrorists inside the Kingdom.[41] Since 2003, the two countries have worked together to reduce radical Islamist terrorist threats.[42]

Yet it is not true, as some have argued, that terrorism "saved" the US–Saudi relationship by providing a new basis for cooperation.[43] Oil was already and continued to serve as the fundamental basis for the relationship. After 9/11, but before Saudi Arabia suffered the first of several terrorist attacks on its own soil in May 2003, the Saudi regime was lukewarm at best to the US interest in combating terrorism. During that time, oil alone served as the primary common interest between the two countries, and already leaders in both countries worked to repair the cooperation. For instance, the Arab–Israeli peace initiative launched by Crown Prince Abdullah in 2002 was in large part an effort to improve US–Saudi relations.[44] The profoundly sympathetic and conciliatory public statement by Abdullah on the one-year anniversary of the 9/11 attacks was a further step to ameliorate the relationship. Further, although the Saudi regime could not publicly support the US-led war against Iraq in March 2003, it did quietly provide significant assistance to the US air campaign that facilitated the campaign's success.[45] As such, the relationship was already well on its way to recovery before the Saudi regime got serious about the fight against terrorism.

In the latter half of the period 2000–2010, Saudi Arabia was deeply concerned about Iran's influence in the region and its suspected nuclear

[41] B. Riedel, 2007; M. Hafez, 2008.
[42] A. Prados and C. Blanchard in N. Tollitz, 2005.
[43] R. Bronson in P. Aarts and G. Nonneman, 2006.
[44] J. Kostiner in P. Aarts and G. Nonneman, 2006.
[45] P. Aarts in P. Aarts and G. Nonneman, 2006; T. Hegghammer, 2010.

weapons development program. Although publicly the Saudi regime rarely spoke directly about Iran's nuclear program, in private it urged its American allies to consider all options, including military ones, to eliminate the threat. Most famously, King Abdullah urged the United States to "cut off the head of the snake," according to leaked US diplomatic cables.[46] As usual, however, the Kingdom itself avoided direct conflict with Iran, not only militarily but also diplomatically. Saudi Arabia was not prepared to accept the risks associated with open interstate conflict.

In other areas, Saudi Arabia's foreign policy in this period was generally non-aggressive and focused on diplomatic initiatives to promote international cooperation. In 2003, the International Energy Forum (IEF) opened its headquarters in Riyadh, with Saudi Arabia as its largest financial supporter. The IEF's mission is to promote dialogue between energy producers and consumers. The Saudis also worked toward peace between Israel and the Palestinians. Although the Arab Peace Initiative initially stalled politically in 2002 due to a major attack by Hamas, the Arab League again endorsed the plan in 2007. As oil prices rose in 2005–2008, the Kingdom increased its foreign aid budget for development projects. The Saudi regime also worked to shut down some of the cross-border funding for international terrorist groups stemming from members of wealthy Saudi citizens.

Operation of causal mechanisms

How did the non-revolutionary character of Saudi Arabia shape its foreign policy?

The Saudi monarchy was not revolutionary in the period 1945–2010. Since Abdul Aziz established the modern state and left it to his sons after his death in 1953, the regime has been primarily focused on preserving its hold on power and developing the state economically. The Saudi kings had good reason to focus on consolidating their power, as they faced various attempts to unseat them from power. There were multiple coup attempts (e.g., 1955, 1969), assassination attempts (including the successful attempt in 1975), and violent insurgencies (including the rebellion in the Eastern Province in 1979, and multiple

---

[46] *Guardian*, 2010a.

terrorist attacks in 2003–2006). Given their general risk-aversion, the risk of overthrow led successive kings to be mindful of their domestic situation. Furthermore, unlike revolutionary leaders, the Saudi royals were dedicated to preserving the integrity of the existing state and its dynastic tradition. The kings were relatively uninterested in initiating interstate conflicts or expanding their territory. In comparison to the revolutionary leaders already studied, the Saudi kings had risk-averse, non-aggressive foreign policy preferences.

The Saudi king faced almost no formal institutional constraints. The Saudi king formally has supreme power over the country. In practice, the kings delegate much of this power to the senior princes in the Council of Ministers. For instance, each branch of the military is controlled by a different senior prince, and the king has direct control over the National Guard. The Council of Ministers has direct authority in budgetary matters, where the king formally has the final decision-making power.

There are, however, two important political actors that have some influence over the king's political decisions. The first is the possibility of "impeachment" or removal from office by other members of the Saudi family. This is a very real possibility, as indicated by the forced abdication of King Saud in 1964. All of the kings since Saud have been careful to consult extensively with senior members of the family, especially those in the Council of Ministers. Second, by long-standing tradition, the king is expected to consult the *ulema*, the senior members of the Muslim clergy in Saudi Arabia. The influence of the *ulema* should not be overstated; it is not decisive for the king's decisions.[47] Still, many important political decisions made by the king are authorized by *fatwas* (formal religious statements).[48] For instance, when the Holy Mosque of Mecca was under siege in 1979, King Khalid summoned the *ulema* to request an opinion authorizing under *shariah* law an attack on Juhayman al-Utaybi and his supporters in the mosque.[49] Without religious authorization, the king's decisions are at increased risk of severe domestic criticism.

These influences can be observed most vividly by the exception that proves the rule: the 1990 decision by King Fahd to invite US troops into the Kingdom. In contrast to normal practice, King Fahd

---

[47] G. Gause, in R. Hinnebusch and A. Ehteshami, 2002.
[48] C. Kurzman, 2003.   [49] A. Brown, 1999: 348.

made this decision swiftly after he met in person with US Secretary of Defense Dick Cheney and General Norman Schwarzkopf.[50] Fahd took this extraordinary decision only because of the acute danger, as shown in satellite photos of Iraqi troops massing on the border of Saudi Arabia. He later said this was the *only* decision he had ever taken in his long public life, as prince or king, that did not involve first building a consensus.[51] Still, Fahd later convened 350 members of the *ulema* to retroactively authorize the decision, and they extracted considerable concessions from the king in exchange for this *fatwa*, including increased domestic authority for their religious police, the *mutaween*.[52] In normal circumstances, the Saudi kings seek to build consensus within the Council of Ministers and religious authorization by the *ulema* to legitimate their political decisions before they are taken and announced. The exceptional danger in 1990 reversed this pattern by forcing Fahd to make the decision first, and then build political support for it.

Thus two significant political actors have some power to influence the Saudi kings' ability to make foreign policy decisions. These actors serve as a constraint against foreign policy aggression, for the following reason: to the extent that the king and the other actors have heterogeneous preferences, compromise is necessary, which in general is likely to produce less radical outcomes. The Saudi leadership, "pushed and pulled in various directions, will try to find a middle ground, a consensus position that will minimize pressures and risks."[53] However, when the king, the Council, and the *ulema* are aligned, such as in the 1973 oil embargo, the Kingdom's foreign policy can be quite aggressive. Indeed, in 1973, it was the king that acted as the moderating influence, rather than the other actors.

Did oil generate conflict-enhancing incentives?

One key component of the theory developed in Chapter 2 is that oil provides petrostate leaders with increased political autonomy. This political autonomy can increase the state's probability of initiating international conflict, because it reduces the probability that a leader

---

[50] R. Bronson, 2006; T. Lippman, 2004.
[51] T. Lippman, 2004: 301.
[52] N. Obaid, 1999.   [53] W. Quandt, 1981: 83.

will be removed from office in the event of an international defeat. When coupled with a leadership with aggressive, risk-tolerant preferences, this political autonomy increases the state's probability of initiating international conflict.

As described above, Saudi kings had formal authority and enjoyed considerable political autonomy by offering the *ulema* and the general population the benefits derived from the country's oil income. This political autonomy means that the Saudi kings have been able to make some deeply unpopular decisions over time, such as Faisal's decision to provide education to girls and Fahd's decision to allow US troops into the Kingdom in 1990. Oil also allowed Saudi Arabia to make extensive military purchases and acquire advanced weaponry, thus expanding its ability to initiate international conflicts. However, in Saudi Arabia the leadership has generally not had aggressive foreign policy preferences, in part because of the powerful incentives for international cooperation (see below). Consequently, while the incentive is present, the leadership has not sought to take advantage of the reduced risk involved with international conflict.

Did oil generate conflict-reducing incentives?

Saudi Arabia's financial health rests on its oil export sales, which generates a powerful incentive to avoid international conflict that could compromise those exports. Saudi Arabia's leaders perceived these incentives and consequently sought to avoid interstate conflict. Consider three examples illustrating the operation of these incentives in practice. First, Abdul Aziz proved in his early life that he had no qualms about waging war, but in the late 1940s, he sought to avoid conflict with United States over the issue of Palestine precisely because he did not want to jeopardize his oil income. The US Minister to Saudi Arabia reported in 1947 that "fortunately for us, the King is a realist and recognizes that his immediate economic interests are bound up with the United States. He himself has repeatedly stated that he will not permit anything, even our Palestine policy, to bring about a breach of relations with us."[54]

Second, in 1973, oil played a significant role in reducing conflict between Saudi Arabia and other states, despite the October War. Saudi

---

[54] J. Rives Childs, quoted in A. Brown, 1999: 187.

Arabia largely stayed out of the direct military conflict against Israel, in part to protect its oil interests. (Saudi Arabia was also less involved in the conflict because it does not have a contiguous border with Israel, but geography alone does not explain the outcome. Saudi territory is much closer to Israel than Libya, Morocco or Cuba, all of which supplied front-line troops for the conflict.) Also, Saudi oil money during the 1970s helped heal the rifts in its relationship with Egypt and Yemen. And finally, Saudi Arabia's oil interests provided strong incentive for Faisal to maintain covert cooperation with the United States even in the face of a public oil embargo. Moreover, as soon as the embargo ended, both countries acted swiftly to repair the US–Saudi relationship.

A third example of the conflict-reducing incentives generated by oil is King Abdullah's willingness to repair the US–Saudi relationship and work towards a diplomatic solution for Palestine in the wake of the second *intifada* in 1999–2001. As demonstrated by his letter to President Bush in August 2001, Abdullah felt strongly that the United States was ignoring severe injustices perpetrated by Israel. Moreover, the Saudi *ulema* and general public was strongly opposed to the actions by Israel, and by extension, the United States. Yet the relationship rapidly recovered and, within four years, Abdullah and Bush walked hand-in-hand at the president's ranch in Crawford, Texas. Again, the primacy of the oil interests for Saudi Arabia's financial health provided a strong incentive for Saudi Arabia (and the United States) to maintain a cooperative partnership.[55]

The political impact of oil in the US–Saudi relationship can also be observed in the continuity of the cooperation over more than six decades, despite multiple wars and geopolitical upheaval. It is especially striking that at least two Saudi kings, Faisal and Abdullah, who were quite anti-American in their views prior to coming to power, nonetheless decided once in office to cooperate extensively with the United States. Similarly, some US presidents (e.g., Kennedy) initially sought to move away from the Saudi regime and court other Arab allies, but quickly accepted that the Saudis were indispensable partners.[56] This has led to remarkable consistency in US policy towards Saudi Arabia, as a policy memo written in 1951 by the State Department outlines the

[55] J. Barnes and A. Jaffe, 2006.   [56] R. Bronson, 2006.

principles of US engagement that are unchanged even today.[57] Thus the history of Saudi Arabia provides significant support for the theory that oil generates financial incentives to avoid interstate conflict.

The difference a revolution makes

The study of Saudi Arabia in this chapter, and the earlier study of Libya, facilitates a comparison that illustrates the importance of domestic politics in understanding the impact of oil income. The two countries were in many respects similar in the 1960s, until Muammar Qaddafi led his revolutionary coup in Libya in 1969. Analytically, the initial similarity of the two countries is helpful in that it allows us to consider one country as having a received a "treatment" (Libya, which had a revolutionary government) and another country that did not receive the treatment (Saudi Arabia, which continued under a non-revolutionary monarchy). Given that controlled experiments are not possible in world politics, this paired-comparison is one of the strongest analytical tools available for social science.

In the 1960s, Libya and Saudi Arabia were similar on multiple dimensions. Both countries had small populations (in 1965, 4.8 million in Saudi Arabia and 1.6 million in Libya), which were almost entirely Arab and Muslim. Both countries were ruled by monarchies that sought to overcome the traditional tribal and provincial cleavages within their territory. Both states were relatively young, although Saudi Arabia was somewhat older: Libya gained independence in 1951, whereas modern Saudi Arabia was unified in 1932. Both countries were economically very poor and far from modernization: slavery was still legal in Saudi Arabia until 1962, and in both states poverty was extensive. Both countries included significant populations of nomadic Bedouin tribes. Perhaps most critically, the central governments in both countries were highly dependent on oil revenues. By the mid 1960s, oil revenues funded the vast majority of each government's expenditure. Thus the two countries were economically underdeveloped, Arabic, Muslim, monarchical petrostates.

During the 1960s, oil played a similar role politically in both Libya and Saudi Arabia. In both countries, American and other Western companies were invited to develop the oil sector in exchange for a

---

[57] T. Lippman, 2004: 279–282.

share of the oil revenue. Concomitantly, both countries were politically allied to the West and largely depended on the United States to
guarantee their national security. Libya and Saudi Arabia were both
in the Arab League's conservative bloc, and resisted radical moves by
Egypt and others. The oil revenue created common interests in peaceful international trade between the two petrostates and their Western
partners, and during the 1960s, neither state wanted to jeopardize this
relationship. As the oil revenues grew, both countries also began to use
them to fund foreign policy initiatives.

The key moment of divergence in the paths of Saudi Arabia and
Libya came in late 1969, when Qaddafi seized power and revolutionized Libya. Qaddafi's revolution led to a highly aggressive foreign policy, financed by Libya's oil income. In Saudi Arabia, by contrast, the
non-revolutionary character of the regime's leadership led to a continued aversion to interstate conflict, despite the sometimes significant
tensions between Saudi Arabia and the Western world. While there are
some similarities in the behavior of the two states – for example, in the
use of oil income to fund foreign insurgents and purchase weapons for
the national military – the differences are even more striking.

The divergent paths of Libya and Saudi Arabia was perhaps most
evident in their approach to the 1973 war against Israel. United by the
common Arab opposition to Israel's position in Palestine, both states
were involved in the war, but on markedly different terms. On one
hand, Saudi Arabia was approached by Egypt and somewhat reluctantly brought into the war, primarily as a financier. We now know
that Saudi Arabia continued to secretly supply the US military with
oil despite its own embargo against the United States.[58] Thus Saudi
Arabia had a contradictory and limited role in the war. By contrast,
Qaddafi enthusiastically endorsed the war, despite being offended that
he was left out of the decision to declare it. Libya had spent more
than $1 billion in 1971–1973 helping Egypt modernize its military,
and during the war Libya sent armed forces including Mirage fighter
planes to the front lines. Libya was also the most aggressive actor in
the oil embargo: Libya was the first to impose restrictions and the
last to remove them. Thus while oil provided financial and military
resources to both Libya and Saudi Arabia, the net impact of those
resources depends critically on the character of the state's leadership.

[58] R. Bronson, 2006.

Conclusion

Over the last half century, Saudi Arabia pursued a complex and multifaceted foreign policy. Two central themes run throughout: the incentives for international cooperation generated by oil, and the checkbook diplomacy made possible by oil income. Four events illustrate the powerful incentives for cooperation generated by mutual interests in the oil trade: the creation of the US–Saudi oil-for-security partnership after World War II; the re-building of the Saudi–US (and Saudi–West) alliance after the 1973 oil embargo; the protection offered by the United States to Saudi Arabia in the 1980s and 1990s, especially against Iraq; and the survival of the Saudi–US relationship in 2001 in the face of significant political differences stemming from the Israeli conflict and the 9/11 attacks. Similarly, four major events illustrate Saudi Arabia's propensity to use checkbook diplomacy to pursue foreign policy goals rather than direct interstate conflict: its funding for Yemeni fighters in the 1960s; its support for Arab resistance groups and the "front-line states" against Israel since 1967; its significant financial assistance in the fight against Communism in states ranging from Afghanistan to Angola; and its massive expenditures during and after the 1991 war against Iraq. In all of Saudi Arabia's major foreign policy decisions, oil has figured prominently.

Consistent with the theoretical expectations, Saudi Arabia has largely avoided militarized interstate disputes. Its aggression has largely been limited to funding foreign insurgents, notably in Afghanistan. While significant, on its own this activity does not constitute significant aggression. This behavior diverges sharply from revolutionary petrostates such as Libya under Qaddafi's leadership. This chapter thus highlights the multiple effects of oil on foreign policy, determined by the interaction with the domestic politics of the petrostate.

10 | *Does oil cause revolution?*

A revolution is an idea which has found its bayonets.

– Napoleon Bonaparte

This chapter addresses the question of whether oil causes revolutionary government, that is, whether revolutions are more likely to occur in petrostates than in non-petrostates. This question is important because up to this point, I have treated the emergence of a revolutionary government as an independent, exogenous event. If this premise is not true, it could significantly alter our understanding of how oil leads to international conflict. Although a comprehensive investigation into the causes of revolutions is far outside the scope of this book, some exploration of the specific relationship to oil income is well worth the effort.

I first consider the question theoretically. I argue that while the idea is plausible, the extant literature does not provide a simple or unambiguous prediction about how oil might affect the incidence of a revolutionary government. The question therefore begs for empirical analysis. I then present the results of an initial investigation using both quantitative and qualitative approaches, to probe whether there is evidence of a causal link. Finding no such evidence, I conclude that oil and revolutionary governments can be treated as variables that are (mostly) independent of each other.

Is oil linked to revolution in theory?

There is a substantial body of research linking oil to civil war and violent domestic conflict, and it is plausible that such uprisings could generate opportunities for revolutions to occur.[1] For instance,

---

[1] P. Collier and A. Hoeffler, 2004; T. Dunning and L. Wirpsa, 2004; J. Fearon and D. Laitin, 2003; M. Humphreys, 2005; M. Ross, 2012. See also T. Dunning, 2005; B. Smith, 2004.

revolutionary leaders could be motivated in part by what some scholars call "greed, not grievance."[2] As discussed in Chapter 2, one of the central characteristics of oil income is that it is easily controlled by the central government. In an autocratic or weakly institutionalized regime, this gives the state leader access to considerable wealth. A resident of a petrostate who is interested in enriching himself and his coterie of followers therefore has a significant material incentive to try to seize control of the government.

However, the theoretical basis for the proposition that oil causes revolutions is not as clear as one might think. First, let us clarify the terminology. Some scholars have used the term "revolution" when they really mean a coup or overthrow by civil war. But revolution, according to the definition laid out in Chapter 2, implies more than simply replacing one leader with another; instead, it requires significant upheaval of the fundamental political, economic, and social institutions of the state. Thus when some scholars argue that oil leads to increased revolution, they are using the term "revolution" in a much different sense than the way it is used here.[3] This is important because, at least at present, there is no systematic theory linking oil to the emergence of the kind of revolutionary government described in this book. Even if oil creates "greed" incentives for coups or civil wars, it does not necessarily follow that revolutions will be the result.

More recent research provides several reasons to doubt the proposition that revolutions are more likely to occur in petrostates. Much scholarly attention has focused on how the resource curse creates incentives for rebels to fight their governments, but less attention has been paid to how oil affects the behavior of an incumbent government.[4] Oil provides the government with an independent source of financial resources, which in turn generates political and military resources. These resources can be diverted to fight rebels relatively easily, in comparison to the resources available to non-petrostates. For instance, petrostate governments tend to spend more on military arms

---

[2] P. Collier and A. Hoeffler, 2004.

[3] E.g., A. Smith, 2008.

[4] A. Smith's (2008) work is a partial exception, as he explains how unearned revenues can shape the response of the government to a rebel threat. Yet Smith never explicitly states how he expects unearned revenues to alter the probability of rebel victory. Also see R. Snyder and R. Bhavnani, 2005, though they focus on diamonds and conflict.

and personnel than non-petrostates.[5] Furthermore, to the extent to which the material rewards of holding office in a petrostate motivate individuals to fight for office, these rewards presumably affect incumbents just as much as rebels. Thus oil income provides both the resources and the motivation for incumbents to mightily resist regime overthrow.

Indeed, there is evidence to suggest that rebels in petrostates are *less* successful at ousting incumbent leaders, as compared to rebels in non-petrostates, even accounting for the fact that the onset of intrastate violence is more frequent in petrostates.[6] Petrostate governments typically have more resources to fight insurgencies than non-petrostates, and therefore lose less often. Partly as a consequence, incumbent leaders in petrostates tend to have longer tenure in office than leaders in non-petrostates, even if one accounts for the differences in regime type.[7] Further, petrostates may also have more durable regimes than non-petrostates.[8] Thus the empirical evidence generates conflicting conclusions about whether oil leads to greater political stability (e.g., longer leadership and regime tenure) or instability (e.g., more frequent civil wars). Consequently, there is no clear reason to believe that revolutionary governments are more likely to arise in petrostates than non-petrostates.

It is perhaps not surprising, then, that even the proponents of the "greed not grievance" claim have come to modify their position over time. Writing in 2004, Paul Collier and Anke Hoeffler state:

This analysis considerably extends and revises our earlier work (Collier and Hoeffler, 1998). In our previous theory, we assumed that rebel movements incurred net costs during conflict, so that post-conflict pay-offs would be decisive. The core of the paper was the derivation and testing of the implication that high post-conflict pay-offs would tend to justify long civil wars. We now recognize that this assumption is untenable: rebel groups often more than cover their costs during the conflict.[9]

[5] S. Chan, 1980; M. Ross, 2001.
[6] J. Colgan, "Oil, Domestic Conflict, and Opportunities for Democratization."
[7] J. Colgan, 2011a; B. Smith, 2004. See also Chapter 3.
[8] K. Morrison, 2009.
[9] P. Collier and A. Hoeffler, 2004.

Their explanation is a significant corrective: whereas in their previous work they assumed that the anticipated financial pay-off after victory was responsible for the increased frequency of civil war onsets in petrostates, Collier and Hoeffler now place more emphasis on the role of rebel funding during the conflict. In other words, they suggest that petrostates have a higher rate of civil wars than non-petrostates because the oil industry lowers the net costs of the fighting itself for rebels, as they make money by stealing oil or ransoming hostages from the oil industry. There is no robust evidence that rebel greed (for a post-conflict pay-off) has any independent causal impact on the probability of civil wars, as they originally hypothesized.

For all these reasons, there is no theoretical reason to assume that oil causes revolution by providing financial motivation to revolutionary leaders. Still, it is possible that oil makes revolution more likely in some other way. It could be, for instance, that the economic volatility associated with the oil industry causes social disruptions that create conditions ripe for revolutions. Alternatively, it could be that the oil generates or exacerbates corruption in the regime and therefore generates revolutionary grievances. Or that foreign meddling in regimes promotes the incidence of revolutions. On the other hand, the effect of oil could just as plausibly be in the opposite direction. For instance, it could be that revolutions are less likely in petrostates because foreign consumers have an interest in avoiding revolutionary governments, and thus intervene to ensure that revolutions do not succeed. The intervention of the United States and the UK in Iran in 1953 is an example of such intervention. In sum, the question is sufficiently complex that theory fails to provide an unambiguous prediction about whether revolutionary governments are more or less common in non-petrostates.

There is, however, a way to get some leverage on this question. The new dataset on revolutionary governments, as described in Chapter 3, provides the basis for a quantitative empirical investigation. In that chapter the dataset was used to measure an independent variable, but the dataset can now be used to examine revolutionary governments as a dependent variable. While not a comprehensive model of revolutions, this preliminary investigation of the correlation between petrostates and revolutions provides some revealing evidence.

Quantitative evidence suggests no link between oil and revolution

There is little evidence that an oil economy plays a causal role in the incidence of revolutionary leaders.[10] Revolutionary leaders have led petrostates in almost precisely the same proportion of state-years as in non-petrostates: 15.8 percent for petrostates, and 15.6 percent for non-petrostates.[11] This difference is not statistically significant. To explore the issue further, I use logit regression models to analyze the probability of the incidence of revolutionary government. One advantage to this kind of regression analysis is that it can be used to reduce the likelihood of omitted variable bias, which could lead to faulty inferences based on just the raw proportion of revolutionary state-years. In the regression models, I use many of the same variables that were used in Chapter 3. Table 10.1 shows the results.

The regression results suggest that petrostates are not strongly correlated with revolutionary governments, throwing any hypothesized causal relationship into doubt. Model AA is a basic bivariate regression, using only the *Petrostate* variable. This simple regression shows no correlation between petrostates and revolutionary governments. In Model BB, the state's GDP per capita, population, and Polity score are added as control variables, as well as the *Cold War* variable, the Muslim percentage of the population, and regional dummy variables. Again, the coefficient for *Petrostate* is close to zero and statistically insignificant. The results indicate that poorer, more populous, and more autocratic countries are more likely to experience revolutionary governments. Notably, the coefficient for the Middle East region (not shown in Table 10.1) is also positive and strongly significant. Model CC is similar but includes country-fixed effects; again, the results fail to reject the null hypothesis. While these results do not represent a comprehensive causal model of the incidence of revolutionary governments,

---

[10] The incidence of revolutionary government, rather than its onset, is most interesting for the purposes of this book because the incidence of revolutionary government is what (potentially) affects the analysis in Chapter 4.

[11] These figures are for developing countries (non-OECD) only. However, OECD states are included in the regression analyses. Clearly, these numbers represent cross-national averages: some states such as Cuba and Libya have been led by revolutionary leaders for as much as 80 percent of the years under investigation, while others have not seen any revolutionary leaders.

Table 10.1 *Correlates of revolutionary governments*

	Model AA	Model BB	Model CC
	Bivariate	Basic	FE
Petrostate	0.208	–0.286	–0.714
	0.223	0.339	–0.396
GDP / cap, log		–0.593	**–1.106**
		0.116	0.149
Population, log		**0.983**	**3.066**
		0.073	0.268
Polity IV		**–0.230**	**–0.241**
		0.014	0.016
Coldwar		0.169	**1.251**
		0.158	0.215
Muslim, %pop.		0.843	
		0.702	
Fixed Effects	No	No	Yes
N	6,838	6,246	2,551
Log-likelihood	–1,616	–1,231	–897

Notes: All models use logit regression analysis for time-series panel data. For each variable, standard errors are given below the coefficients. Coefficients in bold: p<0.05. *Regional dummies are included but not shown, except in model AA.*

they suggest that there is no correlation between petrostates and revolutionary governments.

Thus this prima facie investigation suggests that oil probably does not cause revolutions. Rather, it is the interaction between a revolutionary government and significant oil income that is the key driver in explaining why petrostates launch so many militarized interstate disputes.

A closer examination of specific cases

As a final test of the potential causal role of oil in revolutions, we can consider the qualitative evidence associated with some specific country cases. While the quantitative evidence already suggests that there is no correlation between oil and the incidence of revolutionary governments in the aggregate, further investigation provides a different vantage point from which to check our inferences. Consider in turn each of four hypothesized causal mechanisms identified previously.

First there is the claim that the financial rewards of being a pet-rostate leader provide additional incentive for revolutionary leaders to succeed in overthrowing the government. The claim does not appear to hold up when the actual leaders in question are examined. The precise motivations of individuals are of course inherently unobservable, making them difficult to analyze by the standards of social science. Yet the observable behaviors of leaders often form patterns that provide the basis for at least tenuous conclusions. On this basis, it is difficult to see how the claim of financial greed can be sustained.

Consider any of the petro-revolutionary leaders whose behavior is analyzed in this book. It hardly seems plausible that the Ayatollah Khomeini was interested in revolution for financial gain: he was an ascetic who lived frugally, ate sparingly, and spent much of his time in prayer. Khomeini's words and actions appear to be those of a man who was devoted to the cause of reshaping the moral and political character of his country according to his vision, not someone who set out to enrich himself. Similarly in Libya, Muammar Qaddafi quite explicitly modeled his revolution in emulation of the one led by his idol Gamal Nasser. For decades, Qaddafi exhorted his people to trans-form their behavior, to pursue the goals of pan-Arabism, and even to rid society of the very idea of property itself. Over time, Qaddafi did acquire considerable wealth for the benefit of his family. Yet it seems unreasonable to believe that, in 1969, personal financial gain was a significant motivation in Qaddafi's effort to overthrow Idris.[12] A some-what stronger case can be made for Saddam Hussein, who admittedly used his position to enrich himself. Still, it is again hard to believe that personal financial gain was among Saddam's primary motives for seiz-ing power: Saddam has consistently been described by his biographers as obsessed with power, not money.[13]

In all three cases, it is worth reflecting on a useful thought-experiment: would Khomeini or Qaddafi or Hussein have been less motivated to seize power if his state had no oil? I believe the answer is no. Perhaps if these men had faced the choice of seizing power in two states, only one of which had oil, he would have gone after the petrostate – but

[12] See Chapter 6 for more details.
[13] C. Coughlin, 2002; E. Karsh and I. Rautsi, 2003; L. Yahia and K. Wendl, 1997.

that is not the choice a revolutionary leader (typically) faces.[14] Instead, an individual such as a young Hussein or Qaddafi has the opportunity to lead a revolution in only one country, his home, and the choice of whether to act as a revolutionary leader does not appear to be often motivated by personal financial gain. If that were the case, we might expect a revolutionary to live a lifestyle at least as lavish as the leaders of non-revolutionary petrostates. Yet in comparison to the leaders of many non-revolutionary petrostates (e.g., Saudi Arabia, Equatorial Guinea), the petro-revolutionary leaders appear to be relatively frugal.

A second possibility is that oil causes economic dislocation and volatility, which is often accompanied by social upheaval, thereby creating the grievances which might motivate a revolutionary movement. This claim is most often made in connection with the Iranian Revolution, which occurred at the end of the turbulent 1970s. Oil revenues certainly did contribute to Iran's economic transformation during the 1970s, as well as a good deal of the corruption in the Shah's court. The oil industry was also strongly associated with foreigners, especially the British and Americans, who were treated differently than Iranians and were typically paid higher salaries. Thus if one looks solely at Iran, it is tempting to point to the oil industry as an explanatory factor to the grievances that motivated the revolution and the institutional weakness in the regime that tried to respond to it.

However, a broader, more comparative perspective yields three reasons to think differently. First, even though Iran did experience significant social and economic change in the 1970s, so did many other petrostates such as Saudi Arabia, Venezuela, and Indonesia, and they did not succumb to revolution during this period. Some petrostates, including Saudi Arabia, experienced considerable domestic unrest, but for a variety of reasons the leaders in other states were more capable of holding onto power than was the Shah of Iran. Second, revolutions also occurred in the 1970s in countries that did not have any oil at all, such as Cambodia, Nicaragua, and Ethiopia. This suggests that the causes of unrest and economic dislocation are complex, and cast doubt on the notion that oil is the determining factor. Third, while revolutions have occurred in petrostates during times of economic

---

[14] One might imagine transnational revolutionaries who could face such a choice, but I consider these rather rare cases.

volatility linked to the oil industry, such as the 1970s, they have also occurred during periods of relative stability in the oil industry, such as Iraq's decade of revolutionary turmoil 1958–1968. We should therefore not be too quick to jump to the conclusion that economic volatility and social transformation linked to oil revenues are the key factor in explaining the onset of revolution.[15]

A third potential link between oil and revolution is the idea that oil causes corruption and other grievances, even if one sets aside the economic volatility associated with the industry. This is certainly plausible, as corruption is an endemic problem in most petrostates. The corrupt activities and excessive patronage in the court of King Faisal of Iraq or King Idris in Libya were explicitly used by revolutionary leaders to inspire their followers and justify their seizure of power. Moreover, corruption is especially incendiary when connected to foreign corporations and interests. Yet it is again worth considering whether revolutions in petrostates are in fact different in this regard. Just a few years before Faisal was overthrown in Iraq, a revolution in Egypt removed King Farouk for many of the same reasons: he was perceived as a corrupt leader who allowed foreign interests, especially the British, too much influence over the country. Similarly, the revolution in Cuba expelled President Batista from office because of his notoriously corrupt and self-serving deals with American business interests. Thus incumbent corruption is a common denominator in revolutions, regardless of whether the state has oil. Further, corruption is insufficient on its own to explain a revolution: numerous leaders, from Trujillo to Franco to Stroessner, have been able to remain in office for decades even when their corruption was widely known.

A fourth potential cause of more frequent revolutions in petrostates is foreign meddling. Oil reserves in petrostates give oil-consuming countries an interest in the type of regime that governs those reserves, and one could imagine that powerful oil-consuming states might seek to fund opposition groups or seed a revolution in the hopes of furthering those interests. This argument is given superficial plausibility by the fact that the US government encouraged Iraqis to rise up against

---

[15] This is not to argue that oil played *no* role in the specific case of the Iranian Revolution. Instead, I am making the more modest point that it is unlikely that oil makes revolution *systematically* much more likely in general. Further, I doubt that oil was the determining factor even in the case of Iran in 1979.

Iraq in 1991, and appears to have given at least tacit permission to a coup attempt against Hugo Chávez in Venezuela in 2002.[16] Yet neither case should be exaggerated: at most, the US government gave verbal support to an opposition group, but did not actually intervene materially in any way. (Also, a revolution did not actually occur in either case.) Just as importantly, most of the time foreign powers seem to have precisely the opposite view of revolutions: i.e., that a revolution could bring significant instability and uncertainty that would be harmful to their interests because it would disrupt global oil markets. The US government's desire to have stability in Saudi Arabia is one reason that it shares intelligence with the Saudi monarchy about its domestic opposition groups, despite US policymakers' nominal desire to see democracy in the Kingdom. Britain also sought in the past to put down insurrections or opposition movements in the name of stability in the Middle East, most famously in Iran in 1953.

In sum, a brief examination of evidence in connection with four plausible causal mechanisms casts doubt on the proposition that oil plays a causal role in revolutions. It is always possible that there exists some other mechanism linking oil to revolution, other than the four already considered. Yet at the very least, this investigation shifts the burden of proof. Those who suspect that oil causes revolution must overcome the considerations and evidence just presented.

Conclusion

This short chapter examined whether oil causes revolutions. Although at first glance this seems quite plausible, closer examination of the issue reveals that theory does not provide us with a clear, unambiguous prediction about the impact of oil on the incidence of revolutions. The quantitative analysis presented here – which is not a full causal model, but a useful inquiry nonetheless – suggests that revolutionary governments are no more (or less) likely to occur in petrostates than in non-petrostates. Closer investigation of specific country cases also fails to provide systematic evidence that oil plays a major causal role in revolutions.

[16] Democracy NOW! 2004; E. Vulliamy, 2002.

11 | *Conclusion and policy implications*

Nothing has taken me aback more as Secretary of State than the way that the politics of energy is – I will use the word "warping" – diplomacy around the world.

– Condoleezza Rice

The academic and policy discourse about the role of oil in world politics has traditionally been dominated by a single narrative about resource competition.[1] One contribution of this book is to highlight how narrow this narrative is. Resource-hungry countries do sometimes go to war in part to secure better access to oil reserves, but that is not the only or even necessarily the most important way in which oil plays a role in international relations. As the evidence in Chapter 1 demonstrates, states that have oil are not just the targets of conquest; they are quite often the ones instigating the conflict. Only recently have scholars begun to systematically identify the full set of causal mechanisms linking oil to international conflict and security, and that work is ongoing.[2] This book seeks to elucidate one especially important mechanism, which I call petro-aggression.

Over the last half-century, petro-aggression has become a prevalent feature of the international political system. Iraq under Saddam Hussein started two major wars and engaged in numerous low-level conflicts. Libya instigated or participated in an array of armed international conflicts, with opponents ranging from neighbors Chad and Egypt to more distant enemies in Tanzania, Israel, and the United States. Iran has been aggressive in one form or another against Israel, Iraq, Afghanistan, the United Arab Emirates, and others. Hugo Chávez

[1] W. Engdahl, 2004; J. Ghazvinian, 2008; R. Goralski and R. Freeburg, 1987; M. Klare, 2002, 2004, 2008; R. Mandel, 1988; E. Osnos, 2006; S. Pelletiere, 2004; S. Randall, 2007; B. Russett, 1981; C. Singer, 2008; A. Westing, 1986; D. Yergin, 2008 [1991]; A. Zalloum, 2007.
[2] J. Colgan, "The Pathways from Oil to War"; C. Glaser, 2011.

transformed Venezuela from a once-peaceful and cooperative state to one that frequently antagonizes its neighbors. Across the Middle East and beyond, petro-aggression is an international phenomenon of the first rate.

This last chapter opens a conversation about how to understand this phenomenon in the contemporary world. The first section of this chapter summarizes the core findings of this book, and applies them retrospectively to the situation in Iraq in the summer of 1990. The second section moves forward by two decades to consider the 2011 Arab Spring, a major political transformation that was unfolding as I wrote this book. The third section identifies a set of outstanding research questions that would benefit from additional attention in the future. Finally, the fourth section turns to the policy implications of my work. While I do not offer direct policy recommendations, I try to provide signposts for those who would apply my research to energy policy and foreign policy.

Summary of key findings

This book takes some of the first steps towards understanding the international dimensions of the resource curse. Traditionally, the resource curse has been thought of as a negative political and economic phenomenon that affects oil-producing states. This book shows that the political interaction between oil and revolutionary government has consequences for international security. The real cost of the resource curse is therefore borne not only by the producers of oil, but also by those states that interact with them. The heavy presence of the US military in the Middle East, which exists in part as a consequence of the United States' desire to maintain order and stability in this vital oil-producing region, is a vivid illustration of the cost of this international dimension of the resource curse.[3]

Quantitatively, the link between oil and international conflict is striking. On average, petrostates initiate militarized interstate disputes (MIDs) at a rate almost twice as high as non-petrostates. Yet

---

[3] The cost of US military deployments in the Middle East alone has been estimated at $28–36 billion per year in the 1980s, and $30–51 billion per year in the 1990s and early 2000s. J. Duffield, 2007: 182; figures quoted are in constant 2006 US dollars.

this average rate masks important variation within the group of petrostates. Non-revolutionary petrostates initiate such disputes at a rate about the same as non-petrostates – a fact that contradicts the common claim that oil and war necessarily go hand-in-hand. Rather, it is actually the small group of petro-revolutionary states that drive the overall figures, because these states initiate international conflicts at a rate two-and-a-half times higher than the typical non-petrostate.

The overall effect of oil income thus depends greatly upon domestic institutions and practices. The qualitative studies presented in Chapters 5–9 support the quantitative results, and provide richer detail on the interaction between oil and domestic politics. Iraq under Hussein, Libya under Qaddafi, and Iran under Khomeini are examples of highly revolutionary states in terms of their domestic politics, and as expected by the theory, they were also highly aggressive in their foreign policy. More moderate revolutionary governments, such as Venezuela under Chávez or Iran after Khomeini's death, tend to be somewhat aggressive in their foreign policy, without necessarily instigating a major international war. Saudi Arabia was non-revolutionary throughout the period under analysis, and remarkably for the Middle East, the Kingdom largely avoided direct interstate military conflicts.

While this book emphasizes the importance of the domestic politics of the petrostate, other factors are important, such as regional dynamics. Indeed, any particular state sits within a web of relationships with other states that can be highly significant for both the degree of aggressiveness in the state's foreign policy actions and for the manner in which this aggression is expressed. One reason that petro-aggression in Iraq looks very different than petro-aggression in Venezuela is due to regional differences and the feasibility with which Venezuela can act aggressively against larger and more powerful neighbors. Thus a state's behavior is affected by its position, both in space and in time, within the web of international politics.[4] Still, while regional factors are important in shaping particular outcomes, this book highlights the robust impact of two variables, oil and revolutionary government, for a state's foreign policy.

[4] P. Diehl and G. Goertz, 2001; P. Hensel, 1999; M. Ward and K. Gleditsch, 2002.

The theory in practice: Iraq, July 1990

The findings of this book suggest that revolutionary states, especially petro-revolutionary ones, ought to be considered high-risk candidates for initiating international conflict. This insight should change how policymakers react to the information available to them. For instance, in the weeks that preceded the Iraqi invasion of Kuwait in August 1990, US policymakers observed conflicting signals of Iraq's intentions and debated their meaning. While the Department of Defense reported that there was a high probability of an attack on Kuwait, the Department of State was not nearly so sure. President Bush received mixed signals. Seeking more information, the US Ambassador April Glaspie met with Saddam Hussein on July 25. That meeting was interrupted by a phone call from Egyptian President Mubarak, which Hussein took in private. When he returned, Hussein reported to Glaspie that the Crown Prince of Kuwait would come to Baghdad for direct one-on-one negotiations with Hussein no later than Monday, July 30. Hussein assured Mubarak, and Glaspie, that "nothing will happen until the meeting, and nothing will happen after the meeting if the Kuwaitis will give us some hope." All smiles, Glaspie congratulated Hussein on the good news. The next morning Glaspie sent a jubilant cable back to Washington: "Saddam has blinked. As far as Iraq's government-directed media on July 26 are concerned, the dispute with Kuwait was a 'summer cloud.' Gone are the headlines outlining Kuwaiti misbehavior; gone are the *ad hominem* attacks on Kuwaiti Foreign Minister al-Sabah; gone are the editorials outlining Iraq's case." Hussein was not going to invade after all.[5]

As it turned out, of course, Glaspie got it wrong. The fact that she got it wrong was eminently excusable: there was a jumble of mixed signals; crises and wars are inherently difficult to predict; and probably few if any diplomats or analysts at the time could have done better in her situation. Nonetheless, this book suggests that policymakers in the future ought to shift their prior beliefs about revolutionary and petro-revolutionary leaders and consider them as high-risk candidates for initiating international conflict. In 1990, the Department of Defense's warnings were based on its observations of Iraqi troop movements near the border of Kuwait, which became increasingly suspicious at the end of July. A signal such as a rapid troop mobilization

---

[5] C. Alfonsi, 2006: 36.

in a region known historically for conflicts, when combined with the evidence of this book about the propensity of certain types of states for aggression, ought to provide future policymakers with a considerable sense of foreboding in a similar situation in the future.

Knowing that a state is a high-risk candidate for conflict could have real consequences in sorting out the mixed signals in a crisis situation. If it had been clear to Washington policymakers in 1990 that the Iraqi invasion was coming, they would have had more time to consider the appropriate US response to such an invasion before it occurred. With more time and more information, they might have concluded that, yes, the United States was willing to go to war in defense of Kuwait. And had they been armed with such a consensus, Washington might have been able to convey to Hussein in clear and unambiguous terms the consequences of his planned invasion, before he invaded. History might have taken a very different course.

Considering the Arab Spring "revolutions"

In 2011, as I was working on this book, a wave of political movements swept through the Middle East, collectively becoming known as the Arab Spring. Long-standing autocratic rulers were challenged and in some cases overthrown. The movements began in Tunisia, swiftly followed by Egypt, and eventually Libya, Yemen, Jordan, Bahrain and Syria each experienced serious revolts. Where the protest movements were successful in overthrowing the government, they were often called revolutions.

What are the implications of the Arab Spring for international security? This book is about oil and revolutionary governments, and at first glance the Arab Spring seems to satisfy both those conditions – and thus one might expect a high risk of international conflict.

Yet it is not so clear that the Arab Spring movements are actually revolutions, in the sense used in this book. I do not wish to diminish the accomplishments of those who fought against Ben Ali, Mubarak, or Qaddafi. They are indubitably rebellions, and some of them have been successful, in the sense of ousting the incumbent leader. Yet in the language of political science, especially in the context of this book, the term revolution has a more precise meaning. A mere change in government leadership does not necessarily signify a revolution. Instead, a deeper transformation of political, economic, and/or social institutions and practices is required. It is not yet clear, at least at the time of writing, that such changes are underway in most of the Arab Spring countries.

Moreover, most of the places that experienced the strongest political transformations – i.e., the greatest departures from their past – are the ones that have the least oil. Tunisia and Egypt produce only a modest amount of oil; Bahrain's industry principally exports Saudi oil; Jordan has no oil industry. The exception – the only unambiguous petrostate to experience real political upheaval – is Libya, and it is not yet clear whether the downfall of Qaddafi will result in a genuine revolution. By contrast, most of the oil-rich countries in the Middle East – Saudi Arabia, Kuwait, Qatar, etc. – largely escaped the destabilizing effects of the Arab Spring, at least to date. As Michael Ross argued in *Foreign Affairs*, oil had the effect of "drowning" the Arab Spring in those countries.[6] Given what the existing research shows about the durability of petrostate regimes, this is not surprising.[7] Overall, then, the Arab Spring will not necessarily generate any petro-revolutionary states (or even any revolutionary non-petrostates) that endanger international security.

The other reason to be partially optimistic about the international consequences of the Arab Spring is that not all revolutions are the same, and not all revolutions cause war. Revolutionary leaders and governments have a higher propensity for international conflict than non-revolutionary governments – *on average*. But some revolutions, and the governments that emerge from them, are not conflict-prone. Consider the wave of democratizing revolutions in Eastern Europe in 1989–1992, which produced a set of post-revolutionary regimes that were not aggressive in their foreign policy. Looking only at the post-Cold War experience, one might suspect that democratizing revolutions are rather good for international peace, though that conclusion is part of an ongoing debate among scholars.[8] My own research suggests that revolutions that put personalist dictators in power are the most dangerous for international peace.[9] Revolutions that lead to improvements in political freedom and democracy,

---

[6] M. Ross, 2011.
[7] K. Morrison, 2009; M. Ross, 2012.
[8] E. Mansfield and J. Snyder, 2005; V. Narang and R. Nelson, 2009.
[9] J. Colgan and J. Weeks, 2011.

on the other hand, do not seem to lead to international conflicts – though many revolutions claim to be democratizing, and identifying which ones are truly democratizing is difficult to do except in retrospect.

This is not to suggest that the Arab Spring will necessarily result in a flowering of liberal democracy in the region, or that regional peace is assured. Nonetheless, there is no reason to think that the Arab Spring makes interstate conflict inevitable.

Further research questions

It would be nice if this book neatly solved all of the relevant intellectual issues, but research does not work that way. As with any complex topic, there are always some questions left unanswered, and some issues that could benefit from closer examination.

The first has to do with revolutionary non-petrostates. As I described in Chapter 3, I chose to focus my historical case studies on petrostates, to better understand how revolutionary politics affected their dynamics and led to aggressive foreign policy. The price of this choice is that my research relies more heavily on the quantitative analysis of Chapter 4. Figure 11.1 (drawn from the analysis in Chapter 4) illustrates that while revolutionary states generally instigate more international conflict than non-revolutionary states, oil income tends to amplify this effect. Ideally, future research could use cross-national historical analysis to compare revolutions in non-petrostates to those in petrostates. For instance, one might be able to compare Egypt under Nasser or China under Mao to the petro-revolutionary cases, and ask the difficult counterfactual question: what would the Nasserite or Maoist regimes have been like if they had had oil? While such a study might reveal new insights, the difficulty of completing it should not be underestimated. It is much more difficult to compare revolutionary governments across states than it is to compare different governments of the same state (which was the aim of the case studies in this book). The cross-national comparison involves multiple differences associated with the shift in context (at minimum a different national culture, different geography, different historical legacy, and different revolutionary environment), potentially weakening any inferences drawn from the analysis.

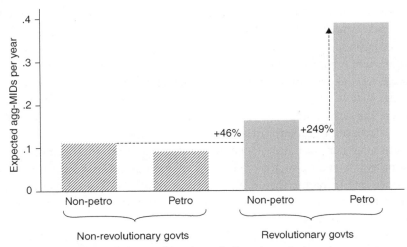

Figure 11.1 Effect of the combination of oil and revolutionary governments on MIDs

Still, if these obstacles can be overcome, additional lessons might be learned about how non-oil sources of revenue might have similar or different effects as oil. For instance, the Cuban Revolution under Castro benefited from massive foreign aid from its patron, the Soviet Union. This external revenue enabled the Cuban regime to be far more militarily aggressive than one would normally expect from a small island nation. In this sense, one might think of foreign aid as having a similar effect as oil income in the Cuban case. Yet it seems likely that there are differences, as well: unlike oil income, foreign aid comes with a donor, and donors have desires and goals of their own. This means that Cuba's military interventions, especially those in Africa, were partially shaped and conditioned by the extent to which the Soviet Union approved of them and was willing to supply weapons and materials.

Another question which could benefit from additional research is the extent to which the interaction between oil and revolutions generalizes to any valuable natural resource.[10] In Chapter 4, I conducted a very preliminary investigation of this question, and found no evidence of a similar pattern of aggressive foreign policy. This negative finding might simply be due to a small-n problem, in the sense that there are

---

[10] The relationship between water and international relations is already the subject of research, for example K. Conca, 2005.

fewer countries that are as dependent on a non-oil resource as there are petrostates, and the subset of revolutionary states that are dependent on a non-oil resource is even fewer. On the other hand, it could be that there is something genuinely special about oil. I discuss some possible reasons why in Chapter 3. One further possibility is that oil provides such large revenues that a state can be both heavily dependent on them (as a percentage of GDP) and made rich by them (and thus able to purchase large quantities of advanced weaponry). While it is not unusual for a poor state to be highly dependent on another non-tax source of revenue, such as diamonds or foreign aid, it is rare for the same state to be made rich by it. Thus it might be that oil income is uniquely dangerous, in combination with revolutionary governments, for international security.

Doubtless one could identify additional research questions to explore, and I earnestly hope that scholars will do so. My wish is to further that conversation, and to offer in this book some useful material as a foundation for research.

Policy implications in a changing world

This book develops and tests a new theory. The work of applying that theory within the context of specific policy problems remains to be done. My findings suggest that the elevated conflict propensity of petro-revolutionary states should be taken seriously, perhaps more seriously than it has in the past (e.g., with Iraq in July 1990); but how exactly the United States or any other country should respond to such challenges depends greatly on the specific circumstances.

Still, the research presented here can contribute to the framework by which policy is developed. At a minimum, this book adds to the growing list of reasons why economic dependence on oil is a negative force in the world. Oil income funds petro-revolutionary states, which fuels their aggression and creates international conflict. It is no coincidence that the United States and its allies spend a substantial amount of public wealth – and human lives – in military deployments that are directly or indirectly connected to the global oil industry.[11] When added to the other negative consequences of the global oil industry – which include environmental degradation, economic volatility, political corruption,

[11] J. Duffield, 2007.

and more frequent civil wars in oil-producing countries[12] – the findings of this book raise a host of political, economic, and moral questions about the world's continued dependence on petroleum as a primary source of energy. For all these reasons, policies and technologies that create incentives for alternatives to oil, especially those that are based on renewable sources, have potentially very positive consequences for global affairs.

Consequently, my research provides support and rationale for two broad policy initiatives. The first is to end our over-reliance on oil as a form of energy, especially in the transportation sector. Energy independence, properly conceived, is both desirable and feasible for the United States in the medium- to long-term. Energy independence emphatically does not require energy autarky – that is, that a country should try to achieve self-sufficiency in energy. I use the term energy independence to mean minimizing the harmful externalities associated with energy production and consumption, and reducing the risk of supply disruptions to a managerial rather than strategic problem. In practical terms, this requires an end to the stranglehold that petroleum has on the transportation sector. Energy independence is probably possible only when there are commercially viable alternatives to petroleum as a fuel for transportation. There are technologies in existence, and more being developed, that could help with this goal. Plotting a strategy towards genuine energy independence, as I mean the term, lies far beyond the scope of this book.[13] There is no doubt that releasing the transportation sector from the grip of the oil industry will require significant investments in technological innovation and in infrastructure. I do not claim to know which investments need to be made. What I do know is that those investments have the potential to contribute to international peace. And surely that is a pay-off that should not be lightly dismissed.

Nonetheless, oil is going to be a vital part of the global economy for at least a few more decades, and probably longer.[14] As a consequence, we need a set of policies to address the harmful geopolitical consequences of the oil sector during that period of transition. Moreover,

---

[12] P. Le Billon, 2005; S. Brown and H. Huntington, 2010; P. Collier and A. Hoeffler, 2004; J. Fearon and D. Laitin, 2003; P. Leiby 2007; M. Ross, 2012.
[13] Others are working on this problem – see, for example, A. Korin and G. Luft, 2009; D. Sandalow, 2007.
[14] K. Crane *et al.*, 2009; J. Deutch and J. Schlesinger, 2006.

changes in the energy markets that are already underway – stemming from geological constraints, new consumption patterns, global climate change, and a production shift away from democratic countries – will alter the relationship between oil and international security. To keep up with a changing world, we must change our ways of thinking about the geopolitics of oil.

This leads to the second policy implication of my research, which is support for the effort to better manage the resource curse in oil-producing countries. Efforts by developed countries to alleviate the resource curse typically are seen as altruistic or humanitarian: they aim to help poor oil-producing countries to develop economically and avoid civil wars. Yet my research suggests that developed countries should recognize that these efforts serve their own interests. The same mechanisms that underlie the resource curse, namely the tendency of oil to reduce the domestic accountability on state leaders, has serious consequences for international security in the form of petro-aggression. Left unchecked, the resource curse can become petro-aggression when a revolutionary government comes to power, with the nearly inevitable consequence that developed countries feel compelled to address its consequences. It is not by accident that the United States spends billions of dollars per year on its military presence in the Middle East and North Africa. Therefore efforts to manage the resource curse, by putting in place institutions, norms, and practices to better manage the inflow of oil income and enhance domestic political accountability, are in everyone's interest. Efforts such as Publish What You Pay or the Extractive Industries Transparency Initiative are probably necessary though insufficient steps toward that goal.[15] In sum, preventing the resource curse is not just in the interests of developing countries; it is in the national security interests of developed countries, especially the United States.

The resource curse and by extension the issue of petro-aggression could become even more significant in the coming years due to a shift in the geopolitical conditions of petroleum production. Increasing worldwide demand is likely to cause increased oil production in autocratic and sometimes politically unstable regions of the world. (North American oil production is also increasing rapidly thanks to the boom

---

[15] The Natural Resources Charter is a promising step toward a more comprehensive approach.

shale oil production, but on its own North America is unlikely to be able to supply all of the net increase in world demand.) By one estimate, more than half of future supply potential is projected to come from just three countries: Saudi Arabia, Iraq, and Iran.[16]

With this shift in the global market, the amount of oil income that flows into autocratic and weakly-institutionalized states is set to increase. These are precisely the countries that are the most likely sites of future revolutionary governments. If a revolutionary government were to emerge in Saudi Arabia or Iraq, it could have disastrous consequences. Of course, it is impossible to predict with any certainty which specific states are most likely to have revolutionary governments in the future. Nonetheless, one of the great lessons of my research is that revolutionary government and large oil incomes are a toxic combination for international peace and security. We might therefore expect further turbulence and political violence in oil-producing regions in the future.

Since the Arab oil embargo in 1973, almost a quarter of the world's militarized interstate disputes have involved at least one petrostate.[17] Localized resource abundance, which produces petro-aggression, has proven to be as important a threat to international peace as global resource scarcity. The problem of oil and war thus extends far beyond intellectual inquiry. For scholars as well as policymakers, oil and energy deserve to be seen as central to issues of modern international peace and conflict.

---

[16] M. El-Gamal and A. Jaffe, 2010: 156. Note that even if this is true, it is still also likely that many African states will become significant oil producers, as discussed in Chapter 1. The problem is thus both wide and deep.

[17] Correlates of War database, based on F. Ghosn *et al.*, 2004. Author's analysis.

References

Aarts, Paul, and Gerd Nonneman, eds. 2006. *Saudi Arabia in the Balance*. London: Hurst and Company.

Abrahamian, Ervand. 2008. *A History of Modern Iran*. New York: Cambridge University Press.

Aburish, Said K. 2001. *Saddam Hussein: The Politics of Revenge*. New edn. London: Bloomsbury UK.

Acemoglu, D., S. Johnson, J. A. Robinson, and P. Yared. 2008. "Income and democracy." *American Economic Review* 98(3): 808–842.

Agence France Presse. 2007. "Uribe: Chávez wants a Marxist FARC government in Colombia." http://afp.google.com/article/ ALeqM5h38LF1xlbHKvSwV8pfmsfWV93Ddw.

Alfonsi, Christian. 2006. *Circle in the Sand: Why We Went Back to Iraq*. New York: Doubleday.

Al-Rasheed, Madawi. 2002. *A History of Saudi Arabia*. Cambridge University Press.

Amirahmadi, Hooshang. 1990. *Revolution and Economic Transition: The Iranian Experience*. Albany: SUNY Press.

Andersen, J. J., and Silje Aslaksen. n.d. "Oil and political survival." *Working paper*.

Anderson, Lisa. 1986. *The State and Social Transformation in Tunisia and Libya, 1830–1980*. Princeton University Press.

Baburkin, S., A. C. Danopoulos, R. Giacolone, and E. Moreno. 1999. "The 1992 coup attempts in Venezuela: causes and failure." *Journal of Political and Military Sociology* 27(1): 141–154.

Bakhash, S. 1982. *The Politics of Oil and Revolution in Iran: A Staff Paper*. Washington, DC: Brookings Institution Press.

Barbieri, Katherine. 2005. *The Liberal Illusion: Does Trade Promote Peace?* Ann Arbor: University of Michigan Press.

Barma, Naazneen, Kai Kaiser, Tuan Minh Le, and Lorena Viñuela. 2011. *Rents to Riches? The Political Economy of Natural Resource-Led Development*. World Bank Publications.

Barnes, Joe, and Amy Myers Jaffe. 2006. "The Persian Gulf and the geopolitics of oil." *Survival* 48(1): 143–162.

BBC. 2002. "Chávez accused of fostering militia links." http://news.bbc.
co.uk/2/hi/americas/2038827.stm (accessed October 30, 2008).

2006. "Storm over Venezuela oil speech." http://news.bbc.co.uk/2/hi/
americas/6114682.stm (accessed March 4, 2010).

2008. "Colombia calls for Chávez charges." http://news.bbc.co.uk/2/hi/
americas/7277313.stm.

BBC Mundo. 2008. "48 horas frenéticas." http://news.bbc.co.uk/hi/spanish/
latin_america/newsid_7274000/7274806.stm.

Bearce, D.H., and J.A. Laks Hutnick. 2011. "Toward an alternative explanation for the resource curse: natural resources, immigration, and democratization." *Comparative Political Studies* 44(6): 689.

Beblawi, Hazem, and Giacomo Luciani. 1987. *The Rentier State*. Croom Helm.

Beck, N., J. N. Katz, and R. Tucker. 1998. "Taking time seriously: time-series-cross-section analysis with a binary dependent variable." *American Journal of Political Science* 42: 1260–1288.

Bellin, Eva. 2004. "The robustness of authoritarianism in the Middle East." *Comparative Politics* 36(2): 139–157.

Bill, James A. 1989. *The Eagle and the Lion: The Tragedy of American-Iranian Relations*. New Haven: Yale University Press.

Le Billon, P. 2005. *Fuelling War: Natural Resources and Armed Conflict*. London: Routledge for the International Institute for Strategic Studies.

2007. "Geographies of war: perspectives on 'resource wars'." *Geography Compass* 1(2): 163–182.

Blainey, Geoffrey. 1988. *The Causes of War*. 3rd edn. New York: Free Press.

Boix, Carles, and Susan Carol Stokes. 2007. *The Oxford Handbook of Comparative Politics*. New York: Oxford University Press.

Bond, R. D. 1977. *Contemporary Venezuela and its Role in International Affairs*. New York University Press.

Bowen, Wayne H. 2008. *The History of Saudi Arabia*. Westport: Greenwood Press.

Braut-Hegghammer, Malfrid. 2008. "Libya's nuclear turnaround: perspectives from Tripoli." *Middle East Journal* 62(1): 55–72.

Bronson, Rachel. 2006. *Thicker than Oil: America's Uneasy Partnership with Saudi Arabia*. New York: Oxford University Press.

Brown, Anthony Cave. 1999. *Oil, God, and Gold: The Story of Aramco and the Saudi Kings*. Boston: Houghton Mifflin.

Brown, S. P. A., and H. Huntington. 2010. "Reassessing the oil security premium." *Discussion Paper DP10–05*.

Bueno de Mesquita, B., A. Smith, R. M. Siverson, and J. D. Morrow. 2004. *The Logic of Political Survival*. Cambridge, MA: MIT Press.

Bulloch, John, and Harvey Morris. 1991. *Saddam's War: The Origins of the Kuwait Conflict and the International Response*. London: Faber & Faber.

Bunce, Valerie. 1981. *Do New Leaders Make a Difference? Executive Succession and Public Policy Under Capitalism and Socialism*. Princeton University Press.

Burrell, Robert Michael, and Alvin J. Cottrell. 1974. *Iran, Afghanistan, Pakistan: Tensions and Dilemmas*. Beverly Hills: Sage Publications.

Byman, D. L., and K. M. Pollack. 2001. "Let us now praise great men: bringing the statesman back in." *International Security* 25(4): 107–146.

Chan, Steve. 1980. "The consequences of expensive oil on arms transfers." *Journal of Peace Research* 17(3): 235–246.

Chaudhry, Kiren Aziz. 1997. *The Price of Wealth: Economies and Institutions in the Middle East*. Ithaca: Cornell University Press.

Cheon, Andrew, and Johannes Urpelainen. 2012. "Oil prices and energy technology innovation: an empirical analysis." *Global Environmental Change* 22(2): 407–417.

Chiozza, Giacomo, and H. E. Goemans. 2011. *Leaders and International Conflict*. New York: Cambridge University Press.

Choucri, Nazli, and Robert North. 1975. *Nations in Conflict: National Growth and International Violence*. San Francisco: W. H. Freeman & Co.

Christensen, Thomas J. 1996. *Useful Adversaries*. Princeton University Press.

Chubin, Shahram, and Charles Tripp. 1988. *Iran and Iraq at War*. London: I. B. Tauris.

Chubin, Shahram, and Sepehr Zabih. 1974. *The Foreign Relations of Iran: A Developing State in a Zone of Great-Power Conflict*. Berkeley: University of California Press.

Clouston, Eric. 1992. "King with no crown defies Gadafy." *Guardian*. http://news.bbc.co.uk/onthisday/hi/dates/stories/september/1/newsid_3911000/3911587.stm (accessed March 19, 2009).

CNN. 2005. "US dismisses call for Chávez's killing." www.cnn.com/2005/US/08/23/robertson.Chávez/ (accessed February 10, 2008).

2008. "Chávez: take FARC off terror list." www.cnn.com/2008/WORLD/americas/01/11/Chávez.farc/.

Colgan, Jeff D. 2010. "Oil and revolutionary governments: fuel for international conflict." *International Organization* 64(4): 661–694.

2011a. "Changing oil revenue, persistent authoritarianism." In MPSA Annual Meeting.

2011b. "Oil and resource-backed aggression." *Energy Policy* 39: 1669–1676.

2011c. "Venezuela and military expenditure data." *Journal of Peace Research* 48(4): 547–556.

2012. "Measuring revolution." *Conflict Management and Peace Science* 29(4): 444–467.

Colgan, Jeff D., and Jessica Weeks. 2011. "Revolution, personalist dictatorships, and international conflict." Peace Science Society (International) Meeting, Los Angeles, CA.

Collier, David, and Henry E. Brady. 2004. *Rethinking Social Inquiry: Diverse Tools, Shared Standards.* Lanham: Rowman & Littlefield Publishers.

Collier, Paul, and Anke Hoeffler. 2004. "Greed and grievance in civil war." *Oxford Economic Papers* 56(4): 563–595.

Collins, S. D. 2005. "Breaking the mold? Venezuela's defiance of the neoliberal agenda." *New Political Science* 27(3): 367–395.

Conca, Ken. 2005. *Governing Water: Contentious Transnational Politics and Global Institution Building.* 1st edn. The MIT Press.

Congressional Research Service. 2008. *Venezuela: Political Conditions and US Policy.* Washington, DC: Congressional Research Service.

Cooper, A. S. 2008. "Showdown at Doha: the secret oil deal that helped sink the Shah of Iran." *The Middle East Journal* 62(4): 567–591.

Cordesman, Anthony H. 2003. *Saudi Arabia Enters the Twenty-First Century: The Political, Foreign Policy, Economic, and Energy Dimensions.* Westport: Praeger.

2004. "The proliferation of weapons of mass destruction in the Middle East."

2007. "Iran's Revolutionary Guards, the Al Quds Force, and other intelligence and paramilitary forces."

Coughlin, Con. 2002. *Saddam: King of Terror.* 1st edn. New York: Ecco.

Crane, K., A. Goldthau, and M. Toman. 2009. *Imported Oil and US National Security.* Santa Monica: Rand Corp.

Crystal, Jill. 1990. *Oil and Politics in the Gulf: Rulers and Merchants in Kuwait and Qatar.* 1st edn. Cambridge University Press.

Dahl, R. A. 1961. *Who Governs? Democracy and Power in an American City.* New Haven: Yale University Press.

Davis, Christina L. 2003. *Food Fights over Free Trade: How International Institutions Promote Agricultural Trade Liberalization.* Princeton University Press.

Deeb, Mary Jane. 1991. *Libya's Foreign Policy in North Africa.* Boulder: Westview Press.

Democracy NOW! 2004. "CIA documents show Bush knew of 2002 coup in Venezuela." www.democracynow.org/2004/11/29/cia_documents_show_bush_knew_of.

Deutch, J. M., and J. R. Schlesinger. 2006. *National Security Consequences of US Oil Dependency.* Council on Foreign Relations Press.

Diehl, P. F. 1985. "Contiguity and military escalation in major power rivalries, 1816–1980." *The Journal of Politics* 47(4): 1203–1211.

Diehl, P. F., and G. Goertz. 2001. *War and Peace in International Rivalry*. Ann Arbor: University of Michigan Press.

Diwan, Kristin. 2009. "Sovereign dilemmas: Saudi Arabia and sovereign wealth funds." *Geopolitics* 14(2): 345–360.

Downes, Alexander B. 2008. *Targeting Civilians in War*. Ithaca: Cornell University Press.

2009. "How smart and tough are democracies? Reassessing theories of democratic victory in war." *International Security* 33(4): 9–51.

Doyle, Michael. 1986. "Liberalism and world politics." *American Political Science Review* 80(December): 1151–1169.

Von Drehle, David, and R. Jeffrey Smith. 1993. "U.S. strikes Iraq for plot to kill Bush." *Washington Post*: A01.

Duffield, John. 2007. *Over a Barrel: The Costs of U.S. Foreign Oil Dependence*. Stanford Law and Politics.

Dunning, T. 2005. "Resource dependence, economic performance, and political stability." *Journal of Conflict Resolution* 49(4): 451–482.

2008. *Crude Democracy: Natural Resource Wealth and Political Regimes*. Cambridge University Press.

Dunning, T., and L. Wirpsa. 2004. "Oil and the political economy of conflict in Colombia and beyond: a linkages approach." *Geopolitics* 9(1): 81–108.

The Economist. 2010. "Carats and sticks," April 3, p. 68.

El-Gamal, Mahmoud A., and Amy Myers Jaffe. 2010. *Oil, Dollars, Debt, and Crises: The Global Curse of Black Gold*. 1st edn. Cambridge University Press.

Ellner, Steve. 2008. *Rethinking Venezuelan Politics: Class, Conflict, and the Chávez Phenomenon*. Boulder: Lynne Rienner.

El Mundo. 2008. "Colombia se disculpa ante Ecuador por la incursión 'obligada' en su territorio." www.elmundo.es/elmundo/2008/03/03/internacional/1204512283.html.

El Nacional. 2008. "Piden a Chávez verdaderos cambios y no rotaciones."

El Tiempo. 2008. "Venezuela Especial: En los confines de Colombia."

El Universal. 2004. "Chávez advierte a Bush sobre nuevos Vietnam."

El Universal. 2006. "Chávez anunció núcleos endógenos militares para la resistencia." www.eluniversal.com/2006/01/18/eco_art_18202C.shtml.

El Warfally, Mahmoud G. 1988. *Imagery and Ideology in U.S. Policy Toward Libya, 1969–1982*. University of Pittsburgh Press.

Engdahl, F. William. 2004. *A Century of War: Anglo-American Oil Politics and the New World Order*. 1st edn. London: Pluto Press.

Enterline, Andrew J. 1998. "Regime changes and interstate conflict 1816–1992." *Political Research Quarterly* 51(2): 385–409.

Evera, Stephen Van. 1997. *Guide to Methods for Students of Political Science*. Ithaca: Cornell University Press.

1999. *Causes of War: Power and the Roots of Conflict*. Ithaca: Cornell University Press.

Farouk-Sluglett, Marion, and Peter Sluglett. 1987. *Iraq since 1958: From Revolution to Dictatorship*. London: I. B. Tauris.

Fearon, J. D. 1995. "Rationalist explanations for war." *International Organization* 49(3): 379–414.

Fearon, J. D., and D. D. Laitin. 2003. "Ethnicity, insurgency, and civil war." *American Political Science Review* 97(1): 75–90.

Felter, Joseph, and Brian Fishman. 2008. *Iranian Strategy in Iraq: Politics and "Other Means."* Military Academy West Point.

Fenno, Richard F. 1978. *Home Style: House Members in their Districts*. New York: Longman.

Fesharaki, Fereidun. 1976. *Development of the Iranian Oil Industry: International and Domestic Aspects*. New York: Praeger.

Filson, D., and S. Werner. 2004. "Bargaining and fighting: the impact of regime type on war onset, duration, and outcomes." *American Journal of Political Science* 48(2): 296–313.

Forero, Juan. 2008a. "FARC computer files are authentic, Interpol probe finds." *The Washington Post*. www.washingtonpost.com/wp-dyn/content/article/2008/05/15/AR2008051504153_pf.html.

2008b. "U.S. links 3 Chávez aides to guerrillas." *The Washington Post*. www.washingtonpost.com/wp-dyn/content/article/2008/09/12/AR2008091201328_pf.html.

Fortna, Virginia Page. 2004. *Peace Time: Cease-Fire Agreements and the Durability of Peace*. Princeton University Press.

2008. *Does Peacekeeping Work? shaping Belligerents' Choices after Civil War*. Princeton University Press.

Fox, J. 1994. "The difficult transition from clientelism to citizenship: lessons from Mexico." *World Politics* 46(2): 151–184.

Frachon, Alain. 1986. "Les defauts de l'armure du colonel." *Le Monde*.

Fravel, M. Taylor. 2008. *Strong Borders, Secure Nation: Cooperation and Conflict in China's Territorial Disputes*. Princeton University Press.

Fundacion de Justicia y Democracia. 2008. *Regalos del Gobierno de Venezuela al Mundo*.

Gabbay, Rony. 1978. *Communism and Agrarian Reform in Iraq*. London: Croom Helm.

Gartzke, E. 2000. "Preferences and the democratic peace." *International Studies Quarterly* 44(2): 191–212.

2007. "The capitalist peace." *American Journal of Political Science* 51(1): 166–191.

Gasto Publico Anunciado por el Gobierno Venezolano en el exterior. 2007. Centro de Investigaciones Economicas.

Gause, F. Gregory. 1990. *Saudi-Yemeni Relations: Domestic Structures and Foreign Influence*. New York: Columbia University Press.

  1994. *Oil Monarchies: Domestic and Security Challenges in the Arab Gulf States*. New York: Council on Foreign Relations Press.

Gelpi, Christopher F., and Joseph M. Grieco. 2008. "Democracy, Interdependence, and the Sources of the Liberal Peace." *Journal of Peace Research* 45(1): 17–36.

George, Alexander L., and Andrew Bennett. 2005. *Case Studies and Theory Development in the Social Sciences*. Cambridge, MA: MIT Press.

Gerring, John. 2012. *Social Science Methodology: A Unified Framework*. 2nd edn. Cambridge University Press.

Ghazvinian, John. 2008. *Untapped: The Scramble for Africa's Oil*. Orlando: Houghton Mifflin Harcourt.

Gholz, Eugene, and Daryl G. Press. 2010. "Protecting 'the prize': oil and the US national interest." *Security Studies* 19(3): 453–485.

Ghosn, F., G. Palmer, and S. A Bremer. 2004. "The MID3 data set, 1993–2001: procedures, coding rules, and description." *Conflict Management and Peace Science* 21(2): 133.

Gilpin, Robert. 1981. *War and Change in World Politics*. Cambridge University Press.

Giraldo, Jeanne K., and Harold A. Trinkunas. 2007. *Terrorism Financing and State Responses: A Comparative Perspective*. Stanford University Press.

Glaser, Charles L. 2010. *Rational Theory of International Politics: The Logic of Competition and Cooperation*. Princeton University Press.

  2011. "Reframing energy security: the international security implications of energy dependence and vulnerability." ISA Annual Meeting, Montreal.

Gleditsch, Kristian Skrede, Idean Salehyan, and Kenneth Schultz. 2008. "Fighting at home, fighting abroad: how civil wars lead to international disputes." *Journal of Conflict Resolution* 52(4): 479–506.

Gleditsch, N. P. 1998. "Armed conflict and the environment: a critique of the literature." *Journal of Peace Research* 35(3): 381.

Goemans, Hein Erich. 2000. *War and Punishment: The Causes of War Termination and the First World War*. Princeton University Press.

Goemans, Hein, and Mark Fey. 2008. "Risky but rational: war as an institutionally induced gamble." *Journal of Politics* 71(1): 35–54.

Goemans, Henk E., Kristian Skrede Gleditsch, and Giacomo Chiozza. 2009. "Introducing archigos: a dataset of political leaders." *Journal of Peace Research* 46(2): 269–283.

Goertz, Gary, and James Mahoney. 2012. *A Tale of Two Cultures: Qualitative and Quantitative Research in the Social Sciences.* Princeton University Press.

Goldberg, Ellis, Erik Wibbels, and Eric Mvukiyehe. 2008. "Lessons from strange cases: democracy, development, and the resource curse in the U.S. states." *Comparative Political Studies* 41(4–5): 477–514.

Goldgeier, Professor James M. 1994. *Leadership Style and Soviet Foreign Policy: Stalin, Khrushchev, Brezhnev, Gorbachev.* The Johns Hopkins University Press.

Goldstein, Joshua S. 2011. *Winning the War on War: The Decline of Armed Conflict Worldwide.* New York: Dutton Adult.

Goldstone, Jack A. 1997. "Revolution, war, and security." *Security Studies* 6(2): 127–151.

Goldthau, Andreas, and Jan Martin Witte. 2011. "Assessing OPEC's performance in global energy." *Global Policy* 2: 31–39.

Goralski, Robert, and Russell W. Freeburg. 1987. *Oil & War: How the Deadly Struggle for Fuel in WWII Meant Victory or Defeat.* 1st edn. New York: William Morrow and Company, Inc.

Gott, Richard. 2005. *Hugo Chávez: The Bolivarian Revolution in Venezuela.* London: Verso.

Gowa, Joanne. 2000. *Ballots and Bullets: The Elusive Democratic Peace.* Princeton University Press.

Guardian. 2008. "Venezuelan troops mobilise as FARC dispute nears boiling point." www.guardian.co.uk/world/2008/mar/04/colombia.venezuela?gusrc=rss&feed=networkfront.

2010a. "US embassy cables: Omani official wary of Iranian expansionism." www.guardian.co.uk/world/us-embassy-cables-documents/165127 (accessed April 15, 2011).

2010b. "US embassy cables: Saudi king urges US strike on Iran." www.guardian.co.uk/world/us-embassy-cables-documents/150519 (accessed February 27, 2011).

Gurr, Ted R. 1970. *Why Men Rebel.* Princeton University Press.

1988. "War, revolution, and the growth of the coercive state." *Comparative Political Studies* 21(1): 45.

Haber, Stephen, and Victor Menaldo. 2011. "Do natural resources fuel authoritarianism? A reappraisal of the resource curse." *American Political Science Review* 105(1): 1–26.

Hafez, Mohammed M. 2008. "Radicalization in the Persian Gulf: assessing the potential of Islamist militancy in Saudi Arabia and Yemen."

Dynamics of Asymmetric Conflict: Pathways toward Terrorism and Genocide 1(1): 6.

Halliday, Fred. 1979. *Iran: Dictatorship and Development.* Harmondsworth: Penguin.

1999. *Revolution and World Politics: The Rise and Fall of the Sixth Great Power.* Durham, NC: Duke University Press Books.

Hart, Gary. 2004. "My secret talks with Libya, and why they went nowhere." *Washington Post.*

Hawkins, K. A., and D. R. Hansen. 2006. "Dependent civil society: the Círculos Bolivarianos in Venezuela." *Latin American Research Review* 41(1): 102–132.

Hegghammer, Thomas. 2009. "Jihad, yes, but not revolution: explaining the extraversion of Islamist violence in Saudi Arabia." *British Journal of Middle Eastern Studies* 36(3): 395–416.

Hegghammer, Thomas, and Stéphane Lacroix. 2007. "Rejectionist Islamism in Saudi Arabia: the story of Juhayman al-Utaybi revisited." *International Journal of Middle East Studies* 39(1).

2010. *Jihad in Saudi Arabia: Violence and Pan-Islamism since 1979.* 1st edn. New York: Cambridge University Press.

2011. "The rise of Muslim foreign fighters: Islam and the globalization of jihad." *International Security* 35(3): 53–94.

Hegre, H., and N. Sambanis. 2006. "Sensitivity analysis of empirical results on civil war onset." *Journal of Conflict Resolution* 50(4): 508.

Hensel, P. R. 1999. "An evolutionary approach to the study of interstate rivalry." *Conflict Management and Peace Science* 17(2): 175.

Herb, Michael. 1999. *All in the Family: Absolutism, Revolution, and Democracy in the Middle Eastern Monarchies.* Albany: State University of New York Press.

2004. "Princes and parliaments in the Arab world." *The Middle East Journal* 58(3): 367–384.

Hertog, Steffen. 2010. *Princes, Brokers, and Bureaucrats.* Ithaca: Cornell University Press.

Hinnebusch, Raymond A., and Anoushiravan Ehteshami. 2002. *The Foreign Policies of Middle East States.* Boulder: Lynne Rienner Publishers.

Hiro, Dilip. 1985. *Iran under the Ayatollahs.* London: Routledge & K. Paul.

Homer-Dixon, T. F. 1999. *Environment, Scarcity, and Violence.* Princeton University Press.

Horowitz, Michael, Rose McDermott, and Allan C Stam. 2005. "Age, regime type, and violence." *Journal of Conflict Resolution* 49(5): 661–885.

Howell, William G., and Jon C. Pevehouse. 2007. *While Dangers Gather: Congressional Checks on Presidential War Powers*. Princeton University Press.

Human Rights Watch. 2006. *Venezuela: Human Rights Overview*. www.hrw.org/legacy/english/docs/2006/01/18/venezu12258.htm (accessed November 10, 2008).

Humphreys, M. 2005. "Natural resources, conflict, and conflict resolution: uncovering the mechanisms." *Journal of Conflict Resolution* 49(4): 508.

Humphreys, Macartan, Jeffrey Sachs, and Joseph E. Stiglitz. 2007. *Escaping the Resource Curse*. New York: Columbia University Press.

Huntington, S. P. 1968. *Political Order in Changing Societies*. New Haven: Yale University Press.

1996. *The Clash of Civilizations and the Remaking of World Order*. New York: Simon & Schuster.

Huth, Paul K. 1998. *Standing Your Ground: Territorial Disputes and International Conflict*. Ann Arbor: University of Michigan Press.

Huth, Paul K., and Todd L. Allee. 2003. *The Democratic Peace and Territorial Conflict in the Twentieth Century*. Cambridge University Press.

Ikenberry, G. J. 1986. "The irony of state strength: comparative responses to the oil shocks in the 1970s." *International Organization* 40(1): 105–137.

Jensen, N., and L. Wantchekon. 2004. "Resource wealth and political regimes in Africa." *Comparative Political Studies* 37(7): 816.

Jentleson, Bruce W. 1986. *Pipeline Politics: The Complex Political Economy of East-West Energy Trade*. Cornell University Press.

Jervis, Robert. 1976. *Perception and Misperception in International Politics*. 1st edn. Princeton University Press.

Johnston, Alastair Iain. 1998. *Cultural Realism: Strategic Culture and Grand Strategy in Chinese History*. Princeton University Press.

Jones, Bart. 2008. *Hugo! The Hugo Chávez Story from Mud Hut to Perpetual Revolution*. Hanover: Steerforth.

Jones, D. M., S. 'A. Bremer, and J. D. Singer. 1996. "Militarized interstate disputes, 1816–1992: rationale, coding rules, and empirical patterns." *Conflict Management and Peace Science* 15(2): 163.

Jones, T. C. 2006. "Rebellion on the Saudi periphery: modernity, marginalization, and the Shia Uprising of 1979." *International Journal of Middle East Studies* 38(2): 213–233.

Kaldor, Mary, Terry Karl, and Yahia Said. 2007. *Oil Wars*. London: Pluto Press.

Kalyvas, S. N. 2006. *The Logic of Violence in Civil War*. Cambridge University Press.

Karimi, Nasser. 2007. "Hugo Chávez receives Iran's highest honor." *Associated Press.*

Karl, T. L. 1997. *The Paradox of Plenty.* Berkeley: University of California Press.

Karsh, Efraim, and Inari Rautsi. 2003. *Saddam Hussein.* New York: Grove Press.

Katzenstein, Peter J., ed. 1996. *The Culture of National Security: Norms and Identity in World Politics.* New York: Columbia University Press.

Kechichian, Joseph A. 2001. *Succession in Saudi Arabia.* New York: Palgrave Macmillan.

Keddie, Nikki R. 2006. *Modern Iran: Roots and Results of Revolution, Updated Edition.* New Haven: Yale University Press.

Kemp, Geoffrey. 2010. *The East Moves West: India, China, and Asia's Growing Presence in the Middle East.* 2nd edn. Washington, DC: Brookings Institution Press.

Keohane, Nannerl O. 2010. *Thinking about Leadership.* Princeton University Press.

Keohane, Robert O., and Joseph S. Nye. 1977. *Power and Independence.* Boston: Little Brown.

Kerr, M. H. 1971. *The Arab Cold War: Gamal Abd al-Nasir and His Rivals, 1958–1970.* London: Oxford University Press.

Khalil, Samir. 1990. *Republic of Fear: The Inside Story of Saddam's Iraq.* New York: Pantheon Books.

King, Gary, Robert O. Keohane, and Sidney Verba. 1994. *Designing Social Inquiry.* Illustrated edn. Princeton University Press.

Kirshner, J. 2000. "Rationalist explanations for war?" *Security Studies* 10(1): 143–150.

Kissinger, Henry. 2000. *Years of Renewal.* New York: Simon & Schuster.

Kitschelt, Herbert, and Steven Wilkinson. 2007. *Patrons, Clients, and Policies.* Cambridge University Press.

Klare, Michael T. 2002. *Resource Wars: The New Landscape of Global Conflict.* New York: Holt Paperbacks.

  2004. *Blood and Oil: The Dangers and Consequences of America's Growing Dependency on Imported Petroleum.* 1st edn. New York: Metropolitan Books.

  2008. *Rising Powers, Shrinking Planet: The New Geopolitics of Energy.* 1st edn. New York: Metropolitan Books.

Korin, Anne, and Gal Luft. 2009. *Turning Oil Into Salt: Energy Independence Through Fuel Choice.* Charleston: BookSurge Publishing.

Kraul, C., and M. Mogollon. 2007. "Presidents of Iran, Venezuela plan $2-billion project fund." *LA Times.*

Kupchan, Charles. 2010. *How Enemies Become Friends: The Sources of Stable Peace*. Princeton University Press.

Kurzman, Charles. 2003. "Pro-US fatwas." *Middle East Policy* X(3): 155–166.

2004. *The Unthinkable Revolution in Iran*. Cambridge, MA; Harvard University Press.

Lai, B., and D. Slater. 2006. "Institutions of the offensive: domestic sources of dispute initiation in authoritarian regimes, 1950–1992." *American Journal of Political Science* 50(1): 113–126.

Layne, C. 1994. "Kant or cant: the myth of the democratic peace." *International Security* 19(2): 5–49.

Legro, J. 2005. *Rethinking the World: Great Power Strategies and International Order*. Ithaca: Cornell University Press.

Leiby, P. N. 2007. "Estimating the energy security benefits of reduced US oil imports." *ORNL/TM-2007/028*.

Levy, J. S. 1988. "Domestic politics and war." *Journal of Interdisciplinary History* 18(4): 653–673.

Library of Congress. 1990. *Iraq, a Country Study*. Federal Research Division, Library of Congress, U.S. Government.

Libya: A Country Study. 1989. United States Government Printing Office.

Lieberman, Evan S. 2005. "Nested analysis as a mixed-method strategy for comparative research." *American Political Science Review* 99(3): 435–452.

Lippman, Thomas. 2004. *Inside The Mirage: America's Fragile Partnership With Saudi Arabia*. Boulder: Basic Books.

Lipson, Charles. 2003. *Reliable Partners: How Democracies Have Made a Separate Peace*. Princeton University Press.

Lo, Nigel, Barry Hashimoto, and Dan Reiter. 2008. "Ensuring peace: foreign-imposed regime change and postwar peace duration, 1914–2001." *International Organization* 62(4): 717–736.

Love, Kennett. 1953. "Royalists oust Mossadegh: Army seizes helm." *New York Times*. http://partners.nytimes.com/library/world/mideast/082053iran-army.html.

Lujala, P. 2010. "The spoils of nature: armed civil conflict and rebel access to natural resources." *Journal of Peace Research* 47(1): 15.

Luong, Pauline Jones, and Erika Weinthal. 2010. *Oil Is Not a Curse: Ownership Structure and Institutions in Soviet Successor States*. 1st edn. Cambridge University Press.

Mahdavy, Hussein. 1970. "The patterns and problems of economic development in rentier states: the case of Iran." In *Studies in Economic History of the Middle East: From the Rise of Islam to the Present Day*. London: Oxford University Press, pp. 428–467.

Mahoney, James, and Gary Goertz. 2006. "A tale of two cultures: contrasting quantitative and qualitative research." *Political Analysis* 14(3): 227–249.

Mandel, Robert. 1988. *Conflict over the World's Resources: Background, Trends, Case Studies, and Considerations for the Future.* New York: Greenwood Press.

Mansfield, Edward D., and Jack Snyder. 2005. *Electing to Fight: Why Emerging Democracies Go to War.* Cambridge, MA: MIT Press.

Maoz, Zeev. 1989. "Joining the club of nations: political development and international conflict, 1816–1976." *International Studies Quarterly* 33(2): 199–231.

1996. *Domestic Sources of Global Change.* Ann Arbor: University of Michigan Press.

Maoz, Zeev, and B. Russett. 1993. "Normative and structural causes of democratic peace." *American Political Science Review* 87(3): 624–638.

Marcano, Cristina, and Alberto Barrera Tyszka. 2007. *Hugo Chávez: The Definitive Biography of Venezuela's Controversial President.* New York: Random House.

Mares, David R. 2001. *Violent Peace: Militarized Interstate Bargaining in Latin America.* New York: Columbia University Press.

Marr, Phebe. 2003. *The Modern History of Iraq.* 2nd edn. Boulder: Westview Press.

Martin, Lisa L. 1993. *Coercive Cooperation.* Princeton University Press.

Maxwell, John W., and Rafael Reuveny. 2000. "Resource scarcity and conflict in developing countries." *Journal of Peace Research* 37(3): 301–322.

Meagher, John B. 1985. *The Jebel Akhdar War Oman 1954–1959.* US Marine Corps Command and Staff College. www.globalsecurity.org/military/library/report/1985/MJB.htm (accessed April 20, 2011).

Meierding, Emily. 2010. "Locating the oil wars." ISA Annual Meeting.

Menashri, David. 1990. *Iran: A Decade of War and Revolution.* New York: Holmes & Meier.

Milani, Mohsen M. 1994. *The Making of Iran's Islamic Revolution: From Monarchy to Islamic Republic.* Boulder: Westview Press.

2011. "Iran and Saudi Arabia square off." *Foreign Affairs.* www.foreignaffairs.com/articles/136409/mohsen-m-milani/iran-and-saudi-arabia-square-off (accessed February 9, 2012).

Moin, Baqer. 2000. *Khomeini: Life of the Ayatollah.* New York: Macmillan.

Molavi, Afshin. 2005. *The Soul of Iran: A Nation's Journey to Freedom.* Revised edn. New York: W. W. Norton.

Morrison, Kevin. 2009. "Oil, non-tax revenue, and the redistributional foundations of regime stability." *International Organization* 63: 107–138.

Morrow, J. D. 1989. "Capabilities, uncertainty, and resolve: a limited information model of crisis bargaining." *American Journal of Political Science* 33(4): 941–972.

Morsbach, G. 2002. "Chávez accused of fostering militia links." *BBC*. http://news.bbc.co.uk/2/hi/americas/2038827.stm.

Mueller, John. 1989. *Retreat from Doomsday: The Obsolescence of Major War*. 1st edn. Basic Books.

Murphy, John. 2008. *Ali Khamenei*. New York: Chelsea House.

Murray, S. K. 2006. "Private polls and presidential policymaking." *Public Opinion Quarterly* 70(4): 477–498.

Narang, V., and R. M. Nelson. 2009. "Who are these belligerent democratizers? Reassessing the impact of democratization on war." *International Organization* 63(2): 357–379.

New York Times. 1975. "Libyan leader Col. Muammar el-Qadhafi."

Niblock, Tim. 2006. *Saudi Arabia*. London: Routledge.

Norton, Augustus Richard. 2009. *Hezbollah: A Short History*. 1st edn. Princeton University Press.

Noticias 24. 2008. "RCN confirma que una llamada de Chávez permitió ubicar a Raúl Reyes." www.noticias24.com/actualidad/noticia/12585/rc n-confirma-que-una-llamada-de-Chávez-permitio-ubicar-a-raul-reyes/.

Obaid, Nawaf. 1999. "The power of Saudi Arabia's Islamic leaders." *Middle East Quarterly* VI(3): 51–58.

Obeidi, Amal. 2001. *Political Culture in Libya*. Richmond: Routledge.

O'Grady, Mary Anastasia. 2008. "Opinion: FARC's 'human rights' friends." *wsj.com*. http://online.wsj.com/article/SB121538827377131117.html (accessed March 4, 2010).

O'Kane, R. H. T. 2000. "Post-revolutionary state building in Ethiopia, Iran and Nicaragua: lessons from terror." *Political Studies* 48(5): 970–988.

O'Neal, John R., and Bruce Russett. 2001. *Triangulating Peace: Democracy, Interdependence, and International Organizations*. 1st edn. New York: W. W. Norton & Co.

De Onis, Juan. 1974. "A multibillion purchase of Treasury issue due." *New York Times*. http://select.nytimes.com/gst/abstract.html?res=F60F15FA 3F59137B93C5A91782D85F408785F9 (accessed October 6, 2009).

Organski, A. F. K., and J. Kugler. 1981. *The War Ledger*. University of Chicago Press.

Osnos, Evan. 2006. "The coming fight for oil." *Chicago Tribune*.

Owen, John M. 1997. *Liberal Peace, Liberal War: American Politics and International Security*. Ithaca: Cornell University Press.

Packer, G. 2005. *The Assassins' Gate: America in Iraq*. New York: Farrar, Straus, and Giroux.

Pelletiere, S. C. 2004. *America's Oil Wars*. Westport: Praeger Publishers.

Penaloza, Pedro Pablo. 2006. *Chávez es derrotable*. [Venezuela]: Editorial Libros Marcados.

Pew Research Center. 2007. *The Pew Global Attitudes Project: 47-Nation Pew Global Attitudes Survey*. Washington, DC.

Pinker, Steven. 2011. *The Better Angels of Our Nature: Why Violence Has Declined*. New York: Penguin.

Pollack, Kenneth M. 2002. *Arabs At War: Military Effectiveness, 1948–1991*. Lincoln, NE: University of Nebraska Press.

2004. *The Persian Puzzle: The Conflict between Iran and America*. New York: Random House, Inc.

Post, Jerrold M., and Alexander George. 2004. *Leaders and Their Followers in a Dangerous World: The Psychology of Political Behavior*. Ithaca: Cornell University Press.

Powell, R. 1999. *In the Shadow of Power: States and Strategies in International Politics*. Princeton University Press.

"Press conference of General Óscar Naranjo, Director of the National Police." 2008. http://embajadadecolombiaoslo.axesnet.com/english/asp_noticia.asp?ite_id=18009&pla_id=1&cat_id=2232&cat_nom=3.%20Political%20and%20social%20information (accessed March 4, 2010).

PressTV. 2010. "Iran oil exports top 844mn barrels." http://previous.presstv.com/detail.aspx?id=130736&sectionid=351020102 (accessed January 14, 2011).

Putnam, R. D. 1988. "Diplomacy and domestic politics: the logic of two-level games." *International Organization* 42(3): 427–460.

Quandt, William B. 1981. *Saudi Arabia in the 1980s – Foreign Policy, Security and Oil*. Washington, DC: Brookings Institute.

Rabinovich, Abraham. 2005. *The Yom Kippur War: The Epic Encounter That Transformed the Middle East*. New York: Schocken.

Rajaee, Farhang. 1993. *The Iran-Iraq War: The Politics of Aggression*. Gainesville: University Press of Florida.

Ramazani, R. K. 1987. *Revolutionary Iran: Challenge and Response in the Middle East*. Baltimore: The Johns Hopkins University Press.

Ramsay, K. 2011. "Revisiting the resource curse: natural disasters, the price of oil, and democracy." *International Organization* 65(3): 507–529.

Randall, Stephen J. 2007. *United States Foreign Oil Policy Since World War I: For Profits and Security*. 2nd edn. Montreal: McGill-Queen's University Press.

Reed, Stanley. 2006. "Surprise: oil woes in Iran." *BusinessWeek: Online Magazine*.www.businessweek.com/magazine/content/06_50/b4013058.htm (accessed March 22, 2010).

Reiter, Dan, and Allan C. Stam. 2002. *Democracies at War*. Princeton University Press.

Renshon, Stanley, ed. 1993. *The Political Psychology of the Gulf War: Leaders, Publics, and the Process of Conflict*. 1st edn. University of Pittsburgh Press.

Reuters. 2007b. "Argentina's Fernandez calls U.S. cash probe 'garbage'." www.reuters.com/article/worldNews/idUSN1351149120071213?feed Type=RSS&feedName=worldNews&rpc=22&sp=true.

2007a. "Oil Nationalization Threatens Output, Investment." http:// en.epochtimes.com/news/7-2-15/51769.html (accessed March 4, 2010).

2008. "Courts freeze Venezuela assets in Exxon row." http://uk.reuters. com/article/idUKN0740865020080207 (accessed March 4, 2010).

Riedel, Bruce. 2007. "Al Qaeda strikes back." *Foreign Affairs* 86: 24.

Rosato, S. 2003. "The flawed logic of democratic peace theory." *American Political Science Review* 97(4): 585–602.

Rosen, Stephen Peter. 2007. *War and Human Nature*. Princeton University Press.

Ross, Michael L. 2001. "Does oil hinder democracy?" *World Politics* 53(3): 325–361.

2006. "A closer look at oil, diamonds, and civil war." *Annual Review of Political Science* 9: 265–300.

2011. "Will oil drown the Arab Spring: democracy and the resource curse." *Foreign Affairs* 90(5): 2–7.

2012. *The Oil Curse: How Petroleum Wealth Shapes the Development of Nations*. Princeton University Press.

Russett, B. 1981. "Security and the resources scramble: will 1984 be like 1914?" *International Affairs* 58(1): 42–58.

1994. *Grasping the Democratic Peace: Principles for a Post-Cold War World*. Princeton University Press.

Sachs, J. D., and A. M. Warner. 1995. *Natural Resource Abundance and Economic Growth*. National Bureau of Economic Research.

Saeidi, A. A. 2001. "Charismatic political authority and populist economics in post-revolutionary Iran." *Third World Quarterly* 22(2): 219–236.

Salehyan, Idean. 2009. *Rebels Without Borders: Transnational Insurgencies in World Politics*. Ithaca: Cornell University Press.

Sanchez, Alex. 2008. "Venezuela's military in the Hugo Chávez era." *Council on Hemispheric Affairs*. www.coha.org/2008/09/ venezuela%E2%80%99s-military-in-the-hugo-Chávez-era/.

Sandalow, David. 2007. *Freedom From Oil: How the Next President Can End the United States' Oil Addiction*. 1st edn. New York: McGraw-Hill.

Saunders, Elizabeth N. 2011. *Leaders at War*. Ithaca: Cornell University Press.

Schultz, Kenneth A. 2001. *Democracy and Coercive Diplomacy*. Cambridge University Press.

Schweller, Randall L. 2006. *Unanswered Threats: Political Constraints on the Balance of Power*. Princeton University Press.

Sciolino, Elaine. 1991. *The Outlaw State: Saddam Hussein's Quest for Power and the Gulf Crisis*. New York: Wiley.

Senese, Paul Domenic, and John A. Vasquez. 2008. *The Steps to War: An Empirical Study*. Princeton University Press.

Simmons, Beth A. 1997 [1994]. *Who Adjusts? Domestic Sources of Foreign Economic Policy during the Interwar Years*. Princeton University Press.

Simons, Geoffrey Leslie. 2003. *Libya and the West*. Oxford: I. B. Tauris.

Sindi, A. 1980. "King Faisal and Pan-Islamism." In *King Faisal and the Modernisation of Saudi Arabia*, ed. Willard A. Beling. London: Croom Helm, pp. 184–201.

Singer, Clifford. 2008. *Energy and International War: From Babylon to Baghdad and Beyond*. Hackensack: World Scientific.

Skocpol, T. 1979. *States and Social Revolutions: A Comparative Analysis of France, Russia and China*. Cambridge University Press.

    1982. "Rentier state and Shi'a Islam in the Iranian revolution." *Theory and Society* 11(3): 265–283.

    1988. "Social revolutions and mass military mobilization." *World Politics: A Quarterly Journal of International Relations* 40(2): 147–168.

Smith, Alastair. 2008. "The perils of unearned income." *The Journal of Politics* 70(3): 780–793.

Smith, B. 2004. "Oil wealth and regime survival in the developing world, 1960–1999." *American Journal of Political Science* 48(2): 232–246.

Snyder, Jack L. 1991. *Myths of Empire: Domestic Politics and International Ambition*. Ithaca: Cornell University Press.

Snyder, R. S. 1999. "The US and third world revolutionary states: understanding the breakdown in relations." *International Studies Quarterly* 43(2): 265–290.

Snyder, Richard, and Ravi Bhavnani. 2005. "Diamonds, blood, and taxes." *Journal of Conflict Resolution* 49(4): 563–597.

de Soysa, I., E. Gartzke, and T. G. Lie. 2011. "Oil, Blood, and Strategy."

Spector, Leonard S. 1990. *Nuclear Ambitions: The Spread of Nuclear Weapons, 1989–1990*. Boulder: Westview Press.

Squassoni, S. 2007. "Iran's Nuclear Program: Recent Developments." Washington, DC: Congressional Research Service, Library of Congress.

St. John, Ronald Bruce. 2002. *Libya and the United States, Two Centuries of Strife*. Philadelphia: University of Pennsylvania Press.

    2008. *Libya: From Colony to Independence*. Oxford: Oneworld Publications.

Stam, Allan C. 1999. *Win, Lose, Or Draw: Domestic Politics and the Crucible of War*. Ann Arbor: University of Michigan Press.

Stempel, John D. 1981. *Inside the Iranian Revolution*. Bloomington: Indiana University Press.

Stevens, P., and E. Dietsche. 2008. "Resource curse: an analysis of causes, experiences and possible ways forward." *Energy Policy* 36(1): 56–65.

Stinnett, Douglas M., and Paul F. Diehl. 2001. "The path(s) to rivalry: behavioral and structural explanations of rivalry development." *The Journal of Politics* 63(3): 717–740.

Talmadge, C. 2008. "Closing time: assessing the Iranian threat to the Strait of Hormuz." *International Security* 33(1): 82–117.

Tammen, R. L., J. Kugler, D. Lemke, A. C. Stam III, M. Abdollahian, C. Alsharabati, B. Efird, and A. F. K. Organski. 2000. *Power Transitions: Strategies for the 21st Century*. New York: Chatham House Publishers.

Tarver, H. M., H. M. T. Denova, and J. C. Frederick. 2005. *The History of Venezuela*. Westport: Greenwood Publishing Group.

Telesur. 2007. "Uribe acusa a Chávez de ser expansionista" y de apoyar a la guerrilla en Colombia." www.telesurtv.net/secciones/noticias/nota/21184/uribe-acusa-a-Chávez-de-ser-expansionista-y-de-apoyar-a-la-guerrilla-en-colombia/.

Terhalle, M. 2009. "Revolutionary power and socialization: explaining the persistence of revolutionary zeal in Iran's foreign policy." *Security Studies* 18(3): 557–586.

Thies, Cameron G. 2010. "Of rulers, rebels, and revenue: state capacity, civil war onset, and primary commodities." *Journal of Peace Research* 47(3): 321–332.

Tilly, Charles. 1978. *From Mobilization to Revolution*. Reading: McGraw-Hill Companies.

1996. *European Revolutions: 1492–1992*. 1st paperback edn. Oxford: Wiley-Blackwell.

Timmerman, Kenneth R. 1992. *Weapons of Mass Destruction: The Cases of Iran, Syria & Libya*. Los Angeles: Simon Wiesenthal Center.

Tollitz, Nino P. 2005. *Saudi Arabia: Terrorism, U.S. Relations and Oil*. New York: Nova Publishers.

Tomz, Michael. 2007. *Reputation and International Cooperation: Sovereign Debt across Three Centuries*. Princeton University Press.

Tripp, Charles. 2002. *A History of Iraq*. Cambridge University Press.

Trofimov, Yaroslav. 2007. *The Siege of Mecca: The Forgotten Uprising in Islam's Holiest Shrine and the Birth of al-Qaeda*. New York: Doubleday.

Tsebelis, George. 2002. *Veto Players*. Princeton University Press.

Tyler, P. 2004. "Two said to tell of Libyan plot against Saudi." *The New York Times.*

Ulfelder, J. 2007. "Natural-resource wealth and the survival of autocracy." *Comparative Political Studies* 40(8): 995.

United States Department of State. 2002. *A Review of U.S. Policy Toward Venezuela November 2001 – April 2002.* Washington, DC.

US Government. 2002. "White House Briefing." www.whitehouse.gov/news/releases/2002/04/20020412–1.html.

US Government, Energy Information Agency. 2010. "Iran-Country Analysis Brief." www.eia.doe.gov/cabs/Iran/Oil.html (accessed March 22, 2010).

Vandewalle, Dirk. 1998. *Libya Since Independence: Oil and State-Building.* Ithaca: Cornell University Press.

2006. *A History of Modern Libya.* New York: Cambridge University Press.

Vasilev, A. M. 1998. *The History of Saudi Arabia.* London: Saqi Books.

Vasquez, John A. 2000. *What Do We Know about War?* Annotated edn. Lanham: Rowman & Littlefield Publishers, Inc.

Vicente, Pedro C., and Leonard Wantchekon. 2009. "Clientelism and vote buying: lessons from field experiments in African elections." *Oxford Review of Economic Policy* 25(2): 292–305.

Victor, David G. 2007. "What resource wars?" *The National Interest* 92: 48–55.

Vitalis, Robert. 2007. *America's Kingdom: Mythmaking on the Saudi Oil Frontier.* Palo Alto: Stanford University Press.

Vulliamy, Eric. 2002. "Venezuela coup linked to Bush team." *Observer.* www.guardian.co.uk/world/2002/apr/21/usa.venezuela.

Walt, Stephen M. 1996. *Revolution and War.* Ithaca: Cornell University Press.

1997. "Rethinking revolution and war: a response to Goldstone and Dassel." *Security Studies* 6(2): 174–196.

Ward, Michael D., and Kristian Skrede Gleditsch. 2002. "Location, location, location: an MCMC approach to modeling the spatial context of war and peace." *Political Analysis* 10(3): 244–260.

Weeks, Jessica. 2008. "Autocratic audience costs: regime type and signaling resolve." *International Organization* 62(1): 35–64.

2012. "Strongmen and straw men: authoritarian regimes, domestic politics, and international conflict." *American Political Science Review* 106(2): 326–347.

Westing, A. H. 1986. *Global Resources and International Conflict: Environmental Factors in Strategic Policy and Action.* Oxford: A SIPRI Publication.

Wilpert, Gregory. 2006. "The meaning of 21st century socialism for Venezuela." *ZNet Magazine*. www.zmag.org/content/showarticle. cfm?ItemID=10620.

  2007. *Changing Venezuela: The History and Policies of the Chávez Government*. London: Verso.

Woods, Kevin M., Williamson Murray, Elizabeth A. Nathan, Laila Sabara, and Ana M. Venegas. 2011a. *Saddam's Generals: Perspectives on the Iran-Iraq War*. Alexandria: Bernan Assoc.

Woods, Kevin M., David D. Palkki, and Mark E. Stout. 2011b. *The Saddam Tapes: The Inner Workings of a Tyrant's Regime, 1978–2001*. Cambridge University Press.

Wooldridge, J. M. 2002. *Econometric Analysis of Cross Section and Panel Data*. Cambridge, MA: MIT Press.

Wright, Claudia. 1981. "Libya and the west: headlong into confrontation?" *International Affairs* 58(1): 13–41.

Wurmser, Meyrav. 2007. "The Iran-Hamas alliance." *inFocus* 1(2). www. jewishpolicycenter.org/57/the-iran-hamas-alliance (accessed April 15, 2011).

Yahia, Latif, and Karl Wendl. 1997. *I was Saddam's Son*. New York: Arcade Publishing.

Yergin, Daniel. 2008 [1991]. *The Prize: The Epic Quest for Oil, Money & Power*. New York: Free Press.

Yetiv, Steven A. 1997. *The Persian Gulf Crisis*. Westport: Greenwood Publishing Group.

Zalloum, Abdulhay Yahya. 2007. *Oil Crusades: America Through Arab Eyes*. London: Pluto Press.

Index